# THEIR LIVES

## Death Row U.S.A.

Edited by

MARIE MULVEY-ROBERTS

Foreword by Jan Arriens

UNIVERSITY OF ILLINOIS PRESS
URBANA AND CHICAGO

Library of Congress Cataloging-in-Publication Data

Writing for their lives : death row U.S.A. / edited by
Marie Mulvey-Roberts; foreword by Jan Arriens.
    p.   cm.
Includes bibliographical references.
ISBN-13: 978-0-252-02793-2 (cloth : alk. paper)
ISBN-10: 0-252-02793-0 (cloth : alk. paper)
ISBN-13: 978-0-252-07099-0 (pbk. : alk. paper)
ISBN-10: 0-252-07099-2 (pbk. : alk. paper)
1. Death row—United States.
2. Capital punishment—United States.
3. Prisoners' writings, American.
4. Death row inmates—United States—Interviews.
5. Death row inmates—United States—Correspondence.
I. Mulvey Roberts, Marie.
HV8699.U5W75      2007
364.66'0973—dc22      2005022123

*Let no one be discouraged by the belief that there is nothing one person can do against the enormous array of the world's ills, misery, ignorance and violence. Few will have the greatness to bend history; but each of us can work to change a small portion of events, and in the total of all those acts will be written the history of a generation . . . It is from numberless diverse acts of courage and belief that human history is thus shaped. Each time a man stands up for an ideal or acts to improve the lot of others, or strikes out against injustice, he sends forth a tiny ripple of hope, and crossing each other from a million different centers of energy and daring, those ripples build a current which can sweep down the mightiest walls of oppression and resistance.*

—Senator Robert F. Kennedy (1966)

*One area of law more than the others besmirches the constitutional vision of human dignity. . . . The barbaric death penalty violates our Constitution. Even the most vile murderer does not release the state from its obligation to respect dignity, for the state does not honor the victim by emulating his murderer. Capital punishment's fatal flaw is that it treats people as objects to be toyed with and discarded . . . One day the Court will outlaw the death penalty. Permanently.*

—William J. Brennan Jr., retired Supreme Court Justice (1994)

*It is as if the Supreme Court has thrown up its hands and admitted that the only way to have the death penalty is to accept racism, to accept sleeping lawyers and drunk lawyers, to accept the execution of the innocent in the package.*

—Rev. Jesse L. Jackson, Rep. Jesse K. Jackson Jr., and Bruce Shapiro, *Legal Lynching* (2001)

*The very worst use to which you can put a man is to hang him.*

—Edward Bulwer Lytton, *Paul Clifford* (1830)

*The punishment of death is pernicious to society, from the example of barbarity it affords. If the passions, or the necessity of war, have taught men to shed the blood of their fellow creatures, the laws, which are intended to moderate the ferocity of mankind, should not increase it by examples of barbarity, the more horrible as this punishment is usually attended with formal pageantry. Is it not absurd, that the laws, which detest and punish homicide, should, in order to prevent murder, publicly commit murder themselves?*

—Cesare Beccaria, *On Crimes and Punishments* (1764)

# Contents

## 5. SHORT STORIES

# Foreword

Jan Arriens, Founder of LifeLines

One of the most remarkable things about death row is that it does not entirely crush people. On the contrary: some prisoners refer to it as the first period of real stability in their lives. They educate themselves, read widely, and discover abilities that had until then remained hidden. Some are even thankful for being on death row. Most arrive on the row while still young—some are even juveniles—after childhoods of deprivation and abuse that defy belief.

Two intertwined themes therefore often dominate the lives of many of the men and women on death row: the terrifying, traumatic, soul-destroying efforts of the state to take their lives, and the first true flowering of many of them as human beings. Many discover that they are, in fact, intelligent and talented. In the depths of their privation they reach out to others—fellow prisoners and, where possible, people in the outside world. They also turn inside, where they are thrust back utterly on their own resources and, if the system does not overwhelm them, discover depths in themselves they never knew they had.

These two great themes of darkness and light and suffocation and liberation also dominate these pages. In their poetry and prose the prisoners chronicle their innermost feelings, fears, and hopes, their travails, despair, optimism, and joys. The pages are sprinkled with bleakness and humor, the mundane and the profound, rage, anger, remorse, sorrow, and pride—indeed the full range of human emotions, including love. These may be men and women who have committed terrible offenses that have caused huge pain and grief in society, but they also have their stories to tell and are part of that society. In many cases they are the outcome of the very society that has condemned them. Sometimes the poetry may be raw and even clumsy, but it also comes from the heart, has enormous integrity, and has been forged in the crucible of experience. It is a cry from the soul, and deserves to be heard.

# Acknowledgments

I am grateful to all those who have contributed to this volume. My chief inspiration has been Tracy A. Hansen, whose friendship has done more than anything else to keep me in touch with death row. I would like to thank his friends and attorneys for the assistance they have given me. These include Dorothy Paton, Kathleen Lawson, Clive Stafford Smith, O.B.E., Charlie Press, and members of the Parchman Information List group, particularly Jean Foreman, Karin Elsea, Jandara Nitz and Human Writes members, Caroline Dipple and Sally Pringle. My gratitude goes to members of LifeLines, most notably Jan Arriens, Micheala Conway, Sarah Girling, Ann Stevens, and Clare Broom as well as to Jean Peake, Margaret Hodson, Libby Peppiatt, and Paula Ann Davis for their help and support. At Amicus, my thanks are due to Michael Mansfield Q.C., Sophie Garner, and especially to Rupert Skilbeck and Phyllis Guest for reading my introduction so thoroughly and for making such constructive suggestions. I am most appreciative of the help given me by Hannah Lyons for her secretarial assistance, Gayle Conway for her typing skills, and Dick Allen, Phillip Hargreaves, and Jean Wilson for their computer expertise.

Amnesty International has given me invaluable help, especially Ken and Liz Strong and Brian Crowther. Noa Kleinman, North American coordinator for Amnesty International U.K. section, deserves special mention for keeping me up to date with material and for being unfailingly helpful, while Rick Halperin, who is the Texas State Death Penalty Abolition Coordinator and Chair of the Board of Directors of Amnesty International U.S.A., has also been unsparing of his time, energy, and resources in answering my questions. I am indebted to Professor Mike Radelet, Professor Peter Hodgkinson, and his researcher Seema Kandelia at the Centre for Capital Punishment Studies in London, and Jack Payden-Travers, Director of Virginians for Alternatives to the Death Penalty. Indispensable help and support has been given me by

Evonne L. von Heussen-Countryman, M.B.E., Mary Maggard, K. Bandell, William McGeachy, and Bryan Stevenson of the Equal Justice Initiative in Montgomery, Stephen Tumim, R. V. Bailey, U. A. Fanthorpe CBE, Lynn Ferguson, Danielle Guédon, Isabelle Delèze, Traci W. Lister, Tim Newell, ex-governor of Grendon Underwood H. M. Prison, Madge Dresser, Jean and Raymond Hutton, Trevor Hanson, Phyllis Pautrat, Gregg Jackson, Rob Warden, Executive Director, and Prof. Larry Marshall of Northwestern University Law School's Center on Wrongful Convictions, Jennifer Bishop-Jenkins of Murder Victims' Families for Reconciliation, and Arnold Erickson, who is the webmaster for The Other Side of the Wall (see "Organizations and Prison Writing Web Sites").

I am grateful to the Trustees of the Society of Jesus for allowing me to use Sister Ruth Evans's essay, "The Struggle for Spirituality," which was originally published in *The Month* (January 2000), 13–17. The Plough Publishers gave me kind permission to use extracts from the interview of Mumia Abu-Jamal by Allen Hougland, from *Death Blossoms: Reflections from a Prisoner of Conscience* (Robertsbridge E. Sussex: The Plough Publishing House, 1997), 123–150. Traci W. Lister has generously permitted me to reproduce "The Long Walk" by Don Hawkins from the Web site Surviving the System, and Micheala Conway, the editor of *The Wing of Friendship,* has very kindly given me permission to use the following poems: "Oblique Sojourn" by Leroy D. Cropper; "Living Death" by Kevin Brian Dowling; "Words that I Hear" by Edwin Smith; and "Journey to Nowhere" by Ramon Rogers. I am grateful to Chris Bessant of New Clarion Press for giving me permission to reproduce the following material from *Out of the Night: Writings from Death Row*, edited by Marie Mulvey-Roberts: "Working Against the Death Penalty" by Marie Deans; "Scars" by Jarvis Masters; "Surviving an Execution Date" by Dominique Malon; "Recipe for Prison Pruno" by Jarvis Masters; "So Many Times" by Mark Robertson; "To be seen, to be done" by Benjamin Zephaniah; "Red Man" by Shoz Dijiji; "Come Back to Me" by Keith B. Taylor; "For You" by Joan Warren; "Death Row Poets" by U. A. Fanthorpe; "You Hide Where You Can't" by Tracy A. Hansen; and "Burnt Almonds" by Steven King Ainsworth. I thank Sound Portraits Productions for permission to use the transcript of "Witness to an Execution," which can be heard on the Sound Portraits Web site: www.soundportraits.org. To purchase a CD of the documentary, visit the store at www.soundportraits.org/store/.

The full text of Dr. Terry Kupers's report on Parchman, Mississippi, is available on the American Civil Liberties Union National Prison Project Web site. His report on Texas has also been truncated. The full text is not yet available due to pending litigation. The material included here is an extract from an affidavit for *Henry Watkins Skinner v. Steve Carey Staples et al.* I am grateful to Hank Skinner for putting me in touch with Dr. Kupers, and I include Hank's address for correspondence: 99143, Terrel Unit, 3872 FM 350 South Livingston, TX 77351–8580, USA. The entire text of Stephen B. Bright's speech, from which I include extracts, was published in *Notre Dame Law Review,* 71 (1996), 845–60.

Claire Jenkins and Jane Officer must be commended for organizing a splendid launch in the Houses of Parliament for *Out of the Night: Writings from Death Row,* the nucleus of this book. The event took place in an annex of Westminster Hall, where Charles I, who was executed in 1649, was sentenced to death. M.P. Nicholas Scott very kindly hosted the event, which was attended by other Members of Parliament including Claire Short. The Right Honorable Michael Foot wrote the preface to the book and has been a stalwart supporter of it and this latest venture. The support of Nigel Biggs, Marion Glastonbury, Naomi Lester, and William Lammas has remained as important as ever. Finally, I would like to thank my own institution, the University of the West of England, Bristol, for their support, and Willis Regier at University of Illinois Press for his assistance in bringing this book to press. Neither the publisher nor the editor can be held responsible for the material presented by the contributors in this book. The contributions have been lightly edited to correct punctuation and spelling while retaining the original voices of the writers as far as is possible.

# WRITING FOR THEIR LIVES

# INTRODUCTION: DEATH SENTENCES

## Marie Mulvey-Roberts

*Creativity is the last vestige of our humanity in here to remind ourselves that we are living beings.*
  —Death Row inmate at the Polunsky Unit, Texas

On January 11, 2003, a momentous decision was made in the history of the death penalty in the United States. Illinois Governor George Ryan was so concerned about miscarriages of justice that he took the unprecedented step of commuting the death sentences of all the death row prisoners in his state to life imprisonment.

The death penalty dissolves the most fundamental of civil liberties: the right to life. It is maintained by myths—that it deters crime, brings genuine closure for victims' families, punishes only the most heinous criminals, and is administered fairly and impartially. In fact, imposition of the death penalty is determined by place, race, and money and is the product of a collective fear reinforced by ethnic divisions, media competitors, and political ambitions. Capital punishment is a relic of a frontier mentality now so sanitized that the average citizen cannot see the home-grown holocaust buried in the apple-pie image of the American Dream. By refusing to collude with this judicial sham and national shame, Governor Ryan halted the grisly process of state execution, which had been preceded by his moratorium on the death penalty in 2000. The American Bar Association House of Delegates in 1997 adopted a resolution calling for a general moratorium on executions until serious flaws in the nation's capital punishment system are eliminated. Yet the death penalty remains and, in the words of Justice Harry A. Blackmun, is "fraught with arbitrariness, discrimination, caprice, and mistake."[1]

In the 1972 case of *Furman v. Georgia,* the Supreme Court declared the death penalty statutes unconstitutional because the dispensation of death sentencing was so arbitrary. Most of the retentionist states redrafted their statutes and bifurcated capital trials into guilt–innocence and punishment phases, allegedly in order to enhance "fairness." The death penalty was thus deemed constitutional in the case, among others, of *Gregg v. Georgia* and reinstated by a Supreme Court ruling in 1976. Since that date, more than 861 people have been executed in the United States, even though III countries have abolished the death penalty.[2] The United States, while proclaiming itself leader of the free world and a model for human rights, lags far behind.

The United States is one of only three countries that carry out eighty percent of the world's judicial executions.[3] It is the only member of NATO and the single "Westernized" country to uphold the death penalty. This is imposed by forty out of fifty-three jurisdictions (which include the District of Columbia, U.S. government, and U.S. military). The most vigorous of all the "killing states" is Texas, followed by Virginia, Oklahoma, Missouri, Florida, and then the rest of the Southern states, which proudly form the "death belt."

Since 1990, the country that has executed the greatest number of offenders sentenced to death for offenses committed as juveniles is the United States. Iran is the only other country known to have executed juveniles since 1992. Amnesty International has campaigned against America for "sending children to the electric chair."[4] The U.S. even signed the International Covenant on Civil and Political Rights (which under Article 6 prevents the execution of people for crimes committed when under the age of eighteen), although its administration purported to have signed a "reservation" rejecting this part of the treaty—which the U.N. Human Rights Committee has declared to be "unlawful." In short, the U.S. has contravened decrees of human rights organizations worldwide including the Convention on the Rights of the Child and international standards on capital punishment, such as the resolutions taken by the United Nations and the Geneva Convention of August 12, 1949.[5]

Human rights violations also relate to race, which is a determining factor in who gets the death penalty. Even though African Americans are twelve percent of the U.S. population, they constitute forty-one percent of prisoners awaiting execution, while eighty percent of those on federal death row[6] are members of minority groups. Some eighty percent of completed capital cases involve white victims, whereas nationally only fifty percent of homicide victims are white. Prosecutors frequently stack juries with whites and death penalty supporters. An illustration of how the death penalty can be seen as a form of state-sanctioned lynching is evident in the case of William Andrews, who was executed in Utah in 1992.[7] Found in the jury room was a note reading "hang the nigger," along with a drawing of a man hanging from a tree.[8]

People also end up on death row because of poverty. The irony is that if a portion of the cost of incarceration had been spent earlier to provide better education and welfare, these people might well have avoided prison. California spends more money on its prisons than on its schools and universities. It is not common knowledge that for capital offenders, life without parole is more cost-effective than execution. In North Carolina for example, a death penalty case costs tax payers roughly $2.3 million, as opposed to $750,000 to imprison someone in a top-security single cell for life.[9]

By the time of execution, the prisoner facing death may no longer be the same person who committed the crime. Profound personal transformations take place in prison cells. It is important to stress that concern for victims of the death penalty should not detract from compassion for the victims of their crimes. An organization combining both is Murder Victims' Families for Reconciliation, which advocates forgiveness rather than revenge as the way forward. Other less-visible victims of death row are the families of prisoners. Imagine the agony of a mother witnessing the killing of her child after having been denied any physical contact with him for many years. The deprivation of death row prisoners, from whom even life is eventually taken, mirrors the moral impoverishment and political paralysis out in the "land of the free."

It has been argued that the death penalty serves as a deterrent to homicide and other violent crimes. If this is true, why do states that lack the death penalty have fewer murders per capita than those that have it? Premeditated murder is an aggravating circumstance that often attracts a capital sentence, yet by taking years before it kills, the state imitates what it professes to condemn. As Robert Kennedy stated shortly after the assassination of Dr. Martin Luther King Jr., "Whenever any American's life is taken by another American unnecessarily—whether it is done in the name of the law or in the defiance of the law, by one man or a gang, in cold blood or in passion, in an attack of violence or in response to violence—whenever we tear at the fabric of the life which another man has painfully and clumsily woven for himself and his children, the whole nation is degraded."[10]

The United States approves five methods of killing, which it has used against thousands of its own citizens and nearly a hundred foreign nationals. These are electrocution, lethal injection, gas chamber, firing squad, and hanging. Lethal injection has been regarded as the safest of these methods, but, due to gross negligence of protocols surrounding this procedure, it frequently violates the clause in the Eighth Amendment of the American Constitution against "cruel and unusual punishment."[11] Physicians are needed to insert intravenous catheters, rather than unqualified and barely trained prison guards, whose efforts can result in botched executions.[12] Contrary to popular medical advice, Texas believes it is reasonable for inmates to have their last meal two to three hours prior to execution, whereas a gap of at least six to eight hours is needed to ensure that the inmate will not vomit the food and choke to death. The first injection to be administered is sodium thiopental, of which 2.5g is widely regarded by the medical profession as a sufficient dose to ensure that an inmate does not regain consciousness. This is followed by the paralyzing muscle drug of pancuronium bromide and then by potassium chloride, which kills by inducing cardiac arrest. The case for lethal injection as a humane method falls apart completely if the anesthetic fails to work, with horrifying consequences. Few states offer sufficient instructions on dosage to executioners. Unfortunately, Montana stipulates a mere 0.5g of sodium thiopental, "an ultra-short-acting drug," which is only twenty-five percent of the required dose to maintain unconsciousness. An inmate's weight, age, and health are factors that need to be considered in determining the correct dose. But only Florida stipulates that a pharmacist, who is trained to take account of such vital variables, should prepare the lethal injection. If an overdose of pancuronium bromide is injected, the inmate will die slowly of asphyxiation. Mississippi, Florida, Washington, and New Mexico specify a dose over fifty times in excess of the safety margins generally accepted by doctors, while Connecticut stipulates a dose even higher.[13] Of the thirty-six states using lethal injection, only nine stipulate the doses of the chemicals administered while only four of these specify an adequate and effective dosage. Texas, the most virulent state executioner, has had practical problems with about eighty percent of lethal injections, prompting even the inventor of the lethal injection machine it uses, Fred Leuchter, to conclude, "In the final analysis, it looks disgusting."[14]

Days before the sentence is carried out, prisoners are removed from the row and their possessions are taken away from them. They are then taken to a bare holding cell, the "Death House," where they are left in solitary confinement with nothing but a Bible and their legal papers and watched day and night by prison guards. The condemned are systematically stripped of everything,[15] even their dignity, for there is no escape from that watchful gaze. Technically, they are not even allowed to take tranquillizers to numb themselves for the ordeal ahead because regulations insist that prisoners must remain as fully physically and mentally aware as possible. As the end draws near, family members are usually allowed a visit. After they leave, the prisoner's attorney and spiritual advisor, who is often the prison chaplain, remain. Prisoners assigned to electrocution have their heads shaved and also a patch on one leg for the electrodes to be put in place. On the last walk, the spiritual advisor is not allowed to give the so-called dead man walking even the comfort and reassurance of touch.

Prior to execution, the strap-down team will have rehearsed its grisly task with military precision. One member may be assigned an arm to restrain, another a leg. The division of the prisoner into bodily parts helps these prison officers to overlook the fact that they are dealing with a human being. Their militaristic discourse further distances them from the horror of taking a human life.

Language also deflects from the grim reality of death when, for example, a government spokesman refers to certain terrorists as being "eligible for death." Politicians brag of the number of corpses piling up from executions carried out in their states, promising more in the hope of increasing the number of votes in the run-up to an election. President George W. Bush holds the record for personally signing more than one hundred death warrants in Texas. He dismisses the fact that every death row statistic is or was a corresponding human life. In death rows across the United States, more than 3,503 men and women now languish. Their numbers are increasing.

In a book called *In Spite of Innocence* (1992), the authors reveal that in the span of one year during the last decade, 400 people were erroneously convicted of capital or potentially capital crimes.[16] Recently, more advanced methods of DNA testing have exonerated a number of prisoners wrongly convicted, showing that the forensic evidence used against them was flawed. Since some police departments now destroy DNA evidence, it is imperative that defense attorneys obtain a court order to preserve it. It is extraordinary that in January 1993 the United States Supreme Court ruled it was constitutional to execute an innocent person, as long as such a manifest injustice was preceded by something called a "fair trial."[17] Equally disturbing is the dilemma that if a defendant's attorney does not file evidence demonstrating the innocence of the accused in a capital case within a given deadline after the original sentencing, the evidence is inadmissible at the appellate stage. A prisoner in Virginia appealed for the right to introduce new evidence, even though the twenty-one-day deadline had passed. The response of Mary Sue Terry, the state's attorney general was that "evidence of innocence is irrelevant."[18] The reification of the law in this way turns "due process" into an inexorable death knell.[19] Yet there were hopeful developments in 2001–2, such as the Supreme Court's decisions in the cases of *Atkins v. Virginia,* proscribing the execution of the mentally retarded, and *Ring v. Arizona,* mandating that death sentences must be determined by a jury rather than by a judge.

Above all, capital punishment is punishment for those without the capital. The defenses provided by states for the ninety percent of defendants unable to afford a lawyer range from the woefully inadequate to, in eight states, the nonexistent.[20] Court-appointed attorneys are usually inexperienced and underpaid, often working in the states of Alabama, Mississippi, and Louisiana for as little as $11.75 an hour. It is not unknown for incompetent lawyers to be asleep during the capital trial, which can last less than a week—hardly enough time even for a "dream team" to present a good defense. Yet some excellent lawyers do work tirelessly and effectively to save lives, including the British-born U.S.-qualified attorney Clive Stafford Smith, Director of the Louisiana Crisis Assistance Center, and Bryan Stevenson, the distinguished lawyer and Executive Director of the Equal Justice Initiative in Montgomery, Alabama. Profits from this book will be donated to the British organization Amicus, a legal charity supporting lawyers in capital defense in the U.S. This publication will enable prisoners to literally write for their lives in a number of different ways alongside leading death row professionals who have dedicated their lives and words to this cause.

These writings grew out of an earlier book I edited called *Out of the Night: Writings from Death Row* (1994). In the years since this book was compiled, the death penalty has accelerated, scarring more deeply the mental and moral landscapes of "the home of the brave." Ironically, death by electrocution, gassing, and lethal injection has become more deeply embedded in the American way of life at the same time that the inner workings of the killing machine have become more transparent. Since *Out of the Night* was published, at least ten contributors have been killed. For some, the date and method of their execution, details of their last meal, and a transcript of their last words have been posted on certain prison Web sites for all to read.[21] These are a chilling reminder that no privacy exists for those who die in execution chambers across America. The macabre patch of cyber-space is a curious crossroad where twenty-first-century technology intersects with the primitive ritual killing of the citizens of a nation proud of its humanitarian role in the world. But it is the very humanity of those who wait for death, in virtual solitary confinement in cells as small as 6 feet by 9 feet, that emerges most powerfully from this anthology. Here, poets, essayists, and creative writers write from under the executioner's shadow. Their words are a beacon of light arising from a legislative darkness in which revenge, retribution, and the rule of law are authorized by the U.S. legislature to blot out human lives.

In this volume, the writings of prisoners have been brought together with those of anti–death penalty campaigners and death row professionals. These include Stephen B. Bright, the leading death penalty attorney and director of the Southern Center for Human Rights; Dr. Terry Kupers, author of the acclaimed *Prison Madness: The Mental Health Crisis Behind Bars and What We Must Do About It* (1999); the abolitionist and spiritual advisor for death row prisoners Sister Helen Prejean, a Nobel Peace Prize nominee whose book *Dead Man Walking* (1993) was turned into an Oscar-winning film; Marie Deans, a founder of Murder Victims' Families for Reconciliation; and Sister Ruth Evans, a British nun in an enclosed order, who campaigns on behalf of the Scotsman Kenny Richey, held on Ohio's death row. Also included in the book is an interview with Mumia Abu-Jamal, the imprisoned award-winning journalist and celebrated black activist, along with stories about incarceration from Jarvis Masters, the author of *Finding Freedom: Writings from Death Row* (1997), and from prize-winning writers William Van Poyck and Michael Wayne Hunter. Each section presents the material through a different genre—poetry, short stories, journal extracts, and letters, as well as a range of discourses from the anecdotal to the legalistic; each has its own self-contained momentum. For example, in chapter four, a journey is mapped out through poems from a capital trial to the first day on death row to the very last. Even between these painful parameters, hope, joy, and light emerge.

The title of the book, *Writing for Their Lives,* is a statement about the importance of writing as a means of survival. Writing can dispel some of the boredom and terror of life behind bars. Prisoners are not recognized by the system as people with emotional needs, dreams, or goals, but only as "human waste"[22] to be contained in cramped, often windowless rooms for "processing" in grisly and gruesome procedures. Yet, through writing, prisoners can reclaim their inner lives and distance themselves from the pain and suffering around them. Writing can be a route to self-reflection, therapy, and healing. As the chapter on letter and journal writing reveals, writing can serve as a bridge to the outside world. In crossing that bridge, prisoners can expose inhumane living conditions, petty rules, and unreasonable regimes, whereby people are abandoned to die, inch by inch, day by day.

Cruelty has now become increasingly etched into the architecture of prisons. Some death rows resemble "supermaximum security" facilities, which foster an array of mental health problems. As David R. Dow points out, "In Oklahoma, a death sentence means never seeing sunshine again," because prisoners at McAlester are confined underground in a "subterranean tomb."[23] In chapter two, Dr. Terry Kupers describes the devastating effects of conditions at the dehumanized Polunsky Unit in Texas. Even though some state penitentiaries describe themselves as "correctional" facilities, there are no educational or rehabilitation programs on death row. The often illiterate inhabitants of death row are "corrected" by being put to death.[24] This makes reading and writing all the more important as vehicles for self-development, education, communication, and recreation available to the condemned.

Some of the contributions in this book emerged from a British writing competition I organized for death row prisoners in the U.S. with the encouragement of Sister Helen Prejean. The adjudicators were Judge Stephen Tumin, Her Majesty's Inspector of Prisons; Michael Foot, the ex-leader of the Labour Party; R. V. Bailey; and two well-known poets, who have each contributed a poem to this anthology. These were U. A. Fanthorpe, who was recently awarded the Queen's Gold Medal for Poetry, and Benjamin Zephaniah, the Rastafarian rap poet feted by the media. Several entrants had never before attempted creative writing and some entries arrived on bits of paper written in pencil in a barely literate scrawl. By contrast, the winner was a prolific writer called Tracy A. Hansen from Parchman, the Mississippi State Penitentiary, who wrote several unpublished books, as well as *The Adventures of Silly Cat* for children. He became my pen pal for nearly nine years. His letters were a continual source of compassion, care, and concern.

A few years ago, I visited him at Parchman, arriving the day after filming had finished of John Grisham's *The Chamber* (1994). During the flight home I read the novel and failed to recognize any familiar landmarks from the prison. I never saw Tracy again. On July 17, 2002, he was executed by lethal injection. The sorrow of losing such a dear friend became the driving force for this book.

This anthology is not only a reminder to the outside world of those who are subjected to the grim conjunction of life imprisonment and execution, it is also a testimony to how prison writing can be both liberating and empowering.[25] Those who are indeed writing for their lives are affirming the value of life from within the pages of this book, for in the words of Frederick Douglass, "Life is the great primary and most precious and comprehensive of human rights . . . whether it be coupled with virtue, honor, and happiness, or with sin, disgrace and misery, the continued possession of it is rightfully not a matter of volition; . . . [it is not] to be deliberately or voluntarily destroyed, either by individuals separately, or combined in what is called Government."[26]

## Notes

1. U.S. Supreme Court Justice Harry A. Blackmun made this statement while dissenting from the Supreme Court's decision denying review in a Texas death penalty case, *Callins v. Collins,* Feb. 22, 1994.

2. The death penalty is still imposed by eighty-three countries.

3. The other two are China and Iran. Figures for this essay have been supplied by Amnesty International and the Death Penalty Information Centre.

4. *The Voice* 11, no. 1 (Jan. 1992): 6.

5. In March 2005, the U.S. Supreme Court ruled by a vote of five to four that the Eighth and Fourteenth Amendments ban the execution of offenders who were under the age of eighteen when they committed their crime.

6. Terre Haute, Indiana, has housed federal death row prisoners since 1990. Previously they had been confined within a number of federal penitentiaries.

7. Ashanti Chimurengo claims that this statement "reputedly, comes out of the mouth of former U.S. Supreme Court Justice Thurgood Marshall." See "The Shame of the Death Penalty" in *The Machinery of Death: A Shocking Indictment of Capital Punishment in the United States,* ed. Enid Harlow, David Matas, and Jane Rocamora (New York: Amnesty International U.S.A., 1995) 1: 8.

8. The judge refused to have an investigation as to where the note came from—that is, who sent it into the jury room. The suggestion was certainly that someone had sent it as an instruction to the jury, rather than it actually coming from the jury themselves. See also Jesse Jackson, *Legal Lynching* (New York: The New Press, 2001).

9. See *Dallas Morning News,* March 8, 1992.

10. From a speech given to the City Club of Cleveland, Cleveland, Ohio, April 5, 1968. Remembering Robert Kennedy, http://www.rememberingrfk.com/april5speech .html.

11. See Matthew Jury, "The Failure of Lethal-Injection Protocols," *Amicus Journal,* 32 (2003): 20–24. All subsequent details relating to lethal injection are taken from his article. Oklahoma became the first state to adopt lethal injection. The first person to be executed by this method was Charlie Brooks of Texas in 1982.

12. A host of physical reasons including diabetes, nervousness, extreme muscle development or obesity, a history of intravenous drug use, or use of ongoing medication can cause veins to constrict, preventing the insertion of the needle. Executioners sometimes inject instead into oversensitive parts of the body such as the groin, hand, or directly into muscle, which is more painful. In extremis, they resort to the "I.V.-cut down" method of surgically exposing a vein in order to connect the I.V. Catheters can also be wrongly inserted so that chemicals flow against the direction of the heart, thereby impeding absorption.

13. The sufficient and safe dose of pancuronium bromide is 0.04–0.1 mg/kg. Mississippi, Florida, Washington, and New Mexico all specify 50mg, while Connecticut stipulates 100mg.

14. Quoted by Matthew Jury, "The Failure of Lethal-Injection Protocols," 23.

15. Prisoners buried within the grounds of the prison may even have their names taken away from them, as when their prison number instead of their name is inscribed on a simple wooden cross over their graves.

16. See *In Spite of Innocence,* ed. Michael L. Radelet, Hugo Adam Bedau, and Constance E. Putnam (Boston: Northeastern University Press, 1992). This book documents the ordeals of these four hundred individuals.

17. See *Herrera v. Collins,* U.S. Supreme Court, decided January 25, 1993, and Chimurenga, "The Shame of the Death Penalty," 8.

18. See http://www.fdp.dk/, Fight the Death Penalty Web site. Mary Sue Terry was the Attorney General from 1986 to 1994. The deadline of twenty-one days has recently been extended to ninety days in Virginia.

19. President Clinton's "anti-terrorism" bill of 1996 limits the number of federal appeals for death row prisoners to just one within one year of conviction. This new legislation has gutted the oldest fundamental right in the English-speaking world: *habeas corpus,* which allows prisoners to try to prove that they have been wrongfully convicted. If eighty-five of the people released from death row after being wrongfully convicted had been put there after Clinton's bill came into law, many of them would now be dead. Clinton has called appeals by death row prisoners "ridiculous" and "interminable." See http://www.nodeathpenalty.org/fiveReasons.html.

20. In 1996, President Clinton cut federal funding to twenty legal resource centers that provided counsel to poor defendants. As a result, all these centers have been forced to close.

21. Texas has provided all this information while other states tend to be more selective in the information they disseminate.

22. This is an expression that has been used by prison personnel, quoted by Sister Helen Prejean in a speech given at a LifeLines conference held in Birmingham, England, in 1992.

23. *Machinery of Death: The Reality of America's Death Penalty Regime,* ed. David R. Dow and Mark Dow (London: Routledge, 2002), 12.

24. In Jackson, death row is housed within the Georgia Diagnostic Facility. The name conjures up the bizarre concept of prisoners being given a diagnosis for which the treatment is death.

25. The writers' voices have been lightly edited, but their language has been preserved even in cases where it might be grammatically incorrect or seemingly incoherent.

26. See http://www.schr.org.

# 1

## ESSAYS AND SPEECHES ON THE DEATH PENALTY

*Criminals do not die by the hands of the law. They die by the hands of other men. Assassination on the scaffold is the worst form of assassination because there it is invested with the approval of the society. It is the deed that teaches, not the name we give it. Murder and capital punishment are not opposites that cancel one another out but similars that breed their kind.*

　　—George Bernard Shaw

# I WILL NOT STAND FOR IT

## George Ryan, Governor of Illinois

Four years ago I was sworn in as the thiry-ninth governor of Illinois. That was just four short years ago—that's when I was a firm believer in the American System of Justice and the death penalty. I believed that the ultimate penalty for the taking of a life was administrated in a just and fair manner.

Today—three days before I end my term as governor—I stand before you to explain my frustrations and deep concerns about both the administration and the penalty of death. It is fitting that we are gathered here today at Northwestern University with the students, teachers, lawyers, and investigators who first shed light on the sorrowful condition of Illinois' death penalty system. Professors Larry Marshall, Dave Protess, and their students along with investigator Paul Ciolino have gone above the call. They freed the falsely accused Ford Heights Four, they saved Anthony Porter's life, they fought for Rolando Cruz and Alex Hernandez. They devoted time and effort on behalf of Aaron Patterson, a young man who lost fifteen years of his youth sitting among the condemned, and Leroy Orange, who lost seventeen of the best years of his life on death row.

It is also proper that we are together with dedicated people like Andrea Lyon who has labored on the front lines trying capital cases for many years and who is now devoting her passion to creating an innocence center at De Paul University. You saved Madison Hobley's life. Together you spared the lives and secured the freedom of seventeen men—men who were wrongfully convicted and rotting in the condemned units of our state prisons. What you have achieved is of the highest calling—thank you!

Yes, it is right that I am here with you, where, in a manner of speaking, my journey from staunch supporter of capital punishment to reformer all began. But I must tell you—since the beginning of our journey—my thoughts and feelings about the death penalty have changed many, many times. I realize that over the course of my reviews I had said that I would not do blanket commutation. I have also said it was an option that was there and I would consider all options. . . . Having said that I want to share a story with you.

I grew up in Kankakee, which even today is still a small midwestern town, a place where people tend to know each other. Steve Small was a neighbor. I watched him grow up. He would babysit my young children— which was not for the faint of heart since Lura Lynn and I had six children, five of them under the age of three. He was a bright young man who helped run the family business. He got married and he and his wife had three children of their own. Lura Lynn was especially close to him and his family. We took comfort in knowing he was there for us and we for him.

One September midnight he received a call at his home. There had been a break-in at the nearby house he was renovating. But as he left his house, he was seized at gunpoint by kidnappers. His captors buried him alive in a shallow hole. He suffocated to death before police could find him. His killer led investigators to where Steve's body was buried. The killer, Danny Edward, was also from my hometown. He now sits on death row. I also know his family. I share this story with you so that you know I do not come to this as a neophyte without having experienced a small bit of the bitter pill the survivors of murder must swallow. My responsibilities and obligations are more than my neighbors and my family. I represent all the people of Illinois, like it or not. The decision I make about our criminal justice system is felt not only here, but the world over.

The other day, I received a call from former South African President Nelson Mandela who reminded me that the United States sets the example for justice and fairness for the rest of the world. Today the United States is not in league with most of our major allies: Europe, Canada, Mexico, most of South and Central America. These countries rejected the death penalty. We are partners in death with several third world countries. Even Russia has called a moratorium.

The death penalty has been abolished in twelve states. In none of these states has the homicide rate increased. In Illinois last year we had about one thousand murders; only two percent of that thousand were sentenced to death. Where is the fairness and equality in that? The death penalty in Illinois is not imposed fairly or uniformly because of the absence of standards for the 102 Illinois State Attorneys, who must decide whether to request the death sentence. Should geography be a factor in determining who gets the death sentence? I don't think so, but in Illinois it makes a difference. You are five times more likely to get a death sentence for first-degree murder in the rural areas of Illinois than you are in Cook County [Chicago]. Where is the justice and fairness in that? Where is the proportionality?

The Most Reverend Desmond Tutu wrote to me this week stating that "to take a life when a life has been lost is revenge, it is not justice. He says justice allows for mercy, clemency and compassion. These virtues are not weakness."

"In fact the most glaring weakness is that no matter how efficient and fair the death penalty may seem in theory, in actual practice it is primarily inflicted upon the weak, the poor, the ignorant and against racial minorities."[1] That was a quote from former California Governor Pat Brown. He wrote that in his book, *Public Justice, Private Mercy: A Governor's Education on Death Row* (1989); he wrote that nearly fifty years ago—nothing has changed in nearly fifty years.

I never intended to be an activist on this issue. I watched in surprise as freed death row inmate Anthony Porter was released from jail. A free man, he ran into the arms of Northwestern University Professor Dave Protess who poured his heart and soul into proving Porter's innocence with his journalism students. He was forty-eight hours away from being wheeled into the execution chamber where the state would kill him.

It would all be so antiseptic and most of us would not have even paused, except that Anthony Porter was innocent of the double murder for which he had been condemned to die. After Mr. Porter's case there was the report by *Chicago Tribune* reporters Steve Mills and Ken Armstrong documenting the systemic failures of our capital punishment system. Half of the nearly three hundred capital cases in Illinois had been reversed for a new trial or resentencing.

Nearly half! Thirty-three of the death row inmates were represented at trial by an attorney who had later been disbarred or at some point suspended from practicing law. Of the more than 160 death row inmates, thirty-five were African American defendants who had been convicted or condemned to die by all-white juries. More than two-thirds of the inmates on death row were African American. Forty-six inmates were convicted on the basis of testimony from jailhouse informants. I can recall looking at these cases and the information from the Mills/Armstrong series and asking my staff: How does that happen? How in God's name does that happen? I'm not a lawyer, so somebody explain it to me. But no one could. Not to this day. Then over the next few months, there were three more exonerated men, freed because their sentence hinged on a jailhouse informant or new DNA technology proved beyond a shadow of doubt their innocence. We then had the dubious distinction of exonerating more men than we had executed. Thirteen men found innocent, twelve executed. As I reported yesterday, there is not a doubt in my mind that the number of innocent men freed from our Death Row stands at seventeen, with the pardons of Aaron Patterson, Madison Hobley, Stanley Howard, and Leroy Orange.

That is an absolute embarrassment. Seventeen exonerated death row inmates is nothing short of a catastrophic failure. But the thirteen, now seventeen, men are just the beginning of our sad arithmetic in prosecuting murder cases. During the time we have had capital punishment in Illinois, there were at least thirty-three other people wrongly convicted on murder charges and exonerated. Since we reinstated the death penalty there are also ninety-three people—ninety-three—where our criminal justice system imposed the most severe sanction and later rescinded the sentence or even released them from custody because they were innocent.

How many more cases of wrongful conviction have to occur before we can all agree that the system is broken? . . . The facts I have seen in reviewing each and every one of these cases raised questions not only about the innocence of people on death row, but about the fairness of the death penalty system as a whole. If the system was making so many errors in determining whether someone was guilty in the first place, how fairly and accurately was it determining which guilty defendants deserved to live and which deserved to die? What effect was race having? What effect was poverty having?

And in almost every one of the exonerated seventeen, we not only have breakdowns in the system with police, prosecutors, and judges, we have terrible cases of shabby defense lawyers. There is just no way to sugar-coat it. There are defense attorneys who did not consult with their clients, did not investigate the case, and were completely unqualified to handle complex death penalty cases. They often didn't put much effort into fighting a death sentence. If your life is on the line, your lawyer ought to be fighting for you. As I have said before, there is more than enough blame to go around. I had more questions.

In Illinois, I have learned, we have 102 decision makers. Each of them is politically elected, each beholden to the demands of their community and, in some cases, to the media or especially vocal victims' families. In cases that have the attention of the media and the public, are decisions to seek the death penalty more likely to occur? What standards are these prosecutors using? Some people have assailed my power to commute sentences, a power that literally hundreds of legal scholars from across the country have defended. But prosecutors in Illinois have the ultimate commutation power, a power that is exercised every day. They decide who will be subject to the death penalty, who will get a plea deal or even who may get a complete pass on prosecution. By what objective standards do they make these decisions? We do not know, they are not public. There were more than one thousand murders last year in Illinois. There is no doubt that all murders are horrific and cruel. Yet, less than two percent of those murder defendants will receive the death penalty. That means more than ninety-eight percent of victims' families do not get, and will not receive, whatever satisfaction can be derived from the execution of the murderer. Moreover, if you look at the cases, as I have done—both individually and collectively—a killing with the same circumstances might get forty years in one county and death in another county. I have also seen where codefendants who are equally or even more culpable get sentenced to a term of years, while another less culpable defendant ends up on death row.

In my case-by-case review, I found three people that fell into this category, Mario Flores, Montel Johnson, and William Franklin. Today I have commuted their sentences to a term of forty years to bring their sentences into line with their codefendants and to reflect the other extraordinary circumstances of these cases.

Supreme Court Justice Potter Stewart has said that the imposition of the death penalty on defendants in this country is as freakish and arbitrary as who gets hit by a bolt of lightning. For years the criminal justice system defended and upheld the imposition of the death penalty for the seventeen exonerated inmates from Illinois's death row. Yet when the real killers are charged, prosecutors have often sought sentences of less than death. In the

Ford Heights Four case, Verneal Jimerson and Dennis Williams fought the death sentences imposed upon them for eighteen years before they were exonerated. Later, Cook County prosecutors sought life in prison for two of the real killers and a sentence of eight years for a third. What made the murder for which the Ford Heights Four were sentenced to die less heinous and worthy of the death penalty twenty years later with a new set of defendants? . . . As I prepare to leave office, I had to ask myself whether I could really live with the prospect of knowing that I had the opportunity to act, but that I failed to do so because I might be criticized. Could I take the chance that our capital punishment system might be reformed, that wrongful convictions might not occur, that enterprising journalism students might free more men from death row? A system that's so fragile that it depends on young journalism students is seriously flawed.

"There is no honorable way to kill, no gentle way to destroy. There is nothing good in war. Except its ending." That's what Abraham Lincoln said about the bloody war between the states. It was a war fought to end the sorriest chapter in American history—the institution of slavery. While we are not in a civil war now, we are facing what is shaping up to be one of the great civil rights struggles of our time. Stephen Bright of the Southern Center for Human Rights has taken the position that the death penalty is being sought with increasing frequency in some states against the poor and minorities. . . .

Is our system fair to all? Is justice blind? These are important human rights issues. . . . In 1994, near the end of his distinguished career on the Supreme Court of the United States, Justice Harry Blackmun wrote an influential dissent in the body of law on capital punishment. Twenty years earlier he was part of the court that issued the landmark *Furman* decision. The Court decided that the death penalty statutes in use throughout the country were fraught with severe flaws that rendered them unconstitutional. Quite frankly, they were the same problems we see here in Illinois. To many, it looked liked the *Furman* decision meant the end of the death penalty in the United States. This was not the case. Many states responded to *Furman* by developing and enacting new and improved death penalty statutes. In 1976, four years after it had decided *Furman,* Justice Blackmun joined the majority of the United States Supreme Court in deciding to give the states a chance with these new and improved death penalty statutes. There was great optimism in the air. . . .

But twenty years later, after affirming hundreds of death penalty decisions, Justice Blackmun came to the realization, in the twilight of his distinguished career, that the death penalty remains fraught with arbitrariness, discrimination, caprice, and mistake. He expressed frustration with a twenty-year struggle to develop procedural and substantive safeguards. In a now-famous dissent he wrote in 1994, "From this day forward, I no longer shall tinker with the machinery of death."[2] . . . Three times I proposed reforming the system with a package that would restrict the use of jailhouse snitches, create a statewide panel to determine death-eligible cases, and reduce the number of crimes eligible for death. These reforms would not have created a perfect system, but they would have dramatically reduced the chance for error in the administration of the ultimate penalty.

The governor has the constitutional role in our state of acting in the interest of justice and fairness. Our state constitution provides broad power to the governor to issue reprieves, pardons, and commutations. Our Supreme Court has reminded inmates petitioning them that the last resort for relief is the governor. At times the executive clemency power has perhaps been a crutch for courts to avoid making the kind of major change that I believe our system needs.

Our systemic case-by-case review has found more cases of innocent men wrongfully sentenced to death row. Because our three-year study has found only more questions about the fairness of the sentencing; because of the spectacular failure to reform the system; because we have seen justice delayed for countless death row inmates with potentially meritorious claims; because the Illinois death penalty system is arbitrary and capricious—and therefore immoral—"I no longer shall tinker with the machinery of death."

I cannot say it more eloquently than Justice Blackmun.

The legislature couldn't reform it.
Lawmakers won't repeal it.
But I will not stand for it.
I must act.

Our capital system is haunted by the demon of error, error in determining guilt, and error in determining who among the guilty deserves to die. Because of all of these reasons today I am commuting the sentences of all death row inmates. This is a blanket commutation. I realize it will draw ridicule, scorn, and anger from many who oppose this decision. They will say I am usurping the decisions of judges and juries and state legislators. But as I have said, the people of our state have vested in me to act in the interest of justice. Even if the exercise of my power becomes my burden I will bear it. Our constitution compels it. I sought this office, and even in my final days of holding it I cannot shrink from the obligations to justice and fairness that it demands. There have been many nights where my staff and I have been deprived of sleep in order to conduct our exhaustive review of the system. But I can tell you this: I will sleep well knowing I made the right decision. As I said when I declared the moratorium, it is time for a rational discussion on the death penalty. While our experience in Illinois has indeed sparked a debate, we have fallen short of a rational discussion. Yet if I did not take this action, I feared that there would be no comprehensive and thorough inquiry into the guilt of the individuals on death row or of the fairness of the sentences applied.

To say it plainly one more time—the Illinois capital punishment system is broken. It has taken innocent men to a hair's breadth escape from their unjust execution. Legislatures past have refused to fix it. Our new legislature and our new governor must act to rid our state of the shame of threatening the innocent with execution and the guilty with unfairness. In the days ahead, I will pray that we can open our hearts and provide something for victims' families other than the hope of revenge. Lincoln once said: "I have always found that mercy bears richer fruits than strict justice."[3] I can only hope that will be so. God bless you. And God bless the people of Illinois.

Governor George Ryan of Illinois delivered a fuller version of this speech on January 11, 2003, at the Northwestern University School of Law.

### Editor's Notes

1. Edmund G. (Pat) Brown with Dick Adler, *Public Justice, Private Mercy: A Governor's Education on Death Row* (New York: Weidenfeld and Nicolson, 1989), 44. Pat Brown was governor of California from 1959 through 1966 (he died in 1996) during which time he commuted twenty-three death sentences and executed thirty-six people. At the age of eighty-three, he concluded his book on page 163 with these words: " . . . the longer I live, the larger loom those fifty-nine decisions about justice and mercy that I had to make as governor. They didn't make me feel godlike then: far from it, I felt just the opposite. It was an awesome, ultimate power over

the lives of others that no person or government should have, or crave. And looking back over their names and files now, despite the horrible crimes and the catalog of human weaknesses they comprise, I realize that each decision took something out of me that nothing—not family or work or hope for the future—has ever been able to replace." Brown died in 1996.

2. U.S. Supreme Court Justice Harry A. Blackmun, dissenting, *Callins v. Collins,* Feb. 22, 1994.

3. Abraham Lincoln, speech in Washington, D.C. in 1865.

## AMERICA DOES NOT NEED CAPITAL PUNISHMENT

### Michael B. Ross, Death Row, Connecticut

"When we abolished the punishment for treason that you should be hanged and then cut down while still alive, then disemboweled while still alive, and then quartered, we did not abolish that punishment because we sympathized with traitors, but because we took the view that this was a punishment no longer consistent with our self-respect."[1] These words, spoken by Lord Chancellor Gardiner during the 1965 death penalty abolition debates in the British Parliament, illustrate the feeling of most individuals opposed to capital punishment. It's not sympathy toward the murderer that we feel; indeed, most of us feel a great deal of anger and revulsion toward all murderers and their actions. Our objection is that the death penalty is a complete renunciation of all that is embodied in our concept of humanity. More simply put, executions degrade us all.

In today's society, the execution process is far removed from most individual citizens. We may, or more likely may not, be aware of the criminal acts that put an individual on death row—and if we are, it is usually only through sensationalized press accounts—but very few of us know of the human being whom society has condemned to death. Even fewer of us have witnessed, or ever will witness, an actual execution. They are carried out in the middle of the night, in the dark, away from us all, to hide what they really are: a barbaric punishment symbolic of our less civilized past.

The public is kept as far away as possible from the whole process to keep them from seeing that human beings—real flesh and blood, real people—are being put to death. This deliberate dehumanization of the entire process makes it easier for us to distance ourselves from capital punishment and to accept it as "something government does," which in turn allows us to avoid accepting individual responsibility for the consequences of such actions. But we are in fact responsible, for our state and federal government are killing people in our names.

There are acceptable alternatives to capital punishment that are more in line with the values of our supposedly enlightened and humanistic society. The state is supposed to be the pillar of our ideals, and its institutions should emulate the best values of our society. Are not the greatest of these values our compassion, our concern for human rights, and our capacity for mercy? By continuing to conduct executions, aren't we undermining the very foundations of our greatness?

As Zimbabwe poet Chenjerai Hove wrote, "The death sentence is abominable, as abominable as the crime itself. Our society must be based on love, not hatred and victimization. Our penal code must be based on rehabilitation rather than annihilation."[2] For so long as the spirit of vengeance maintains the slightest vestige of respectability, so long as it pervades the public mind and infuses its evil upon the statute books of law, we will make no headway toward the control of crime in our society.

There are suitable alternatives. Individuals who are a danger to society must be removed from society. Society has the right to protect itself; there is no disputing that. If rehabilitation is not possible, or is not a consideration, then that removal must be made permanent, but that permanent removal need not take the form of the death penalty. Those who favor the abolition of capital punishment do not advocate releasing convicted murderers into society. The choice is not between the death penalty and unconditional release, but between the death penalty and meaningful long-term sentences. Life without the possibility of parole, or a natural life sentence, meets the necessary requirements of society without being excessively brutal or barbaric.

Feelings of retribution, vengeance, blood atonement, and the like are difficult to suppress. Perhaps there are some individuals who, in some sense, "deserve" to be executed. But the real question that needs to be asked is, do we really need the death penalty? In light of such suitable alternatives as natural life sentences, is society in general paying too high a price when it executes its own citizens?

It is time for us to acknowledge the death penalty for what it really is—barbaric savagery, pure and simple—and abolish it nationwide by replacing it with natural life sentences. By rejecting the seemingly simple solutions that compromise our values and undermine the fundamental principles of society, we maintain the greatness of our country. It is certainly true that by giving in to our basest emotions, we lower ourselves to the very level of the persons whom we wish to execute and in the process weaken the moral fibers that bind and protect our society.

While it is admittedly difficult at times, when we recognize the humanity of even the vilest criminals—when we acknowledge them as fellow human beings rather than as objects to be discarded—we pay ourselves the highest of tributes and celebrate our own humanity.

### Notes

1. Quoted by Ian Gray and Moira Stanley, *A Punishment in Search of a Crime: Americans Speak Out against the Death Penalty* (New York: Avon, 1989), 19.
2. Quoted by John Dzvinamurungu, "The Death Penalty Is a Violation of Human Rights," Amnesty International Zimbabwe seminar on the death penalty, section 5. Kubatana.net/docs/hr/a121m_deathpenalty_040709.doc.

## MY TURN

### William Van Poyck, Death Row, Virginia

On a quiet day almost twenty years ago, I watched two fellow prisoners at Florida State Prison enter Dana DeWitt's cell and stab him so viciously that his blood painted the walls and ceiling like a Jackson Pollock abstract. Neither the first nor last murder I would witness, I, nevertheless, marked it as one of life's broadening experiences, for it was the first time I personally saw a man confess to a crime he did not commit, and personally saw an innocent man sentenced to death. James "Pop" Agan, possessing a documented history of mental illness and driven by indiscernible imperatives, soon stepped forward. Pop not only confessed to Dana's murder, he insisted on pleading guilty, a strategy his court-appointed attorney, who conducted no independent investigation, fully embraced. At sentencing, Pop vociferously demanded a death sentence, and Judge Green obliged. Many years later the federal appellate court took Pop off the row, not because of his innocence, but based upon his trial attorney's blatant incompetence.

Seventeen years ago, Earl Washington, black, poor, and bearing a borderline I.Q., allegedly signed a confession helpfully typed up for him by police. In it, Earl, unable to read, "admitted" to the brutal rape and murder of a young woman in bucolic Culpeper, Virginia. No other corroborating evidence existed. Earl protested his innocence. But who would listen? Earl was sentenced to death. On the eve of execution, then-Governor Douglas Wilder, troubled by the facts, commuted Earl's sentence to life. Last year, faced with DNA evidence excluding Earl and implicating the true killer, Governor James Gilmore pardoned Earl.

Fourteen years ago, Frank Smith, poor, black, and owning an extensive documented history of mental illness, was arrested for the rape and murder of an eight year-old Fort Lauderdale girl. Though the only evidence was two questionable eyewitness identifications, Frank's trial attorney helpfully pled him not guilty by reason of insanity, a de facto guilty plea because it concedes the defendant committed the crime. Relieved of its burden of proof the state easily convicted and sentenced Frank to death. One eyewitness later recanted, testifying that police pressured her to identify Frank.

In 1972, serving life for a Miami robbery and tutored by an ex-judge doing life for double murder, I dedicated myself to studying law. Infused with the Panglossian confidence of a neophyte and the fervency of a zealot convinced of the inherent justness of the system, I set out on my odyssey. In 1988, my own personal tides propelled me to death row for my part in a botched attempt to free a friend from a prison transport van in downtown West Palm Beach, during which my co-defendant shot a prison guard.

I celled close to Frank Smith for ten years. Crazy as Hamlet, often behaving irrationally, Frank was easily overlooked and looked down upon by prisoners and staff alike. Frank shuffled around Florida State Penitentiary in quiet desperation, convicted of and ostracized for a crime he said he did not commit. In his deepest moments of private pain Frank sometimes came to me, painfully deferential, his taped-up state eyeglasses framing a face without happiness or anticipation of any, clutching tattered legal papers as indecipherable to him as a Mandelstam poem. I would patiently explain the merits of his lawyer's latest motion, even as I blithely assumed his guilt. I should have known better. I can still hear Frank's gravelly voice, like a refrain in a minor key, reaching up through his psychosis, claiming his innocence with the same passionate articulation he employed to proclaim himself a messenger of God. Perhaps he was. People were, Frank assured me, plotting on him. Perhaps they were. Who would listen?

In January 2000, Frank Smith, stricken by cancer, still enduring his own solitude, quietly died on the other side of truth. Ten months later the FBI released its DNA report conclusively excluding Frank. The assistant attorney general, doubtless a dedicated public servant, expressed shock and dismay that she had so earnestly sought the execution of an innocent man for so many years. "I was certain he was guilty," she lamented. The case has been reopened. Who will listen to the voices of those murdered by the true killers while Frank and Earl languished in prison?

Fourteen years after I stood up in a West Palm Beach courtroom to demand the then-nascent DNA testing that could conclusively establish I was not the triggerman, the bloody clothes remain untested. Though the state now belatedly concedes I was not the shooter, they vigorously occupied the opposite position at trial, and I was sentenced to death by a jury and judge that believed them.

You need not study law for twenty-eight years to discern the common threads in the warp and woof of this fabric. Cases like Pop, Earl, and Frank are as common and close as yesterday's *Chicago Tribune,* today's *Newsweek,* or tomorrow's segment of *Nightline.* Between them all lies a continuum of consequences. People inexplicably confess to crimes they did not commit; innocent people occupy death row; DNA tests go unconducted. To remain silent is to speak the lie of acquiescence. Who will listen?

William Van Poyck was transferred to Virginia's Death Row in 1999, following the death row murder of his co-defendant, Frank Valdes, allegedly by a group of prison guards. The guards await trial for murder.

## THE RING DECISION AND WHAT IT MEANS

Richard Rossi, Death Row, Arizona

On Monday, June 24, 2002, the U.S. Supreme Court handed down its decision in the Timothy Ring case. In its simplest terms, this landmark decision has overturned all the death penalty sentences in Arizona, Idaho, Montana, Nebraska, and Colorado. This is approximately 160 death sentences. Four other states will be partially affected.

The Ring case is based on *Apprendi v. New Jersey,* 530 U.S. 466 (2000). The Ring case challenged Arizona's sentencing scheme, claiming it violated the Sixth Amendment's jury trial guarantee by entrusting to a judge the finding of a fact that raises the defendant's maximum penalty. In Arizona, the law allowing a judge rather than a jury to do the sentencing had been upheld in *Walton v. Arizona* 497 U.S. 637 (1990). The Supreme Court has now declared that they erred in Walton and overturned the death penalty sentencing law because it allowed a sentencing judge, sitting without a jury, to find an aggravating circumstance necessary for the imposition of the death penalty. It is now clear that the *jury* must find any such aggravating circumstance, rather than the judge, if the death penalty is to be imposed.

Arizona will now call a special session of the legislature to rewrite the sentencing laws so that the death penalty can once again be imposed on criminal defendants. State Attorney General Janet Napolitano, who unsuccessfully argued the Ring case before the U.S. Supreme Court, has come forward in an attempt at damage control to declare that this decision will affect only 30 of the 127 prisoners on death row who are in the first stages of appeals in the state court. She does not envision any relief for those whose appeals have proceeded past the state court into the federal courts. Her interpretation is that there is no retroactivity available to the rest of us. It should be noted that Ms. Napolitano is running for governor of Arizona.[1] Federal public defender Dale Baich, an assistant, believes all 127 of the state's death row inmates should now be eligible for re-sentencing.

As with so many major court decisions, more questions have been raised than answered. There is the issue of retroactivity; whether the majority of Arizona's death row population who are past the initial stages of the state court appeals will prevail and be allowed a jury sentencing will have to be litigated in the courts. The state does not wish to acknowledge all of its previous mistakes in applying the death penalty, and the politicians certainly don't want to appear weak on crime by acquiescing to the dictates of the U.S. Supreme Court without some grandstanding. There are not many in the state government who will step forward and do what is politically unpopular. The sound bites keep saying that the public should not fear that these dangerous killers will be released back into society.

Even if the state made the decision that we were all to be re-sentenced by a jury, how can this be accomplished? How do you reconstitute old juries, many from decades past? What do you do about witnesses and jurors you can't find or who have died? To empanel new juries would be very expensive. An alternative that would have a jury listen to testimony read from a transcript seems an inadequate remedy. Perhaps the state will do as they did back in the 1970s when the death penalty was declared unconstitutional and simply sentence all the death row prisoners to a life sentence.

Therefore, at this point in time, a clear answer as to what this all means cannot be given. We are certainly in limbo. But what *can* be said is that for the first time since the 1970s, the state of Arizona's death penalty sentencing scheme is in complete ruins and the laws need to be rewritten. And for the first time in many years there is reason to smile, and hope is in the air for a better life. For without hope, there is no life.

### Note

1. Janet Napolitano was elected governor of Arizona in 2002.

## IS THERE SUCH A THING AS CLOSURE?

Richard Rossi, Death Row, Arizona

In June of 1999, the television program *48 Hours* broadcast an episode entitled "My Daughter's Killer." It details Mitzi Johnson Nalley, who was murdered by Jonathan Wayne Nobles in 1986 in Austin, Texas, on her twenty-first birthday. The program revolves around her mother, Paula Kurland, who struggled over the protestations of family and friends who did not understand her desire to meet face-to-face with her daughter's killer. Texas is one of a number of states that provide facilities whereby the prisoner and victim or victim's family members can undergo a series of counseling sessions with a prison counselor that will prepare them for a face-to-face meeting accompanied by the counselor.

The murder was both gruesome and needless. Nobles broke into the house through the back door. Mitzi and some girlfriends had returned from celebrating her twenty-first birthday. Mitzi was stabbed twenty-eight times and died. Her boyfriend, Ron Ross, was sleeping in another room. He awoke and was stabbed nineteen times. He ran outside the house where he collapsed. A neighbor called the police. In the struggle, Nobles was cut. Police followed a trail of blood when witnesses told them that Nobles had asked them for bandages and Band-Aids. Nobles was caught. He confessed on tape. He never showed remorse nor took responsibility for the crime, but rather blamed his bad childhood, mental problems, and drug abuse.

After a month-long trial, the jury took just three hours to find him guilty. He received the death penalty.

For many years Nobles refused to participate in the process that would lead to a face-to-face meeting with Paula Kurland. In the twelve years since the crime, Nobles underwent positive changes. He sincerely found religion. Finally he overcame his denial and agreed to counseling as preparation for a meeting with Paula. A large portion of the program is devoted to chronicling the pain and suffering that Paula went through. A homemade cedar chest serves as a shrine to Mitzi. It holds memories for Paula, who says that she wants to tell Nobles what he has done to her life. How much pain and suffering he has caused. What a monster he is. Then reconciliation and closure can occur.

One begins to suspect her motives of reconciliation and closure when she objects to Nobles's participation in a program that allows prisoners, even on a condemned row, to donate vital organs in return for a reduced sentence. She sees this as a ploy by Nobles, a way to cheat her out of her closure. And worse, by donating organs, there would be more of "him" walking around inside other people. She would thus be taunted. Perish the thought, more Nobles in this world! The day comes when they meet face to face. Paula wears a photo of Mitzi on her dress to remind Nobles of his actions. She gets a blessing from the prison priest. She loudly tells Nobles how he has ruined her life and caused her so much pain. He breaks down in tears and apologizes to her. He acknowledges that he can never comprehend her pain, that death is easy compared to this meeting with her. She breaks down, and they take a break. The entire meeting takes a full day. When she returns, they agree on how much of a monster he was. He states, "If I could give my life to bring her back, I would." She tells him that this is not enough. He is still remorseful, and says, "Sorry is not enough, I brought harm into our life—sorry is cheap." He has tried to change his life. Again he apologizes. She cannot forgive him, but she can give him forgiveness. Her God makes her do this. Forgiveness or not, she tells him she still wants to watch him die.

As execution day approaches, Paula states that she will finally get her life back. And if he does not die, if he gets a commutation, then what? Will her obsession for revenge drive her crazy and cause more pain? This is a possibility because Paula, like so many other victims, lives only in the world of pain caused by the crime. She cannot see the present. Victims and/or their families rarely comprehend that death row prisoners can come to grips with the tragedy and be genuinely remorseful of their crimes. That we can ever be rehabilitated.

Nobles's request to donate organs is turned down. Now Paula worries that Governor Bush may commute his death sentence. He does not. She is going to witness his execution. From his gurney, Nobles tells Paula he loves her and again says how sorry he is. Then he starts singing "Silent Night" until the poison that is flowing into his veins silences him forever. After the execution, she receives an envelope left from him to her. It contains a religious medal. She is shown putting it into the cedar chest that holds Mitzi's memories. The program ends there, but not this article.

Because I am a death row prisoner, some who read the following may assume I am being insensitive to the theory of closure. I plead no contest. In a society that is so fueled by hatred and revenge toward criminals, many victims and their families are told by prosecutors that they are being disloyal to the person who died if they don't want the murderer to die as well. The pressure leads them to believe that killing the killer is somehow going to make them whole again. This is not so. What this does is to allow them to be angry and hateful. When the execution is completed, all of these expectations of instant healing are not realized. Where is the closure? It was only false hope. There can never really be closure simply by killing another human being. We are just compounding the specter of pain and barbarity. The grief must be dealt with individually by the victim.

Execution is not the "magic pill" to right the wrongs of society. Should we stoop to the level of the killer? Are we not better? Closure is a cruel hoax. It is a neologistic term, a new word to give false hope and more pain to victims. It is the "pie in the sky" solution that more often plummets back down to earth so quickly and causes more pain than it ever eases. It is a "crap shoot" thrown with loaded dice. What are we teaching our children when we as a society kill in the name of justice? We only teach them that it is good to hate and kill for revenge. Vengeance by definition is "excessive." The relief sought is sour. The false hopes and jingoistic pronouncements of politicians and prosecutors who seek votes by fueling and fooling victims into clutching onto closure as a resolution of their anguish is a cruel trick. The sooner individuals come to terms with their loss, the sooner they will have peace. To be persuaded to wait years, decades even, in the false hope that the act of execution will end the grief and pain is a crime in itself. Closure does not occur by killing again. Execution is not the solution. Is it not time to end this madness and stop the pain?

## NOT IN MY NAME

### Celeste Dixon, member,
### Murder Victims' Families for Reconciliation

On August 18, 1986, I was in the U.S. Navy, stationed at Roosevelt Roads, Puerto Rico. That was the night my whole world fell apart. It was the night I found out about my mother's death. The devastation I felt was not only because it was so unexpected but also because of how it happened. She was murdered by a man who broke into my parents' home to steal what he could and sell it for money to buy drugs. It was a kind of death beyond my comprehension. Murder is something you read about in the papers: something that happens to people you don't know. It's not something that happens to you personally. How does one cope with murder? I had no idea but I was learning fast.

The first thing I did was fly home immediately for the funeral and to spend time with my family. I was only home for two weeks, though, and then had to go back to Puerto Rico for seven more months before my enlistment was up. Those seven months were probably the longest of my life. Even though I had friends to help me get through those dark days, I was separated from my family by an ocean, and that made me feel very lonely and isolated. The one thing that kept me going was the knowledge that I would be out in time to attend the trial of the man who had murdered her, a man named Michael Richards.

Being there for the trial had started to become very important to me, especially because the prosecutors had told us that they were going to try him for capital murder. One thing I was quickly discovering about murder is that while death due to accident or illness can leave you with nothing to focus your anger on, murder has an object for all the anger and sadness that wells up within you and threatens to overwhelm you. Any other kind of death only leaves you the option to rail against God, if you believe in God, or fate if you don't. But murder gives you a focus for your anger. Looking back after all this time I can understand why capital punishment seems so right at first to many family members of the victims—why it seemed so right to me at the time. Not only did I have someone to blame for my loss, but it also seemed to give some measure of control to us. We can do something to the person who caused us all this pain.

One thing is for sure, having that option made me think about capital punishment, which I had never done before in any serious way. Occasionally when the subject came up I had a vague sense that a life for a life seemed like a fair trade. But I didn't have any firm views on the subject, so I never questioned the prosecutors' decision to seek the death penalty in this man's case, mainly because, the more I listened to them the more I began to believe that his death would be just compensation for the death of my mother. Eventually I came to see it as something we all deserved. Any other outcome was simply unthinkable. So I attended every day of that first trial for two reasons: to hear the judge pronounce the sentence of death and to confront Michael Richards with the reality that Marguerite Dixon had a family that had been left behind to deal with the consequences of his crime. I was so full of anger and hate then that it frightens me now to think of what kind of person I was at the time.

But something totally unexpected happened to me in that courtroom. When Michael Richards's lawyers brought out the fact that he and his siblings had been abused as children, I started to feel some compassion for him. I couldn't help but compare his childhood with mine. If what his sister said was true (and the prosecutors tried to cast doubt on that) then he never knew like I did what it was like to have two parents who loved and cherished him. What I gathered from his sister's testimony was that his father had given him a home filled with abuse and humiliation. It was definitely not a place where anyone would have felt a sense of self-respect. I don't think that is an excuse for what he did, but knowing that, I began to understand how circumstances had made him the kind of person who could do something like that and put him in a place where it was likely to happen. Many times since then I have often wondered how law-abiding I would have grown up to be if I had not had the happy, loving home that I did have.

But when those thoughts began to enter my head I quickly pushed them aside. Not only was I still very angry, I also felt that I wasn't supposed to feel any sympathy for him. I had begun to see him as another human being and that was definitely not how the prosecutors saw him, or wanted us to see him, for that matter. To them, he was a monster who deserved to die. In order to keep us supportive of the death penalty, on their side, so to speak, we had to see him that way too. Not only the prosecutors, but all of society said it was right and natural for us to hate him and want him to die. To think any other way about him would mean that we didn't love our mother.

Even though I tried to keep thinking of him the way the prosecutors wanted me to, as a monster who deserved to die, I simply could not forget what happened in that courtroom. His sister's testimony had touched something in my heart. He became a fellow human being to me, someone who also could experience joy, sadness, pain, and disappointment like the rest of us. I didn't know it then, but that was only the beginning of my journey of healing. The next step came after the trial was over as my family and I were standing in the hallway outside the courtroom congratulating each other on our victory. Although I did feel happy at the time, more than anything else, I felt a sense of relief. I had a sense that justice had been served. That we had only gotten what we deserved.

While we were standing there I happened to see his mother standing a few feet away, momentarily alone, and crying. She wasn't just crying, she was sobbing terribly. My heart went out to her because I realized that the news, which had made us so happy, had broken her heart. We had just heard that the man who had murdered our mother was going to die, but she had just heard that her son was going to die. It also occurred to me that it didn't matter how he died, his family would still feel his loss just as keenly as we had felt the loss of our mother. Without even thinking about it I walked over to her, hugged her and told her I was sorry.

I realize now that I probably never really believed in capital punishment, I just allowed myself to be influenced by the expectations of those around me who naturally assumed I would want this man to die. I didn't change my mind right away about the death penalty. It took me about a year to process all these events and make some sense of them, but by the time I started attending the University of Texas at Austin in the fall of 1988, I had reached the conclusion that capital punishment was wrong. Killing him is not going to bring my mother back. All it will do is bring more grief and suffering to his family. In fact, the more I thought about what capital punishment actually means, the more I hated what it stood for. I found myself actively wishing for another human being to die and I didn't like the way that made me feel. If what he did was wrong, then having the state kill him couldn't be right either. Murder is murder, whether it's done by an individual or by the state.

Once I came to the conclusion that capital punishment was wrong, I thought that I had come to the end of my journey. After all, I no longer wanted this man to die. I thought that was enough. I had even begun to speak to people about my feelings on the death penalty. In every debate about capital punishment the trump card that is supposed to stop those against it in their tracks and win the argument is the statement "You'd feel differently if it happened to someone in your family." Naturally I was now in a position to come back with the information that it had happened to someone in my family and I was still opposed to it. After a while I started to feel a little proud of myself for being able to say that. It's the dangerous, self-righteous "Oh what a good person I am" syndrome. The thing about pride, though, is that if you give into it, sooner or later God usually gives you a lesson in humility. I was missing the point with that approach, because I didn't realize that rejecting the death penalty as punishment for his crime was not the same as forgiving him for what he did. And no matter if I forgave him or not, I shouldn't feel any pride about rejecting the violence of capital punishment considering how my views on the subject developed in the first place.

My humility lesson came six years later while I was on a retreat in 1994. I happened to find a book in the retreat center library about the lives of seven women saints. The main reason I had gone on this retreat in the first place was to try and find some direction for my life. This book looked like it might be helpful, especially since I had a strong feeling at the time that God was calling me to be a nun. All the stories were interesting, but none of them really provided me with any kind of inspiration until I came to the story of Maria Goretti. I had never heard of her, or her story, so I was completely unprepared for the impact it would have on me.

Maria was a young Italian peasant girl who died around the turn of the century. She was stabbed to death by her seventeen-year-old neighbor, Allesandro, when she resisted his attempt to rape her. The doctors did what they could for her, but they could not save her life. The parish priest was called in to bring her communion, administer the last rites, and to wait with her until she died. As he sat by her side, trying to comfort her, the priest asked Maria if she could forgive Allesandro for what he had done to her, just as Jesus had forgiven those who nailed him to the cross. Without hesitation she said yes. Eventually that "yes" would change Allesandro's life. He was sentenced to forty years in prison, where at first he was defiant and unrepentant. Then one night he dreamed that Maria came to him bringing white flowers as a symbol of her forgiveness. From that point on his life was changed. He became a model prisoner and actually had two years taken off his sentence for good behavior. When he got out of prison he went immediately to Maria's mother to ask for her forgiveness as well. She told him that if her Maria could forgive him she could do no less. In a very fitting end to the story, both of them were together in St. Peter's Square in Rome when Maria was canonized as a saint.

As I read this story I was unprepared for the impact it had on me. Before I had even finished I started to cry because I realized how close to home it was. I couldn't help but compare this story to my own experience and immediately began to think about my mother and how her death had affected my life. At first I found myself naturally sympathizing with Maria's mother. After all, who could better understand what she was going through than I? But as I reflected on the story more throughout the weekend, I unexpectedly found myself feeling happy for Allesandro because of the peace Maria's forgiveness brought to him. To my complete surprise, what struck me as the most important part of the story was how Maria's forgiveness allowed him to come to terms with what he had done, which in turn enabled him to forgive himself and find some peace in his life.

With a little help from the nun who was directing the retreat I was able to realize that through Maria's story God was asking me to forgive the man who murdered my mother. As I sat under those trees on the grounds of the retreat center, I found myself filled with an incredible love for him. As I marveled at how I could actually feel that way towards him I realized that God had given me just a tiny glimpse of what his love is like. The love I felt for him was only a reflection of the love God feels for him. Once I understood how much God loves all of us, no matter what we've done, it was simply impossible for me to hate him. I prayed for him that weekend and I still pray for him.

What I have come to understand is that God offered me a chance to forgive him because he wanted to give me the gift of peace that comes with it. It was really for my sake first that I have forgiven this man. Once I let go of my hatred for him I was able to properly mourn for my mother and to reclaim her memory. Hating him had robbed me of that memory because I could never think of her without torturing myself with images of what her death must have been like. Those images kept me from remembering all the good things about her life. Now I don't think about how she died anymore, but about how she lived. I think about all the joy and happiness she brought to my life and count myself blessed for the time I did have with her instead of feeling cheated of the time taken away from me by her death.

The final step in the journey came in the summer of 1997 when I began to work on a book about the impact capital punishment has on victims' family members. My main focus is studying the role forgiveness plays in the healing process for family members dealing with the aftermath of a murder. As I was interviewing family members who either never believed in capital punishment or no longer believed in it, I spoke with several who had actually forgiven the perpetrators, either in person or by letter. All of them urged me to do the same for Michael Richards. Thinking about their experience made me realize that my forgiveness of him had helped me, but it wouldn't help him if I didn't let him know about it. Although it took me several months to compose the letter and actually send it I finally offered my forgiveness to him in January of 1998. We exchanged a few letters but I did not feel a need to correspond with him. Although I did find a very warm, interesting individual the process of communicating with the man who killed my mother proved to be too uncomfortable. It has been enough for me to let him know I forgive him.

The most surprising discovery of all has been that the offer of that forgiveness has not been the end of my journey. The most valuable lesson I have learned in all of this is that forgiveness is not a one-time deal. It is not done and then over with. It is a process that continues every day. Every day I have to continue to forgive Michael Richards and remind myself that he is human like all of us, and that none of us are beyond committing the kind of mistake he made given a particular set of circumstances.

## THE ELECTRIC CHAIR AND THE CHAIN GANG: CHOICES AND CHALLENGES FOR AMERICA'S FUTURE

Stephen B. Bright, Director,
Southern Center for Human Rights

The use of capital punishment in America today presents a number of fundamental moral issues about our society and our system of justice. It is fitting that we address those issues here at Notre Dame Law School, which has a well-deserved reputation for raising moral issues, for a deep commitment to justice, and for responding to human needs with compassion.

Our society and the legal profession are failing to meet the need for legal services of many of those most desperately in need of such services in cases involving the highest stake, life itself. There are, of course, urgent needs in other areas besides capital punishment. These include those accused of crimes which do not carry the death penalty: the poor, people of color, homeless people, people with mental impairments, people who are HIV positive, people in prisons and jails, and many others are without lawyers to represent them in cases which involve their freedom, their shelter, their survival.

Those needs will be greater when you graduate from law school than they are today. But there could be fewer jobs and fewer resources for those who respond. And, as you know, you will be saddled with enormous debts. This presents a challenge, but it should not deter you from responding. Indeed, my message to you is that you have no choice except to respond as the needs and the times demand it.

Let's examine the needs and how individuals and institutions may respond to them. Children and the poor are going to have a tremendous need for your services. The states are increasingly passing so-called welfare reform measures and Congress and the President are about to follow suit with a measure that will "end welfare as we know it." The result of these "reforms" will be to put thousands of children on heating grates to live.

But America's children can still count on their government to fulfill one promise. Both the federal and state governments are committed to spend up to $30,000 a year on every child in the United States. All that child must do to obtain this government support is to try to medicate his depression or despair with illegal drugs or commit some other crime. The state and federal governments are absolutely committed to having a maximum security prison cell for any child who commits a crime, especially if that child is a person of color.

Some of those accused of crimes will be entered in a lottery, a lottery rigged by race and poverty. Out of thousands eligible, about 250 will be condemned to be strapped down and shot, hung, gassed, electrocuted, or injected with lethal drugs. Other industrialized nations have abandoned the death penalty. Recently the Constitutional Court of South Africa unanimously found the death penalty to be cruel, unusual, and degrading punishment under that country's constitution.[1] But we continue to sentence people to death in the United States. The sad fact is that, increasingly, our state and federal governments are offering the young not hope, opportunity, and equality, but the threat of incarceration and execution. Last summer, President Clinton began running television advertisements proclaiming his support for the death penalty and tough sentencing laws. In 1994, he signed into law a crime bill providing for the death penalty for fifty federal crimes.

The federal death penalty was brought back in 1988. Since that time the Justice Department has approved fifty-four capital prosecutions. All but nine have been against people of color. During the Clinton administration, Attorney General Reno has approved twenty-seven capital prosecutions. Twenty were against African Americans. Yet despite this sorry record, even more capital crimes were adopted last year.

In addition to providing for more death, state and federal governments pass new measures each year to provide for more incarceration. Longer prison sentences, mandatory minimum sentences, unreasonable and inflexible sentencing guidelines and other legislation such as "three strikes and you're out" result in more people serving longer periods of time behind bars at enormous cost. The United States now imprisons more people than ever before—over 1.5 million in both prisons and jails—and has the highest incarceration rate of any country in the world.[2] To keep up with the growth in prison population will require the construction of 1,725 new prison beds each week.

And legislatures are moving to make life even more unbearable for those crowded into prisons and jails. Alabama has brought back the chain gang.[3] Its only purpose is degradation and humiliation of human beings for political points. A person cannot get much work done chained to another person. Alabama has also returned to the practice of having prisoners stand in the hot Alabama sun for ten hours a day breaking rocks with ten-pound sledgehammers.[4] This activity serves no practical purpose. There is no need for the crushed rock but apparently it serves political purposes.

Not long ago such barbarism would be seen as just another aberrational act by Alabama. Today, it starts a national trend. Arizona and Florida have already reinstated the chain gang, and other states are contemplating it as well. And the Alabama legislature, continuing its role as the trendsetter, is now considering a bill to return to caning as punishment for crime. Children even as young as thirteen are being prosecuted as adults, not just in Alabama, where fourteen- and fifteen-year-old children are serving sentences of life imprisonment without any possibility of parole, but all across the land.

As prisons and jails become even more overcrowded, conditions deteriorate. Yet legislation proposed in the United States Congress would restrict the ability of federal courts to provide relief for unconstitutional conditions in prisons.[5] This legislation is based on irresponsible assertions by the National Association of Attorneys General and members of Congress that prisoner lawsuits are about nothing more important than soggy sandwiches or being deprived of watching football games on television or the use of electronic games. Nothing is said about the unconscionable degradation and violence in America's prisons that was corrected only by order of federal courts in response to suits brought by prisoners. Judge Frank Johnson ordered the correction of barbaric conditions in Alabama's prisons twenty years ago. Judge Johnson found "horrendous" overcrowding, with inmates sleeping on mattresses in the hallways and next to urinals; prisons were "overrun with roaches, flies, mosquitoes, and other vermin"; mentally disturbed inmates were "dispersed throughout the prison population without receiving treatment"; and robbery, rape, extortion, theft, and assault were "everyday occurrences" among the general inmate population.[6]

Prisons in thirty-nine states and the District of Columbia have been put under some form of court supervision because of the failure of state officials to operate constitutional facilities. For example, a federal judge found that residents of the California State Prison at San Quentin were "regarded and treated as caged animals, not human beings."[7] At a prison in Pendleton, Indiana, the federal court found that inmates were shackled spread-eagle to metal bed frames for up to two-and-a-half days at a time and were "frequently denied the right to use the toilet and had to lie in their own filth."[8] At the Southern Center for Human Rights, our docket of suits on behalf of prisoners is not about melting ice cream but about the most fundamental human rights of people, such as the right to safety and security, to basic medical and mental health care.

It is the threat of punishment and degradation, not the promise of hope and opportunity, that we hold out to children who have the misfortune to be born into poverty, the victims of brutal racism, those who have the misfortune to be born into dysfunctional families, those who are the victims of physical, sexual and psychological abuse, and those who have the misfortune to be born with a deficit in intellectual functioning or some other mental impairment.

One would think that if all we hold out to these children is a prison cell, the chain gang, and the electric chair, at least we could provide a fair procedure with a good lawyer before we take away their lives or freedom and subject them to such suffering and degradation for the suffering and degradation they have caused others. And one would think that, at the very least, we would make sure that racial prejudice, which already puts so many at such a disadvantage, would not influence the severity of their punishment. But both fair procedures and the access to courts through competent and experienced counsel are being taken away even from those with the most desperate needs of all, those facing the executioner. And the courts are completely indifferent to the prominent role that race plays in the criminal justice system.

### Habeas Corpus

Since 1977, Chief Justice Rehnquist has waged a relentless war on the once great Writ of Habeas Corpus, which the Supreme Court described over thirty years ago as "the common law world's 'freedom writ.'"[9] It gives a person the right to go into federal court and assert that he or she has been imprisoned in violation of the Constitution. It gives a life-tenure federal judge the power, where there has been a constitutional violation, not to let the defendant go free, but to require the state to provide a new and fair trial. The Supreme Court once said "there is no higher duty than to maintain it unimpaired."[10]

But the Supreme Court under the leadership of Justice Rehnquist, later Chief Justice Rehnquist, has placed all manner of technicalities in the way of vindication of violations of the Bill of Rights.[11] And now Congress and the President are poised to finish off the Writ. The Anti-Terrorism Bill that has passed the Senate includes provisions which would limit even further the ability of federal judges to set aside an illegally obtained death sentence.[12] It will impose time limits that would treat capital cases like small claims cases.

This legislation would leave enforcement of the Bill of Rights primarily to state court judges. This sounds reasonable, but it overlooks the fact that state court judges in all but a handful of states must stand for election.[13] Those judges are not independent. In high-publicity, high-profile cases, enforcing the law may cost them their jobs. In the present political climate, an elected judge who grants relief in a capital case signs his or her own political death warrant.

Of course the most fundamental element of a fair process is the right to counsel, because without a lawyer, a person untrained in the law has no idea what his rights are or how to assert them. I am sure that many of you were inspired to go to law school, as I was, by Anthony Lewis's marvelous book, *Gideon's Trumpets* (1964). It is the story of Clarence Earl Gideon who was convicted in Florida and then filed his own handwritten petition with the United States Supreme Court saying it just was not fair that he did not have a lawyer at his trial. This ultimately led to the case of *Gideon v. Wainwright*,[14] which held that the poor person accused of a felony is entitled to a lawyer. Anthony Lewis observed after the decision, "It will be an enormous task to bring to life the dream of *Gideon v. Wainwright*—the dream of a vast, diverse country in which every person charged with a crime will be capably defended, no matter what his economic circumstances, and in which the lawyer representing him will do so proudly, without resentment at an unfair burden, sure of the support needed to make an adequate defense."[15]

Over thirty years after Gideon was decided, this dream has not been realized. There is no public defender's office in many jurisdictions; in some jurisdictions, the indigent defense work is assigned to the lowest bidder.[16] It was recently discovered that in Putnam County, Georgia, the local sheriff appointed lawyers to the cases of poor defendants and refused to appoint lawyers who would not agree to the plea dispositions proposed by the sheriff.[17]

Congress cut off all funding in the fall of 1995 for a very modest program to provide some measure of justice to those facing the death penalty—the post-conviction defender organizations or resource centers that had existed in twenty states. The resource centers, created in 1987, were a relatively small program for the size of the problem. All together they had about 200 lawyers to deal with the post-conviction representation of over 3,000 people condemned to death. But the young lawyers who were at the resource centers during their eight years of existence proved what a difference you can make if you tackle a problem, work hard at it, build an expertise, and are committed to justice.

Some of the resource centers' attorneys were right out of law school. Besides building their own expertise and applying it, they recruited lawyers from firms to provide pro bono representation. Many lawyers responded to the call. And they, working with the resource center lawyers, provided the highest quality of representation.

And they made a difference. Walter McMillian, who spent six years on Alabama's death row, is a free man today because the Alabama Resource Center proved that he was innocent of the murder for which he was condemned to die.[18] Lloyd Schlup is alive today because the resource center in Missouri established his innocence.[19] Curtis Lee Kyles is alive today because the resource center in Louisiana marshaled evidence of his innocence.[20]

In addition, these young lawyers, and the pro bono attorneys with whom they worked, exposed constitutional violations in other cases—violations such as failure to disclose exculpatory evidence, racial discrimination, and prosecutorial misconduct. These are not technicalities. These are constitutional violations that go to the very integrity and reliability of the system.

And because these lawyers and these programs made a difference, they came under attack by the National Association of Attorneys General, led by the new Attorney General of South Carolina who ran on a promise to replace the state's electric chair with an electric sofa so that more people could be executed at one time.[21] Apparently the attorneys general consider it a bad reflection on our criminal justice system that innocent people are being sentenced to death. The House and the Senate responded by cutting off all funding [for the Alabama Resource Center] last fall.

Those who depend upon government funding must recognize that a reality of our times is that if they are effective in helping the poor or people of color, there is a very substantial risk that the government will take away or reduce the funding or, as with the federal Legal Services Corporation, which makes legal assistance available to the poor in civil cases, interfere with their ability to help their clients by placing restrictions on their practices. Of course, that has always been the case in many states; the only programs that received funding were the ones that were completely ineffective. But at least the federal government could be counted on for some programs and the federal courts for some measure of justice that could not be obtained in the state courts. But now there is no commitment to access to the courts or to fairness on the part of our national leadership in either party.

The result is that many who most need legal assistance are without it. Many of the 3,000 men, women, and children on death rows throughout the country are without counsel. Many of the lawyers from the capital resource centers who would have provided representation have gone to other jobs in other states. This leaves two choices. One is the states can execute the condemned without providing counsel for the post-conviction stages of review. The Supreme Court has held there is no right to counsel in state post-conviction proceedings.[22] The other choice is to assign a lawyer who knows nothing about post-conviction practices and pay the lawyer a token amount for providing the appearance of some process. Alabama compensates lawyers $600 for handling post-conviction representation. An attorney who devotes the necessary time will be earning less than ten cents an hour. But the fees in Alabama are better than in Georgia, Mississippi, and some other states. They pay nothing.

If the states do provide counsel, we can expect to see the same quality of representation during post-conviction that we see at trial. And the quality of representation at trial in capital cases has been a disgrace to the legal profession.[23] For example, judges in Houston, Texas, have often appointed a lawyer to defend capital and other criminal cases who occasionally falls asleep during trial.[24] When a defendant in a capital case there once complained about his lawyer sleeping, the judge responded that the Constitution guarantees the accused a lawyer, but it does not guarantee that the lawyer must be awake.[25] The trial of a woman facing the death penalty in Alabama had to be suspended for a day because the lawyer appointed to defend her was too drunk to go forward.[26] The judge sent him to jail for a day to dry out and then produced both the client and lawyer from jail and resumed the trial. The client was sentenced to death.

Last month, I handled a post-conviction proceeding in a capital case in Georgia in which the court-appointed lawyers did not make one objection during the entire trial, which lasted only one-and-a-half days.[27] Only one motion was filed prior to trial. One of the attorneys appointed to defend the accused had never heard of two important Supreme Court decisions in Georgia capital cases, *Furman v. Georgia*[28] and *Gregg v. Georgia*,[29] which provide the structure for much of the Eighth Amendment law governing capital trials. Another lawyer who has handled a number of criminal and capital cases in Georgia was asked to name all of the criminal law decisions of which he was aware. He could answer only *Miranda* and *Dred Scott.*[30]

The Alabama Supreme Court affirmed a conviction and death sentence in a case after receiving a brief from the lawyer that was only one page long.[31]

The lawyer did not show up for oral argument. One might have expected the Alabama Supreme Court or the courts in the other cases I have described to call a halt to proceedings where the lawyering was so bad and appoint new counsel, not only to protect the rights of the accused, but also so that the court could do its job. Do these courts care at all about justice? How can a court decide a capital case based on a one-page brief and without oral argument? But the Alabama Supreme Court affirmed without ever having adequate briefing or any argument. The client was eventually executed.

Poor people do not choose their lawyers. They are assigned lawyers by state court judges, many of whom are elected and are more concerned about the next election than the Bill of Rights. We must ask, is it morally right to assign a poor person a lawyer who does not know the law, who does not care enough to investigate, who is incapable of properly handling such a serious case, and then penalize the poor person for errors made by the lawyer?

Another great moral and legal issue that courts continue to ignore is the role that racial prejudice plays in deciding who dies. Edward Horsley was executed in Alabama's electric chair on February 16, 1996. He was the eleventh African American put to death by Alabama of the fourteen who have been executed since the Supreme Court allowed resumption of capital punishment in 1976. He and his co-defendant were sentenced to death by all-white juries selected in Monroeville, Alabama.

Two African American men sentenced to death by an all-white jury in Utah were executed even though jurors discovered during a lunch recess a note which contained the words "Hang the Nigger's" [*sic*] and a drawing of a figure hanging on a gallows.[32] No court, state or federal, even had a hearing on such questions as who wrote the note, what influence it had on the jurors, or how widely it was discussed by the jurors. William Henry Hance was executed in Georgia without any court holding a hearing on the use of racial slurs by jurors who decided his fate.[33] The racial disparities in the infliction of the death penalty are undeniable,[34] yet courts refuse even to hold hearings on such ugly racial incidents as I have described here.

But even if our system could provide the person facing the death penalty with a fair and impartial judge, a responsible prosecutor who was beyond political influences, a capable defense lawyer, and a jury which represented a fair cross-section of the community, it would not eliminate the discrimination and unfairness in the infliction of the death penalty. No procedure employed by the court during jury selection or trial can eliminate the centuries of racial prejudice and discrimination in our history. Beyond that, the task of deciding who should live and who should die is simply too enormous for our court system. And our courts do not function best when caught up in the politics and passions of the moment, which is almost always the case when a capital trial is taking place.

I am reasonably confident that this sad situation is only going to get worse because no one in a leadership position speaks out against it. That was not always the case. Over thirty years ago, the Attorney General of the United States, Robert F. Kennedy, observed, "the poor person accused of a crime has no lobby." And he did something about it. He, the Attorney General of the United States, became a lobby for the poor person. He found responsible leaders on Capitol Hill who responded to his call. Together they brought about passage of the Criminal Justice Act to give lawyers to poor people accused of crimes in the federal courts. One opportunity that will be open to you upon graduation is to work at one of the federal defender offices all across the country now in existence thanks to the leadership of Attorney General Kennedy. Attorney General Kennedy supported the Criminal Justice Act not because he was soft on crime—Robert Kennedy was a tough prosecutor—but because he believed in fairness. It was as simple as that.

But after the election of 1994, as the state attorneys general and politicians in both parties moved to take away funding for the resource centers to remove the small fig leaf of fairness that did not begin to cover the injustices and inequities in the use of the death penalty, not a word of protest was heard from the White House or the Department of Justice.

Those of us who remember Robert Kennedy hoped that someone might at least say, "Wait, if we are going to have the death penalty, if we are going to kill our own people, even our children, at least we must give lawyers to those accused of crimes." And not just a stable of plug horses that would not be accepted by a decent glue factory, but real lawyers who know what they are doing. It is a matter of fairness. We hoped that someone might say, "Wait, we cannot gut the great writ of *habeas corpus*. Life and liberty are too precious. Even in this material world, life and liberty should have the protection of the federal courts." Our country could have benefited from a lesson in fairness and due process from the president or the attorney general or some of the leaders in Congress.

Those are some of the challenges. What can we do about them? Law schools and human rights organizations must come to the rescue. The legal profession must respond to the challenge. And you as individuals must respond to the problems I have described.

A number of law schools have responded. The University of Texas Law School now has a capital punishment clinic which provides an outstanding experience for students and desperately needed help for lawyers defending capital cases in that state. The Capital Clearinghouse at the Washington and Lee College of Law has helped improve the quality of representation in Virginia. Loan forgiveness programs are making it possible for law school graduates to take jobs which pay very little but allow them to respond to desperate needs. Yale and New York University are among the leaders in providing full loan forgiveness for students who go into public interest careers.

Our program, the Southern Center for Human Rights, has benefited tremendously in the last six years because each year we have had a Skadden Fellow, a new law graduate whose salary and benefits were paid for by the fellowship foundation of the law firm of Skadden, Arps, Slate, Meagher & Flom. Now in its seventh year, the Skadden program provides two-year fellowships for twenty-five law graduates. Thanks to that program, we have had three outstanding lawyers who would not have been with us otherwise. There are clients who are alive today who would be dead were it not for our Skadden Fellows. It is time for other firms to follow Skadden's lead.

Lawyers have a monopoly on access to justice; they have a duty to see that it is not only available to those who can pay. I also urge you to explore creating your own programs, your own nonprofit public interest law projects: not offices where lawyers get rich, but places where people get justice. But to do that, you must settle for less in material rewards than what other lawyers are receiving for their work.

It is easy to lose perspective. Remember that it is no sacrifice to receive the same income as that received by teachers, farmers, workers on the assembly line, and other good, decent working men and women who raise families and contribute to their communities. To the contrary, it is a great privilege to devote one's life to things that are important and about which you care passionately.

You who will someday graduate from law school have the opportunity to become what Martin Luther King Jr., in one of his many great sermons, called "drum majors for justice." Dr. King described the drum major for justice as one who speaks the truth no matter how unwelcome it may be and no matter how uncomfortable it may make the listener and as one who gives his or her life to serving others: to feeding the hungry, clothing the naked, and, particularly important for lawyers, to visiting those who are in prison, and to loving and serving humanity.[35] He described his goal as a drum major for justice: "I just want to be there in love and justice and in truth and in commitment to others, so that we can make of this old world a new world."[36]

Follow the example of a young lawyer who graduated from Howard Law School, opened a practice in Baltimore, and handled civil rights cases and became a great drum major for justice, Thurgood Marshall. Follow the example of a nun who ministered to the poor in the projects of New Orleans and on death row at Angola, Sister Helen Prejean.[37]

I offer my office as an example of what you can do only because it is the one I know something about and we have had some experience in surviving in hard times without much money. We have never received any government money. We must spread very thinly what little money we have to provide justice for those most in need of it. And that requires living a simple life, not letting a lot of material things clutter our existence.

We pay everyone the same, whether secretary, senior lawyer, or junior lawyer. Our annual salaries have been as low as $8,500. Now, everyone makes $23,000. You can live on this amount. I have lived on such a salary for the last thirteen years. But, of course, so have many other people in our society who work at jobs that are not nearly so interesting and fulfilling as what we do.

Consider practicing law not in Washington, New York, or the Bay Area, but in communities where there has never been a lawyer who would question the status quo, who would give African Americans the same representation as white people, who would give the poor the same representation as the rich. You can change that. Those communities are not hard to find. Get a map of any state in the Union. It will be full of them.

We live in a society where it is possible to isolate ourselves from the poverty, the racism, the injustices that affect the lives of so many people. The culture of becoming a lawyer is one in which there is almost overwhelming temptation to take the job that pays the most money to pay those debts; but then it is so easy to fall into a costly culture of BMWs, big houses, and summer homes. There is so much money available and so many good uses we can think of for it, that it is easy to give in to the twin evils of complacency and complicity.

I urge you to commit yourselves today not to do that. As Elie Wiesel said in accepting the Nobel Peace Prize, "Our lives no longer belong to us alone; they belong to all those who need us desperately."[38] I have not had enough time to describe all the desperate needs, only some of what needs to be done to work toward finally realizing the promise of Clarence Earl Gideon's case.

Your time, your talents, and your commitment are urgently needed. Let me give you an example of how much you are needed. Cornelius Singleton, a mentally retarded African American youth on death row in Alabama, went eight years without seeing the lawyer assigned to represent him in post-conviction proceedings. Can you imagine what it must be like to be on death row for eight years and not see a lawyer? Not to know whether you are going to be executed the next day, the next week, the next year? To have no idea what is even happening on your case? Do you see what a difference you could make if you had been Cornelius Singleton's lawyer? Just by going to see him, by counseling him, you would have provided a valuable service.

We cannot solve all the problems, but we can lend a helping hand and our professional skills to those who most need us. Like those who helped slaves escape to freedom as part of the Underground Railroad before the Civil War, we can help people reach safe passage, one at a time, from the injustices which threaten to destroy them.

And what a difference you can make to those individuals whom you help. Last summer, one of my clients, Tony Amadeo, who had been condemned to die by Georgia when he was only eighteen years old but whose death sentence was set aside due to racial discrimination,[39] graduated *summa cum laude* from Mercer University. Do not let anyone tell you that you cannot make a difference as a lawyer. And we can bear witness to the injustices we see until we shake our fellow citizens out of the indifference which we see about us.

I leave you with the challenge issued by Justice Thurgood Marshall, six months before he died, in accepting the Liberty Bell Award in Philadelphia. Justice Marshall was frail. He was in a wheelchair. But by the end of his remarks, it was observed that "his voice was as booming as [it had been] in those magnificent times when he argued before the Supreme Court."[40] Justice Marshall said:

> I wish I could say that racism and prejudice are only distant memories and that liberty and equality were just around the bend. I wish I could say that America has come to appreciate diversity and to see and accept similarity. But as I look around, I see not a nation of unity but of division, Afro and white, indigenous and immigrant, rich and poor, educated and illiterate. We cannot play ostrich. Democracy cannot flourish among fear. Liberty cannot bloom among hate. Justice cannot take root amid rage. We must go against the prevailing wind. We must dissent from the indifference. We must dissent from the apathy. We must dissent from a government that has left its young without jobs, education, or hope. We must dissent from the poverty of vision and an absence of leadership. We must dissent because America can do better, because America has no choice but to do better. Take a chance, won't you? Knock down the fences that divide. Tear apart the walls that imprison. Reach out; freedom lies just on the other side.[41]

That's the challenge. To continue the work which Justice Marshall so nobly advanced in his great career at the bar. Now it's your turn. I hope to see you in the courts.

Lecture presented to law students at the Notre Dame Law School, February 15, 1996

## Notes

1. *The State v. Makwanyane,* Constitutional Court of South Africa, June 6, 1995, reprinted in *Human Rights Law Journal* 16 (1995): 154.

2. "1,725 New Prisons Beds a Week; Biggest 1–Year Spurt in Inmate Population," *Atlanta Constitution* (Dec. 4, 1995): 1A (reporting a Department of Justice announcement that there are 1.1 million inmates in prison and another 484,000 in jails, giving the United States an incarceration rate of 565 per 100,000, higher than even Russia, which had been the world leader).

3. Rick Bragg, "Chain Gangs to Return to Roads of Alabama," *New York Times* (Mar. 26, 1995): 16; Brent Staples, "The Chain Gang Show," *New York Times Magazine* (Sept. 17, 1995): 62.

4. "Alabama to Make Prisoners Break Rocks," *New York Times* (July 29, 1995): 5.

5. Stop Turning Out Prisoners Act, H.R. 667, 104 Cong., 1st Sess. (1995). After some modification, the restrictions were adopted as the Prison Litigation Reform Act by the Congress as a rider to the Omnibus Rescission and Appropriations Act of 1996, Public Law 104–134, and signed into law by President Clinton on April 26, 1996.

6. *Pugh v. Locke,* 406 F. Supp. 318, 322–27 (M.D. Ala. 1976), aff'd as modified, 559 F.2d 283 (5th Cir. 1977), rev'd in part on other grounds, 438 U.S. 781 (1978) (per curiam).

7. *Toussaint v. McCarthy,* 597 F. Supp. 1388, 1400 (N.D. Cal. 1984), aff'd in relevant part, 801 F.2d 1080 (9th Cir. 1986), cert. denied, 481 U.S. 1069 (1987).

8. *French v. Owens,* 777 F.2d 1250, 1253 (7th Cir. 1985), cert. denied, 479 U.S. 817 (1986). These are, of course, only a few of the many examples of unconscionable constitutional violations that could be found in America's prisons before they were corrected by federal lawsuits brought on behalf of prisoners. For an excellent and sobering account of conditions in the Mississippi State Penitentiary over the decades before federal court intervention, see David M. Oshinski, *"Worse than Slavery": Parchman Farm and the Ordeal of Jim Crow Justice* (New York: Simon & Schuster, 1996); see also Nils Christie, *Crime Control as Industry: Toward GULAGS, Western Style?* (New York: Routledge, 1993) (a description of failures of the American prison system by an eminent Norwegian criminologist); Susan P. Sturm, "The Legacy and Future of Corrections Litigation," 142 *University of Pennsylvania Law Review* 639 (1993) (describing reforms accomplished through corrections litigation).

9. *Smith v. Bennett,* 365 U.S. 708, 712 (1961).

10. Ibid., 713 (quoting *Bowen v. Johnson,* 306 U.S. 19, 26 [1939]).

11. The Court has limited the availability of the Writ to vindicate constitutional rights by adopting strict rules of procedural default; see, for example, *Smith v. Murray,* 477 U.S. 527, 533–36 (1986); *Engle v. Isaacs,* 456 U.S. 107, 130–34 (1982); *Wainwright v. Sykes,* 433 U.S. 72, 88–91 (1977); Timothy J. Foley, "The New Arbitrariness: Procedural Default of Federal Habeas Claims in Capital Cases," 23 *Loyola of Los Angeles Law Review* 193 (1989); by excluding most Fourth Amendment claims from habeas corpus review, *Stone v. Powell,* 428 U.S. 465 (1976); by requiring deference to fact-finding by state court judges, see, for example, *Patton v. Yount,* 467 U.S. 1025 (1984); *Sumner v. Mata,* 439 U.S. 539 (1981), after remand, 455 U.S. 591 (1982), after second remand, 464 U.S. 957 (1983); by making it more difficult for a petitioner to obtain an evidentiary hearing to prove a constitutional violation, *Keeney v. Tamayo-Reyes,* 504 U.S. 1 (1992); by adopting an extremely restrictive doctrine regarding the retroactivity of constitutional law, *Teague v. Lane,* 489 U.S. 288 (1989); James S. Liebman, "More than 'Slightly Retro:' The Rehnquist Court's Rout of Habeas Corpus Jurisdiction in *Teague v. Lane,*" *New York University Review of Law and Social Change* 18 (1991): 537; by reducing the harmless error standard for constitutional violations recognized in federal habeas review, *Brecht v. Abrahamson,* 507 U.S. 619 (1993); and by restricting when a constitutional violation may be raised in a second habeas petition, *McCleskey v. Zant,* 499 U.S. 467 (1991).

12. The Antiterrorism and Effective Death Penalty Act of 1996, signed into law by President Clinton on April 24, 1996, Public Law 104–132, requires deference by federal courts to decisions of state courts unless the decision is "contrary to, or involved an unreasonable application of, clearly established Federal law," ibid. § 104(3); establishes a statute of limitation for the filing of habeas corpus petitions, ibid. § 101; further restricts when a federal court may conduct an evidentiary hearing, ibid. § 104(4); and adds new barriers to hearing a successive habeas corpus petition, ibid. § 105; see David Cole, "Destruction of the Habeas Safety Net," *Legal Times* (June 19, 1995), 30.

13. Stephen B. Bright and Patrick J. Keenan, "Judges and the Politics of Death: Deciding Between the Bill of Rights and the Next Election in Capital Cases," 75 *Boston University Law Review* (1995): 759, 779 n.89 (in 32 of the 38 states that have the death penalty, state court judges must stand for periodic election or retention).

14. 372 U.S. 335 (1963).

15. Anthony Lewis, *Gideon's Trumpet* (New York: Random House, 1964), 205.

16. For a description of the lack of indigent defense systems and the state of indigent defense, see Stephen B. Bright, "Counsel for the Poor: The Death Sentence Not for the Worst Crime but for the Worst Lawyer," 103 *Yale Law Journal* (1994): 1835, 1849–55.

17. Judy Bailey, "Does Sheriff Run Putnam's Indigent Defense?" *Fulton County Daily Rep.* (Nov. 10, 1995): 1.

18. Peter Applebome, "Black Man Freed after Years on Death Row in Alabama," *New York Times* (Mar. 3, 1993): A1.

19. See *Schlup v. Delo,* 115 S. Ct. 851 (1995).

20. *Kyles v. Whitley,* 115 S. Ct. 1555 (1995) regards finding a violation of due process by the prosecution due to failure to turn over exculpatory evidence.

21. Marcia Coyle, "Republicans Take Aim at Death Row Lawyers," *National Law Journal* (Sept. 11, 1995): A1, A25, describes the effort of South Carolina's Attorney General and other members of the National Association of Attorneys General to eliminate funding for the post-conviction defender organizations even though the organizations had established the innocence of at least four men condemned to die; David Cole points out that eliminating funding for the capital representation centers would increase the cost of providing representation, but decrease the quality in "Too Expensive or Too Effective? The Real Reason the GOP Wants to Cut Capital-Representation Centers," *Fulton County Daily Report* (Sept. 8, 1995): 6.

22. *Murray v. Giarratano,* 492 U.S. 1 (1989).

23. For a more comprehensive discussion of the problems of deficient representation in capital cases and the reasons for it, see Bright, supra note 25.

24. Paul M. Barrett, "Lawyer's Fast Work on Death Cases Raises Doubts About System," *Wall Street Journal* (Sept. 7, 1994): 1. Barrett describes Houston lawyer Joe Frank Canon, who is known for hurrying through capital trials like greased lightening, occasionally falls asleep, and has had ten clients sentenced to death. Also ex parte Burdine, 901 S.W.2d 456, 457 (Tex. Crim. App. 1995) (Maloney, J., dissenting), which notes testimony of jurors and court clerk that defense attorney slept during trial.

25. John Makeig, "Asleep on the Job; Slaying Trial Boring, Lawyer Said," *Houston Chronicle* (Aug. 14, 1992): A35.

26. Record, 846–49, *Haney v. State,* 603 So. 2d 368 (Ala. Crim. App. 1991), aff'd, 603 So. 2d 412 (Ala. 1992), cert. denied, 113 S. Ct. 1297 (1993).

27. Judy Bailey, "A Poor Example of Indigent Defense," *Fulton County Daily Report* (Jan. 16, 1996): 1. Bailey describes the hearing in *Fugate v. Thomas,* Super. Ct. of Butts Co., Ga., No. 94-V-195 (Jan. 10–11, 1996).

28. *Furman v. Georgia,* 408 U.S. 238 (1972) struck down Georgia's death penalty statute.

29. *Gregg v. Georgia,* 428 U.S. 153 (1976) upholds the death penalty statue enacted by the Georgia legislature in 1973 in response to the Court's decision in Furman.

30. Transcript of Hearing of Apr. 25–27, 1988, 231, *State v. Birt,* Super. Ct. of Jefferson Co., Ga. No. 2360 (1988) (on file with author). The lawyer was referring to *Miranda v. Arizona,* 384 U.S. 436 (1966), and *Dred Scott v. Sandford,* 60 U.S. (19 How.) 393 (1857). Dred Scott was not a criminal case.

31. Brief for Appellant, ex parte Heath, 455 So. 2d 905 (Ala. 1984). The brief is set out in full in Bright, supra note 25, 1860–61 n.154.

32. See *Andrews v. Shulsen,* 485 U.S. 919 (1988) (J. Marshall dissenting from denial of certiorari).

33. See *Hance v. Zant,* 114 S. Ct. 1392 (1994) (J. Blackmun dissenting from denial of certiorari); Bob Herbert, "Mr. Hance's 'Perfect Punishment,'" *New York Times* (Mar. 27, 1994): D17; Bob Herbert, "Jury Room Injustice," *New York Times* (Mar. 30, 1994): A15.

34. For further discussion of the influence of race on the imposition of the death penalty and the failure of legislatures and courts to deal with the problem, see Stephen B. Bright, "Discrimination, Death, and Denial: The Tolerance of Racial Discrimination in the Infliction of the Death Penalty," 35 *Santa Clara Law Review* (1995): 433

35. *Testament of Hope: The Essential Writings of Martin Luther King, Jr.,* ed. James Melvin Washington (New York: Harper & Row, 1986), 259–67.

36. Ibid., 267.

37. See Helen Prejean, C.S.J., *Dead Man Walking: An Eyewitness Account of the Death Penalty in the United States* (New York: Random House, 1993), which describes her work with death row inmates.

38. Wiesel's speech, "This Honor Belongs to All the Survivors," *New York Times* (Dec. 11, 1986): A2.

39. *Amadeo v. Zant,* 486 U.S. 214 (1988).

40. A. Leon Higginbotham Jr., "Justice Clarence Thomas in Retrospect," 45 *Hastings Law Journal* (1994): 1405, 1430.

41. Carl T. Rowan, *Dream Makers, Dream Breakers: The World of Justice Thurgood Marshall* (New York: Little Brown and Co., 1993), 453–54.

# ACCOUNTS OF LIFE
# ON DEATH ROW

*Crime is redeemed by remorse, but not by a
blow of the axe or slipknot. Blood has to be
washed by tears but not by blood.*
   —Victor Hugo

# WORKING AGAINST THE DEATH PENALTY

## Marie Deans, Murder Victims' Families for Reconciliation

Death row, wherever it exists, is purgatory. It is where the people we condemn to death suffer and where some expiate their sins. It is where human beings exist in a state of anticipation of their own predetermined deaths. No matter the conditions, whether relatively good, bad, or indifferent, death row is not and cannot be less than physical torture. There is no way to predict how an individual will react to death row. Sometimes those who appear the strongest are defeated and broken. Sometimes those who appear the weakest find amazing spiritual strength. We kill the broken and reborn alike.

Conditions on death row depend on the prison administration. I began working on death row in South Carolina, where the administration openly opposed the death penalty. The men on death row were viewed as arbitrarily chosen victims. They, their families, friends, and defense teams were treated with kindness and understanding. By the time I moved to Virginia, I had seen harsh conditions on death rows in Texas and Oklahoma, but I was totally unprepared for what I would find in Virginia.

It is difficult to describe the inhumanity of Mecklenburg Correctional Center in the late '70s and early '80s. Men on death row and in segregation were beaten regularly. These beatings were done by teams of guards, suited up for combat and carrying shields and clubs, against individual prisoners. The beatings were relentless—even when men were beaten to the floor, they were then kicked. When word of these beatings began to get out and receive some criticism, the prison started videotaping the beatings. There are hours upon hours of these videotapes, and they defy any sense of humanity. But perhaps the most astounding aspect of these videotapes is the fact that the prison administration was convinced that the tapes would prove that these beatings were justified.

Many of the men were kept on dangerously high doses of psychotropic drugs. I have a letter in my files from a psychiatrist recommending experimenting with hallucinogens on one of the men, because, the doctor says, the man can be kept in his cell and his life will end soon anyway. If the men tried to refuse the drugs, they were beaten, chained down to their bunks, and the drugs were administered by force. Other than beating them and barking orders at them, the guards were not allowed to speak to the men. Rules changed weekly or more often, but the men were not allowed to know what the rules were until they broke them and were punished, either by beatings or being thrown into a strip-cell. In strip-cells they weren't allowed to have anything but a pair of undershorts. That is, no clothing, mattress, blanket, paper, pencil, or toilet paper. They had a choice of sleeping on the concrete floor or steel bunks. Often their water was cut off so that they could not get a drink of water or flush their toilets. Sometimes the men were injured when they were put in strip-cells, and naturally, whether injured or not, they often got sick, but they received no, or grossly inadequate, medical treatment.

The prison administration made every attempt to totally isolate men on death row from all outside assistance. Lawyers and legal assistants had great difficulty getting in to see their clients and were treated so badly when they did get in that most stopped going. Because I was persistent and wouldn't go away voluntarily, I was repeatedly banned from the prison. Once, because a newspaper article quoted a lawyer as saying my counseling of men on death row was invaluable, the prison said I didn't have the right to counsel my clients. Another time I was banned because I was talking to my clients about God. The prison said I wasn't a chaplain and didn't have the right to talk to my clients about religion. On the other hand, clergy who opposed the death penalty and befriended the men were banned as well. Family members and friends were humiliated by strip and partial strip searches (for non-contact visits) and sexually harassed. Often they would spend hours driving to Mecklenburg on a visiting day, only to be told that their family member or friend wouldn't be allowed to visit that day. By the time I got to Virginia, most of the men's families and friends had given up trying to visit. It was understandable. They were going through all this to talk over a phone to their loved one who was locked in a concrete and glass cage.

Even during legal visits men had to wear metal chains with padlocks in the small of their backs, were handcuffed to those chains, and had to wear leg irons as well. Guards sat in the room listening to our conversations, and those conversations, which are guaranteed confidentiality by our Constitution, were reported to the wardens and the attorneys general who work to overcome our legal arguments and have our clients killed. In addition, there were strict orders that no one was allowed to touch a man on death row. A legal visit with a lawyer, law student, and me was once stopped because our client began crying, and after a few moments I couldn't stand it and put my hand on his arm. How do normal human beings reach the point of being able to treat other human beings the way the guards and administration at Mecklenburg were treating these men? We do it through a process of transmogrification. We turn human beings into non-humans, objects, or monsters. We project our fears, frustrations, and dissatisfactions onto them. They become our scapegoats, the embodiment of everything that is wrong with us and our society.

Finally, the facts about the conditions at Mecklenburg were taken to court. A federal judge said that Mecklenburg was in the dark ages and declared the conditions unconstitutional. A new administration was brought in, and conditions improved. Conditions on death row remain unnecessarily strict, and there is an admitted and successful effort to keep the men disoriented and divided. Death row itself is tomblike. Everything is off-white concrete and steel. The predominant sounds are electronic. The ventilation is so poor even the air is deadly still. It looks and feels like a sensory deprivation chamber. In the summer it is like a combination sensory deprivation chamber and oven.

To me the worst condition the men, their families, and friends endure is a complete lack of privacy. Any letter going in or coming out can be read, any phone call or visit monitored. This is extremely destructive to the family relationship. Think of all the things you discuss with your husband, father, brother, favorite cousin, or best friend that you would never discuss in front of strangers. Think of years of carrying around alone all the emotions that go unshared, all the things you want to say that go unsaid, and think of the pain of those unshared emotions and unsaid words after your loved one has been killed. The families and friends of people on death row are truly the unacknowledged, unseen victims of the death penalty.

Several years ago there was an attempt in Virginia to get contact visits for men on death row—they are usual in most of the death penalty states. There was an enormous uproar. Legislators and citizens alike kept repeating the theme that "Why should men on death row be allowed to hold their mothers' hands when their victims would never be able to hold anyone's hand again?" Not once did any of these people say, "Aren't we punishing these mothers enough by killing their sons? What harm would it do to let them hold their sons' hands until we kill them?" Of course, in our use of the death penalty, we have to ignore the families and friends of those we condemn to death. Monsters don't have families and friends. The families and friends are uncomfortable reminders of the humanity of the people on death row, uncomfortable reminders that they, like us, are more than the sum of their worst acts.

The suffering of the families and friends of the condemned is so heart-breaking that if proponents and those who administer the death penalty were to let it in, it would sear their souls. There is a mother who dreams every night that she is forced to plug in the electric chair in which her son is strapped and waiting to be killed. I watched a sister beg a governor's aide for her brother's life. She had been ten and her brother six when their mother ran away and their father began drinking himself into oblivion and beating them every night. Their suffering is caused by—as I said earlier—what many people in my country view as a necessary, though perhaps regrettable, policy upon which reasonable men and women can agree. But having seen all this suffering and so much more, I am unable to see the death penalty as anything but evil.

If you are involved in killing a human being, you have to rationalize that killing. One method of doing so is to convince yourself that the killing serves some good. Once you've done that, more killing must equate with more good. Dr. James Grigson, a psychiatrist in Texas who has been responsible for putting over 200 people on death row and who even Supreme Court Justices refer to as "Doctor Death," has said on national television that he views himself as a savior. The Attorney General of Virginia and those in her office who work on death cases felt that the campaign for a new trial for Joe Giarratano was a personal attack on them. They lobbied *intensely* to have Joe killed. They expressed their feeling that Joe had to be killed in order to *vindicate* them. If the death penalty is good, it doesn't matter who its victims are. Professor Ernest von den Haag argues that the good served by the death penalty far outweighs the harm of killing a few innocent people.

Many sociologists, psychologists, and other scholars say the death penalty brutalizes society because it sends the message that violence solves problems and causes an imitative reaction. Living and working in a killing state, I have come to realize that brutalization is not simply a sociological abstract or theory. The death penalty first brutalizes those who are closest to it, and there it can be measured. I believe there is a dangerous atmosphere in the land when lawmakers and law enforcers are brutalized.

About ten years ago I read an article by a Jewish scholar, a man who had survived one of the Nazi concentration camps. He traced the Holocaust back to Hitler's reintroducing the death penalty in Germany for murder. He argued that once you get people to agree that certain individuals can be killed for certain crimes, you can expand that penalty to include any crime—real or imagined. He pointed out that although the Holocaust was a crime against mankind, by the *legal* expansion of the death penalty in Germany during that time, the killing of criminals, the retarded, gypsies, homosexuals, Jews, and Christian "traitors" was all legal. His is a warning none of us can afford to ignore.

Now working with prisoners on death row in the state of Virginia, Marie Deans joined Murder Victims' Families for Reconciliation after her mother-in-law was murdered in 1972.

## DAILY EVENTS

### Richard Rossi, Death Row, Arizona

The air has been charged with tremendously high levels of stress and uncertainty. There is an electrical charge hanging in the air, a storm waiting to descend on us. The dragons want to eat, and we are ripe for plucking. We are always ripe for plucking. We are always apt targets. We are simply defenseless. It is only a matter of time before the fire breathing begins in earnest. To make sure we do not go off in sympathy for what they just did to another prisoner, a major shake down [search] is imminent.

There is one pod—pod six—where ten misfits are housed. It is right next door to my pod, which is pod five. The men in pod six are there because they do not abide by the rules of the control unit and this is the last resort for them. Although the cells are the same, there are some harsher rules for these men, especially when they are taken out of their cells for any reason. They must strip completely naked and have their clothes searched before being allowed to dress and be cuffed up to exit their cells. Obviously these men do not give a damn about the police or their rules. Yesterday one of these men was out in the exercise area. When he was told to cuff up and be escorted back into the pod, he refused. The police noticed this prisoner had a shank [homemade knife] in his possession. It is hard to understand how he could have a shank in his possession since he was searched upon leaving his cell. Anyway, when he refused to cuff up, the call went out on the radio that they had a problem with a prisoner in pod six who would not cuff up and that he was believed to have a shank. The goon squad was called. Six to eight police were also walking on the roof to look into the exercise yard. The loud barking indicated that the German shepherd attack dog was brought along as well.

When they could not talk this man into complying, the order was given to gas him. Either mace or an Israeli Fogger was used on him. This is when I was awakened. I had been asleep. I was not awakened by the noise, but rather by the residual gas that flows into the vent system and reaches everyone in the other five pods eventually. I started to gasp and cough. I realized that someone must be getting gassed. The eyes start to tear next. The best way to deal with this is to take a towel, wet it down and place it over your mouth and nose. It does not stop the gas, but reduces the effects somewhat.

Eventually the prisoner was subdued. For the next hour we continued to suffer from the gas in the air. When you are locked in a cage, you cannot run away from such intrusions. You are captive prey and suffer needlessly as well. As a result, the only privilege we had, which was to come out of our cells once a week for thirty minutes to clean our cells and the pod area, was terminated. There is no logic to this action. You may ask, why do they do this? It is simply retaliation. Everyone pays for the action of one. So now we do not come out of our cells except for exercise and a shower three times a week. Now we are also subjected to a full body search before we can walk the ten feet or so to the shower stall. Can you believe that! You have no idea how dehumanizing it is to have to get naked in front of another every time you have to leave your cell. You are robbed of your dignity on a daily basis. If you do not comply, you cannot come out of your cell and have a fifteen-minute shower. It is little wonder that there are some men who rebel against such practices, even though the end result is known to be fruitless. It is just the reaction against the madness. And sooner or later you will go mad yourself. Welcome to prison. . . .

## RUNNING IN: CELL EXTRACTION

### Hank Skinner, Death Row, Texas

Things here have gone from bad to worse. Yesterday they ran-in (or "cell extracted") [Richard]. After they subdued him, had him on the floor of the cell handcuffed and shackled, Sergeant ———, 2nd shift, who was the point man (first in) on the team, got on top of [Richard] and began punching him in the face with his fist; according to [Richard] he hit him five times. I saw his face and he's busted up pretty good. Sergeant ——— is a kind of gung-ho type. Even in a cell extraction they're not supposed to beat you with closed fists and especially not after you've been subdued with the capture shield, lying prone on the floor, cuffed behind your back and helpless with a five man extraction team on you, and shackled. Sergeant ——— was up here talking to us the other day and telling us about his workouts. He's a big ol' dude, about 5' 10", 240 pounds, weight-lifter built. But I've never known him to do something like this. Not until now.

This morning they ran-in on [Richard] again. They took him out of the cell after gassing him three times. They took him to the shower—cuffed, clothed, and shackled—to decontaminate him. All they did was get him soaking wet. They did not turn on the gas purge while he was out of the cell. They put him back in the cell with all that gas. Since the gas settles to the floor and he was soaking wet, the effect is worse than having gas sprayed on you and more like being painted with liquid gas. The pepper gas is a skin irritant.

See, what they are supposed to do when they run-in on you is get you out of the cell, put you in the shower and uncuff you through the bean hole, strip you out, and let you wash off the gas. But they're afraid he would've "jacked" (refused to come out of the shower), so they just keep him cuffed and shackled, with the door opened, let two members of the team hold him and run the water on him for a minute, clothes and all. It's an easy way to get drowned. Since you can't use your hands to shield your face and can't move out of the spray, if one of them punches you and makes you gasp, you get a lung full of water, quick. They always come out of there spittin' and sputtering. The gas soaked clothes rubbin' against your skin turns it raw and red. It burns like hell for days afterward and draws blisters which fill up with water. It ain't pretty. They have all kinds of little ways to make it more painful on you, and these kinds of things aren't readily apparent to someone who doesn't know the procedures and doesn't understand the effects of failing to follow them.

When they do it right, within twenty-four hours you'll be half way O.K. again. But when they do it wrong, intentionally, it's what we call a "fuck job," and when they put one of those on you, you're lucky if you get over it in a week or two. That's what they did to [Richard], twice in less than twenty-four hours. As Nietzsche famously said, "Beware all those in whom the urge to punish is very strong." They think a use of force is the answer to everything. You know, when they run-in on you it's understood that it ain't no game. They mean business and one way or another you are going to get subdued. Still there are certain unspoken rules observed. Those officers on a team are "suited up" in riot gear: helmets with visors and caged face shields, gas masks, body armor, chest, knee, and shin guards, stab-proof vest, combat boots. Some of them wear leather drivers' gloves. There are few ways to hurt them. They use a "capture shield" which is a big resin shield that's see-through and concave with handles on the outside edges.

The "point man" (or first man in line) grabs it by the handles and holds it in front of him and to his chest. All the other members of the team line up single-file behind the point man. After they gas you two–three times at five-minute intervals, they line up, and the Sergeant or Lieutenant stands by the door to give the signal to the picket officer to "roll the cell door!" (i.e., to open it. It slides open to the side, doesn't swing on hinges. All the electric mechanism does is release the lock, so the Sergeant has to slide the door on open). When the door opens the team takes off, like a football team off the line of scrimmage, except they're like a train. All the men behind the point man push forward—momentum. They have their shoulders in the posterior of the one before them. Five 200–pound men or more, that's 1,000 pounds of rolling momentum coming at you through the cell door. The idea is to use the capture shield to pin you to a wall, the bunk, the floor. Once they pin you, they throw the shield to the side then grab your arms and wrestle them behind you to cuff you. Then they shackle you at the feet. Each man on the extraction team has a number on the back of his helmet which corresponds to a specific function he is expected to perform once they got you down. They do it like bulldoggin' at the rodeo (steer wrestlin').

What happens when they come through that door is always chaotic. You've got five guys all over you, they've got all the protective gear while you're barefooted and in boxer shorts. Since they don't feel it when they crash and smash all over everything, it might be hard [for them] to tell if they're hurting you. It's much more dangerous than professional football because those guys are on a soft turf open field with no obstacles and still they get hurt bad all the time. Careers get ended in the blink of an eye. In these cells it's concrete and steel with obstacles everywhere. If you slip and fall on the corner of a steel bunk, the table welded to the wall, the stainless steel toilet or sink, you could easily get your skull crushed, your spine severed, chest caved in (as happened to Rick . . . the other day when the tip of the toilet bowl was driven into the center of his chest, when all five of them piled on top of his back and while they were drivin' him to the ground he went into the toilet bowl full force.) In any event, they are there to subdue you and take you out of the cell without hurting you. The unspoken rules are that you can tussle with them but you don't go at them with a weapon; you don't: kick them in the nuts, yank their helmets back, jerk the canister off their gas masks. It's a chase game. You're tryin' to elude the shield and get out the cell door, but you've got to get past the five guys to do it. If you make it out of the cell you consider that "a win." A prisoner who makes it past the tackle is one who knows how to "go hard," who "stays down for his." If you start swinging fists on them, setting up traps in the cell, trip wires, etc., then you're "taking it to the next level." Some of the guys "take off" from different positions in the cell—whatever they believe will give them an edge, an advantage, a better chance.

You can block the windows and lights with paper so they have to run-in in the dark and they can't see you too well. You can wait right by the door crouched down to take off or at the back of the cell or by the toilet, etc. Put shampoo or baby oil on the floor in the doorway to make 'em slip and fall. All this stuff is acceptable. The team is not supposed to kick, stomp, or pound you with fists. But that's what they've been doing. It shows us you've got some guys on the team who hate death row and want to hurt us.

It's escalating and getting worse and worse. It's not necessary. You can pound them with your fists and feet but they don't even feel it. You just bust your knuckles on that protective gear. If one or more of them hits you though, your ass is had because all you've got is your boxer shorts or jumper on. Those fists and boots with knob tread hurt like hell. They kick you, it's likely breaking bones in your face, feet or hands, ribs; they know what to go for—that's part of a "fuck job."

You become numb in here from lack of social interaction. Guys start doing things just to feel something, to get a few minutes of some kind of attention. It's like the guys who cut on themselves. They do it in order to feel something, even if it's only pain and hurt. I've heard it said by psychiatrists that children who get no attention, no love from their parents, will start doing little bad things to get spanked for. Because, to a human, even negative attention is better than no attention at all. It's something similar at work here. All we get is the negative attention. Dysfunctional. The other day, when I got gassed and run-in on, I had no choice. Lieutenant ———— was doing all those retaliatory shakedowns, twenty times in sixteen days. I got tired of it. The only resistance I could offer was to refuse to come out, refuse to comply, make it as hard as possible on them. They'd been tearing up my stuff and taking things they knew they weren't supposed to take: I'd just had all I could stand.

When they ran-in on me after gassing me twice, even though they knocked me smooth out, unconscious, afterward I felt really great. I had my feeling back for a little while. I felt invigorated. All the stress and tension was gone for a little while. Everybody was excited. We talked about it for hours, picked it apart and dissected every action of every participant, every word said. When I finally went to sleep, I slept good. The next day, though, I went right back to numb and miserable like I was before. I tried to get them to run-in on me again but they wouldn't do it. But then they decided to leave me alone so I just decided to be content with that. Like *Fortune News* said, these places (control units) breed monsters. I'm kind of ashamed of how I felt and what I wanted to do. I think I should not feel that way, but this place and the way these people run it make you feel things, whether you want to or not. It's just what they teach, by the reactions they give to whatever you do—it's always something negative or stressful.

It's really weird how they run these levels and discipline overall. They expect you to react to it in relation to the policy, but it's not a human reaction and if you're dealing with an officer or rank who's shooting straight with you, they'll tell you that they would not react the way it's stated either. I say, "So if you admit that you, yourself, wouldn't do it, how can you expect me to?" Then they go right back to, "Well, a jury convicted you and this is how the state and the prison board says we are to treat you, I've got a job to do and so I do it, it's nothing personal" . . . This place . . . it does the same to the officers. They teach them this perverted, anti-human logic, they chant it like a mantra, "It's nothing personal, I've got a job to do." They (the administration) convince them we are not human. Once they buy into that logic they convince themselves and it helps to deal with the human feelings of guilt an officer has from mistreating his fellow human beings this way. Then the officers become hardened and uncaring. From there, it's but a short few steps to sadism and brutality.

It's the scariest thing you could ever imagine to see an officer trying to subdue an out-of-control prisoner with a choke hold, trying his best to break the prisoner's neck. Smiling all the while and telling the prisoner, "Quit resisting" . . . the prisoner is unconscious already.

I talked to Sergeant ———— yesterday, late. He admits that he punched [Richard] but says that [Richard] was not in restraints (cuffs and shackles) when it happened, that "[Richard] was still struggling" when they ran-in on him and "I had to sting him a few times in order to subdue him." He also said, "I was point man on the team. You already know, this ain't no game. If you're still standin' when I come through that door, I'm gonna sting ya a few times til you go down, simple as that." "Sting ya," what kind of euphemism or analogy is that, for "I'm gonna beat your face into pulp with my fist?"

What Sergeant ———— failed to mention here is that, while [Richard] may or may not have been cuffed when it happened, he was still restrained by the four other officers on that team—"still struggling"—[Richard] could not have been "still struggling" unless they'd already taken him down and he had someone to "struggle" with. The other four officers on that team were holding him while Sergeant ———— punched him out.

## CONDITIONS ON DEATH ROW, TERRELL UNIT, TEXAS

### Dr. Terry Kupers, School of Psychology of the Wright Institute in Berkeley

From March 1995 through the summer of 1999, Mr. Hank Skinner was incarcerated at the Ellis Unit of Texas Department of Criminal Justice (TDCJ). Since June 18, 1999, he has been housed in the Terrell Unit, death row. There are approximately 450 prisoners on death row at Terrell (there are approximately 2,900 prisoners in general population at Terrell). Death row has the architectural design and programming of a supermaximum security unit or Security Housing Unit (SHU), very similar to SHUs I have toured, testified concerning, and written about in California, Indiana, Michigan, Pennsylvania, Wisconsin, and other states. The structure is mainly concrete, cinder block, and stainless steel, and prisoners confined on death row are subject to a very closely controlled environment. They are permitted almost no wall decorations and very limited possessions. The environment is stark, and there are lights on at all times. Cell doors are opened and closed by remote control, and prisoners are usually strip-searched, handcuffed, and accompanied by two officers when they leave their area to go to the recreation area, to the shower, to visits, and to medical/dental appointments. There are narrow horizontal windows high on the outside wall of the cells that cannot be opened, and unless the prisoner is fortunate enough to have a view of the parking lot, his view will be limited to an adjoining section of building. The cells have solid doors which contain a food slot and ports for cuffing and so forth.

The prisoners are single-celled and confined to their cells nearly twenty-four hours per day. They are released one at a time to shower or go to the dayroom or the "yard." The dayroom and yard are similar in shape, though the latter lacks a roof. Each are smaller than 300 square feet and contain a chin-up bar. The dayroom also contains a rolled up mat and the yard contains a basketball hoop. The yard in Mr. Skinner's unit is divided in two, and two prisoners are permitted to be on it at once, separated by bars. The prisoners are fed in their cells and there is little if any social interaction. The fourteen cells in a pod are stacked two high in rows of seven, and a prisoner cannot view any other prisoner's cell from his own door. If a prisoner shouts, he can be heard by out-of-view inhabitants of immediately adjacent cells. The officers control the lights and make rounds to effect "counts" at least three times per shift, around the clock.

According to Mr. Skinner, the architecture of the units is "cavernous"; there are no sound-deadening panels, acoustic tiles, nor other effective insulation so that clanging of the metal doors reverberates throughout the unit. Every sound is magnified and echoes badly. When officers conduct counts during the night hours, they bang loudly on metal cell doors demanding the prisoner call out his number, and Mr. Skinner describes the noise as piercing, causing most prisoners to wake instantly. Meanwhile, the prisoners are not permitted to possess fingernail clippers, mirrors, or razors. Yet they are required to conform to a strict code of grooming that includes short hair, shaved faces, and short nails. They must request a razor and nail clippers from officers when they shower, and even then they are not permitted to use mirrors. The officers keep the men's razors in a common storage space; and even though they are supposed to label each razor and make certain it gets to its owner each time, Mr. Skinner believes it often happens that the officers make mistakes and pass out razors to prisoners other than their owners, thus creating a grave and unconscionable risk of transmitting HIV or Hepatitis C.

Prisoners are permitted almost no human contact, except with officers. In fact, this forced isolation is so thorough that when prisoners are taken out of their cells to go to the shower or the yard, they are handcuffed and accompanied by two officers. If they pass another prisoner in the hallway, one of the two prisoners is ordered to step into a side passage and face the wall, so there is not even any casual conversation between prisoners in transit. Further, when the prisoner goes to the shower in a locked section at Terrell, he is strip searched, run through a metal detector, his shower supplies are searched, and he is forced to walk backwards out of his cell. Mr. Skinner experiences these intensive and repeated intrusive searches and routines as humiliating and emasculating, and other prisoners express the same feelings.

According to Mr. Skinner (and other prisoners corroborate his report here as elsewhere):

> Everything here is such an effort that most (prisoners) are withdrawing, showering only every three or four days or washing in the cell. Some guys go to the shower every day still, anything just to get out of the cell for a minute. I guess it depends on your need. I've started to become so apprehensive and anxiety-stressed that I rarely go to recreation, usually only the shower. There is nothing to do in the dayroom, but there is constant observation. You feel like an exhibit at the zoo.

Thus, on the Terrell death row unit, prisoners are relegated to near total isolation and idleness, their movements and activities are very closely controlled, they are repeatedly searched and they are subjected to extremes of noise and sleep deprivation.

While the Terrell Unit is officially designated "death row" and not "super-max," the conditions, policies, and staff practices in effect on the Terrell Unit are remarkably comparable to those in effect on supermaximum security units I have toured in five states. Prior to the move of death row from the Ellis Unit in Huntsville to the Terrell Unit in Livingston, inhabitants of death row were permitted a certain degree of socialization with each other, physical activities on the yard, arts and crafts materials in their cells, and so forth. And some of the prisoners on death row, designated "work capable," were permitted to work at jobs within the prison. With the move came a much more restrictive setting and daily life, with almost no out-of-cell activities, no socialization, and almost no materials in the cells. The category "work capable" seems to have been obliterated, or at least no prisoners on death row would any longer be permitted to work. In other words, all the prisoners were consigned to isolated confinement, with almost total idleness and isolation.

There is no credible penological objective served by instituting such restrictive and harsh policies to punish death row prisoners. The sentence of death is their punishment. On average, death row prisoners are not a serious security risk—they are too busy thinking about their eventual de-mise or working on their appeals to cause much difficulty for the security staff. Of course there are exceptions, some prisoners do break rules and get involved in violent altercations, and there was an escape attempt at the Ellis Unit. Still, the prevalence of rule-breaking and violence is typically lower on a death row unit than elsewhere in the prison system. And instead of punishing all occupants of death row for the misdeeds and rule-breaking of a few, it is possible to mete out specific punishments for individuals who do pose a security threat while leaving the large majority of death row prisoners with their activities and privileges intact. But instead of opting to punish individual offenses with specific punishments and restrictions, the TDCJ decided to place the entire death row population in isolated confinement.

## Use of Force

An example of the ways death row prisoners are punished unfairly involves the use of force in prison, specifically pepper spray and other toxic gasses. At the Terrell Unit death row, officers carry dispensers of pepper spray or some other chemical gas with them as they conduct rounds, and there are many "gassings" and "cell extractions." Cell extractions and the use of gas constitute relatively extreme uses of force and should be reserved for the most extreme situations, after all other remedies have been tried and failed. In addition, in the close quarters of a supermaximum unit such as Terrell, there is "collateral damage," damage that is suffered by prisoners who have not even committed any punishable acts.

Mr. Skinner reported to me that a prisoner on Level three (the highest and most restrictive level—Mr. Skinner was then on Level two) who is quite disturbed was brought to the recreation area adjacent to Mr. Skinner's cell.

> They came in here and gassed him [sprayed him with O.C. gas (Oleoresin capsicum, i.e., pepper spray) or equivalent] in the day cage. He was against the concrete section divider wall when they shot him with "Agent Orange" gas. I stood at my cell door and watched the whole thing. He was kind of crouched down as if to ward off a blow. His silhouette was on the wall. The wall was white and he against it, you could see how the cloud of gas hit him and splattered all over the wall. The gas is heavier than air so it floats to the ground and hovers there. It settled in my sink. After they'd turned on the purge fans and I'd quit coughing and sneezing with my eyes watering, I'd washed my face. Three hours later I got up again to wash my face because it was still burning my skin. The gas had settled in the sink bowl, and when I leaned over into it to wash my face I got a mouth, nose, and lungs full of it. Nearly knocked me down. The little exhaust vent I'd covered with a sheet of plain white typing paper to keep that vent from sucking the gas into the cell. After the gassing and purge, the paper had four orange squares on it, where the gas had penetrated the paper through the vent. The next day those orange squares on the paper crumbled and fell out. The gas ate the paper, literally dissolved it into something resembling oily ashes. I wonder, if it does that to paper, what'll it do to lung tissue, capillaries, mucous membrane, sinus lining, esophagus, etc. Pretty scary to contemplate.

This kind of trauma is not rare on death row at Terrell and causes untold psychiatric damage. Imagine the kind of intense anxiety, not to mention paranoia, that might expectably be induced in the average person undergoing this kind of "collateral damage," even though he had not done anything wrong. And the prisoner who is affected traumatically has absolutely no control over the toxic effects of the gas—he cannot leave the area or even close a vent.

*Excessive and Unfair Punishment*

Mr. Skinner charges the staff with retaliation against him and associated unfair punishments. According to another prisoner: particular officers "would shut Mr. Skinner's outer door for no reason, for hours at a time, turn off the electricity to his cell, leave him like that for hours in heat which could not hardly be tolerated even with a fan and ventilation" sometimes nearly killing him. Another prisoner has stated:

> Skinner was never violent to these officers and I never once saw him actually attempt to hit, hurt, or assault one of them. But they were always accusing him of it. They would stand outside Skinner's cell door, sometimes take turns doing it for hours on end, taunting him, daring him to do something. They would call him all kinds of names, "dicksucker," "asshole," "punk," "motherfucker," say bad things about Skinner's mama, say his sister was a whore, take Skinner's photos of his family in shakedowns then later wave the pictures at Skinner while mock-kissing them and talking trash about Skinner's family and friends. They would shut the outer door to Skinner's cell, leave him in the heat without any electricity to his cell, no fan, no ventilation of any kind. There were air vents in each cell, and these officers would always break the control switch by the door leading out into the hall so that the vents couldn't be turned on again. At one point they left Skinner like that for so long, he was so dehydrated that his skin had turned really pale and he was wrinkled up like a prune. When he came out of the cell he was so weak legged he couldn't stand on his own. The officers had to hold him up by his arms. His legs were just dragging behind him as they took him to the infirmary. Skinner later told me that when he'd ordered copies of his medical records after reviewing them, there was no record of this having ever happened. Skinner was at the infirmary for over four or five hours while they revived him that time. I also remember when a particular officer gassed Skinner for no reason in January, 1999, who bragged that he had used so much gas on Skinner—over 4 ½ oz., two full cans—that they were wondering how Skinner had survived it and was still alive . . .

These are stories of extreme cruel and bizarre events. I am not in a position to determine whether each precise detail Mr. Skinner and other prisoners report is accurate in every regard—determination of such should be left to a fair and impartial hearing in each instance. However, the opinion by the Court in *Ruiz* about use of force in the TDCJ, plus other prisoners' accounts verifying Mr. Skinner's allegations, give more than a little credence to Mr. Skinner's story about ways in which he has been unfairly treated.

It is clear that there is something about the environment on the Terrell Unit that gives prisoners cause to fear they might be the victims of retaliation, that presents officers with many opportunities to act ever more punitively toward the prisoners, and causes the prisoners to fear unpredictable and unprovoked attacks. Whether any particular perceived sign of disrespect on the part of prisoners or officers is an exaggeration or fabrication, and whether and to what degree retaliation does occur (again, this is not for me to determine), the resultant intensified mutual distrust and rage that are clearly present on death row at Terrell Unit quite predictably lead to increasingly uncooperative and aggressive acts on the part of all participants, as the SHU becomes the site of ever escalating irritability, rage, brutality, and violence.

### A Vicious Cycle

There is social science and clinical research establishing the existence in isolated confinement units such as the Terrell Unit death row of a "vicious cycle" of worsening hostility and misunderstanding between staff and prisoners. This is not to downplay the fact that rule violations do occur in such units, and an appropriate and fair disciplinary system must be maintained. But when human beings are deprived of the freedom to control their movements, their activities, the temperature in their cells, the noise level, and other aspects of their environment, and in addition are denied social contact and all means to express themselves in a constructive manner, then it is quite expectable that they (or any reasonable human being) will resort to increasingly desperate acts to achieve some degree of control of their situation and to restore some modicum of self-respect. The prisoners are driven to small acts of resistance, which in turn are likely to be perceived by officers as disrespectful or rule-breaking, and the officers become increasingly punitive or even abusive toward the identified "troublemaker(s)."

### The SHU Syndrome

It has been known for as long as solitary confinement has been practiced that human beings suffer a great deal of pain and mental deterioration when they remain in solitary confinement for a significant length of time. Human beings require social interaction and productive activities to establish and sustain a sense of identity, self-worth, and well-being, as well as to maintain a grasp on reality. In the absence of social interactions, unrealistic ruminations and beliefs cannot be tested in conversation with others, so they build up inside and are transformed into unfocused and irrational thoughts. Disorganized behaviors emerge. Internal impulses linked with anger, fear, and other strong emotions grow to overwhelming proportions.

Prisoners on death row at Terrell Unit are locked alone in their cells all but three or four hours per week, when they are permitted to go to recreation. The environment is totally controlled by the staff, meaning that the prisoners have almost no control of their daily living. Officers bring their food trays, turn the water in their cells on and off, permit them to go to the exercise cell, etc. Officers give orders, refuse many of the prisoners' requests, and sometimes use force against the prisoners. Anxiety and anger mount in the prisoners. The almost total lack of social interaction and meaningful activities means the prisoner has little or no opportunity to test the reality of his worst fears, nor direct the emotional intensity provoked by the harsh environment into productive activities.

Prisoners in this kind of segregation do what they can to cope. Many pace relentlessly, as if this non-productive action will relieve the emotional tension. Those who can read books and write letters do so. But at least forty percent of prisoners nationwide are functionally illiterate, and evidence is accruing that illiterate prisoners fare less well than others in isolated confinement. Other prisoners clean their cells many times each day.

Under these extreme conditions, symptoms begin to emerge. For example, the walls may seem to be moving in on the prisoner. He may begin to suffer from panic attacks wherein he cannot breathe and thinks his heart is beating so fast he is going to die. He may find himself disobeying an order or inexplicably screaming at an officer, when really all he wants is for the officer to stop and interact with him a little longer than it takes for a food tray to be slid through the slot in his solid metal cell door. It is in this context of near-total isolation and idleness that psychiatric symptoms emerge in previously healthy prisoners. In less healthy ones, there is psychosis, mania or compulsive acts of self-abuse, or suicide.

There are very destructive emotional consequences when prisoners are subjected to harsh conditions such as the conditions on the Terrell Unit over time. There is a large body of research literature about isolated confinement and punitive segregation in correctional institutions. There is a minimum of quality social interaction and while there is quite a bit of noise in such units, there is very little meaningful sensory input (some studies employ the term "reduced environmental stimulation"). We know that the social isolation and idleness, as well as the near absolute lack of control over most aspects of daily life, very often lead to serious psychiatric symptoms. This is made even worse by sleep deprivation, which is a frequent occurrence on such units because of just the kinds of constant intrusions all night long by officers conducting counts and the loud banging and closing of metal doors that Mr. Skinner describes.

Harvard Psychiatrist Dr. Stuart Grassian discovered what he terms the "SHU Syndrome" in prisoners confined in punitive segregation environments for a significant length of time.[1] He lists these symptoms as part of the syndrome: massive, free-floating anxiety; hyper-responsiveness including startle; perceptual distortions; derealization experiences; difficulty with concentration and memory; acute confusional states; the emergence of primitive, ego-dystonic aggressive fantasies; ideas of reference and persecutory ideation; motor excitement, often associated with sudden, violent destructive, or self-mutilatory outbursts; and rapid reduction of symptoms upon termination of isolation.

A significant proportion of prisoners housed in isolated confinement units who are prone to mental illness tend to suffer psychiatric breakdowns under the strain. In my tours of isolated confinement units in many states, I have discovered as many as one half of the inhabitants to be suffering from a serious psychiatric disorder requiring immediate treatment. Prisoners who are prone to violence tend to have difficulty controlling their rage, and prisoners prone to suicide tend to become suicidal when kept in segregation for significant lengths of time.

Dr. Craig Haney, a prominent expert on correctional psychology and the psychological effects of prison conditions, toured the Terrell Unit when it was an administrative segregation unit. He told the court about his experience:

> In a number of instances, there were people who had smeared themselves with feces. In other instances, there were people who had urinated

in their cells, and the urination was on the floor . . . These were people who appeared to be in profound states of distress and pain . . . The bedlam which ensued each time I walked out into one of those units, the number of people who were screaming, who were begging for help, for attention, the number of people who appeared to be disturbed, the existence, again, of people who were smeared with feces, the intensity of the noise as people began to shout and ask, "Please come over here. Please talk to me. Please help me." It was shattering.[2]

The court called the picture Dr. Haney painted "harrowing."

From descriptions I have read of the new punitive regime relating to the "Death Row Plan," and from what Mr. Skinner tells me of the daily routine, I liken the Terrell Unit to an administrative segregation or super-maximum security unit. Thus, prisoners on death row, even if they have not violated enough rules to be assigned to administrative segregation, are in fact confined in conditions comparable to those in administrative segregation units within the TDCJ, and in my opinion these conditions of confinement cause great pain, suffering, and psychiatric decompensation or breakdown.

The Terrell Unit has been renamed the Polunsky Unit because the person it was named after, Charles Terrell, did not want to be associated with it. Before 1999, death row used to be at Huntsville, which was reputed to be a more humane unit.

## Notes

1. See S. Grassian, "Psychopathological Effects of Solitary Confinement," *American Journal of Psychiatry* 140, no. 11 (Nov. 1983): 1450–54.
2. Cited in Order, *Ruiz v. Johnson,* June 18, 2001: 10.

## CALIFORNIA'S DEATH ROW

Michael Wayne Hunter, Death Row, California

A considerable amount of mail flows into my cell from people out there in the world asking what it's really like living day-to-day on San Quentin's death row. I'm always tempted to quip, "It's a hell of a lot better than dying here." But then I really don't know if that's true—yet. I answer every letter even if the writer is rabidly pro-death penalty. It's easy for me to understand their attraction to the concept of killing convicted murderers. In the abstract, the death penalty has an elegant Newtonian symmetry—for every action there is an opposite reaction—that easily harmonizes with the Old Testament eye-for-an-eye overtone which strikes a reassuring resonance within a majority of citizens.

### Suicide

Most people already have a fairly clear concept of what it's like when an execution occurs, since an ocean swell of media rolls over totally engulfing and covering San Quentin prison, but they're usually unaware of the other death row prisoners who have died here. Many condemned men have stopped breathing and disappeared with scarcely a ripple in the media pool.

A whistle will pierce through a cell block. "We've got a hanger," booms over the housing unit's loudspeakers. Guards spike open a cell door, handcuff a dead-body's hands before they cut the hangman noose. Tossing the corpse into a bright orange stretcher, the badges haul the remains of the suicide away. The property officer boxes up the deceased man's belongings, trustees hose out the cell, another condemned man is shoved inside the four-by-ten-foot box, and the relentless, mind-numbing daily routine of death row grinds on and on and on. Often it's fairly easy to see the mental deterioration, and how suicide seems inevitable, and it's almost a relief when the condemned man ends his misery-filled existence.

A friend of mine, Ron Fuller, piled all his belongings onto his steel bunk and set them on fire. From six cells away, I could feel the heat radiating on my mind when I stuck my mirror outside my cell bars to see what the commotion was about. Crackling flames roared out of Ron's cell reaching up and licking the tier of cells above us.

Whistles blowing, heavy boots pounding, the guards arrived and brought the blaze under control. Handcuffing Ron, the uniforms yoked him out of his cell. Marching past my cell with a guard on each arm, Ron's unfocused eyes were spinning wildly, the hair on his chest and arms had been singed away, and I could smell charred flesh. After treating his burns, Ron was turned over to the California Department of Corrections' psychologists who opinioned he was faking suicide. You see, the State of California isn't allowed to execute anyone who's insane—it's the law. So the psyches employed by the State of California asserted Ron was playing insane in order to fend off the gas chamber. Prison officials charged Ron a couple of hundred dollars for the cell's fire damage, tossed him inside another four-by-ten-foot box, and pretty much ignored him. Finally, he made a noose, tied it to his bars, stuck his head inside the loop, pulled it tight, and quietly died.

One day, which at first glance seemed no different than any other, I spent a couple of hours playing basketball on an exercise yard. After the game, everyone shook hands, agreed to play again, and one of the players, who I barely knew, went back to his cell and hanged himself. I saw Ron's suicide coming, but this one really stunned me. It's bewildering: how does a guy go from shooting hoops on a fine summer day to suicide in a dark cell within the minuscule time-frame of an hour?

Suicide, killed by another condemned prisoner, shot and killed by a guard, death due to old age or lack of decent medical care, and the condemned man's life passes with scarcely anyone out there in the world noticing. It's not death that brings the media cameras and intense public scrutiny to San Quentin's death row, it's only the executions with their time-honored rituals of last meals, last thirteen steps into the gas chamber, that attracts the interest of taxpayers.

### The Consent Decree

Many citizens believe California's death row simply consists of men-in-cells lined up in a neat row, each awaiting his turn to march into the gas chamber, inhale, and fail to metabolize cyanide gas. Although it was once a lot like that, day-to-day existence has evolved a bit. In response to a federal lawsuit filed by condemned prisoners, San Quentin officials in the early 1980s signed a consent decree agreeing to provide certain living conditions to the men on death row. [On July 11, 1997, the State asked the federal court to terminate the decree under the Prison Litigation Reform Act.] Essentially a contract, the decree guarantees condemned prisoners an opportunity to venture out of their cells to an exercise yard for about five hours each day.

An instructor from San Quentin's Education Department teaches high school courses through a cell-study program. An arts and crafts program is included in the decree. Condemned prisoners have entered art competitions and won prizes in many media. Guards are allowed to sign contracts with condemned men in order to buy their work. It's fairly common for guards and other staff members to bring photos of their families onto death row so a condemned artist can paint their portraits. A phone has been installed on each tier. Condemned men can call collect their friends, families, and the attorneys handling their death sentence appeals.

The death row visiting room is open four days a week and has murals on its walls painted by a condemned artist. This is the only place inside San Quentin where death row prisoners and guards mingle together without bars between them or chains on the condemned. Children run around playing tag between the chairs, a cheerful atmosphere reigns, much more reminiscent of a group of vacationers in a departure lounge waiting to board a charter flight to Hawaii than an annex of the death house.

Since the consent decree was signed, California's death row population has quadrupled to well over four hundred, we've outgrown the original death row, and now there's actually three San Quentin death rows. A fourth death row is located at the California Institute for Women in Frontera where the handful of women condemned by the State of California are housed while their appeals wend through the courts.

### North Seg

North Segregation housing unit is the original death row at San Quentin. Nicknamed "The Old Death Row" or "North Seg," the original death row houses thirty-four men [on] each of its two tiers. Located on the sixth or top floor of the North Block housing unit, many of California's most infamous [prisoners]—Charles Manson and Sirhan Sirhan—spent time locked inside its cells. Now considered the luxury penthouse suite, condemned men must submit a request to the classification committee in order to be considered for housing within North Seg. Carefully screened for their potential to live well with others, if approved for transfer, condemned men are placed on the long waiting list for a cell inside the Old Death Row's friendly confines. During the two years I was housed in North Seg, no one committed suicide, no one died, it was a protected sanctuary far removed from the everyday hazards of prison.

Breakfast and dinner are the two hot meals provided each day. The tier guard pushes a hot cart down the tier, shovels food onto paper trays, and shoves one into each cell. The food isn't terrible, it's better than the food I was served on aircraft carriers during the four years I spent in the United States Navy. Sandwiches, fruit, and chips in a paper bag make up the noon meal.

After breakfast, the guards pull three men from each tier out of their cells, place them in holding cages, so they can conduct cell searches. In theory, the search is for weapons, drugs, and escape paraphernalia. In reality, North Seg is such a quiet, tranquil place, the guards don't have any violence or serious discipline problems to cope with. In their boredom, the badges are reduced to simply counting how many socks and other clothing men have in their cells and taking away any exceeding the limitations imposed by the property regulations.

After the cell searches, the cell doors are unlocked, and the condemned men are allowed to roam the tiers until about 2 P.M. The atmosphere is so relaxed, North Seg prisoners are not even searched coming and going from their cells to the tiers or the exercise yard. On the tiers, there are a couple of tables. Condemned men use them to play cards, study education courses, or work on their art projects. Others simply hang out and talk, or lazily stroll up and down the tier. A green exhaust stack (used to vent cyanide fumes from the execution gas chamber) rises high above the North Block. In the shadow of the exhaust stack on the room of North block there is an exercise yard. Weightlifting equipment, basketball, jump-ropes, heavy and speed punching bags are provided for exercise under the consent decree.

Condemned men on Old Death Row aren't allowed any "'tude"— slang for bad attitude. If 'tude creeps into a condemned man's speech or even his body language, the guards order him to pack up his personal belongings and he's beamed into one of the other two death row housing units.

### East Block

Located inside San Quentin's East Block housing unit is a second death row. It's officially designated "Death Row II," but more commonly, it's simply referred to as East Block. A huge warehouse-type building, many different species of birds nest in its nooks and crannies. Starting their singing with the daylight, they fly onto tiers and scamper around while prisoners share their breakfast with them. Feral stray cats also live inside the housing unit: they hide out during the day and prowl around at night. Although condemned men also feed them, the cats seem to prefer stalking the birds for their meals.

Like North Seg, there are two sides to East Block, the Bay-side and the Yard-side. Each side has five tiers of fifty-four cells (a few less on their first tier where a handful of cells have been converted into administrative offices), more than 250 condemned men live on six of the tiers—dead men stacked up all the way to the rafters. Existence in East Block is far removed from the tranquil serenity of North Seg: noise pumps out of the cells, off the soundtrack to the constant, chaotic bedlam rampaging throughout the cell-block. Most guards in East Block don't sweat 'tude in a prisoner's words or body language. Pretty much the line is drawn at threats of violence directed towards staff members, and, of course, actual violence is frowned upon.

Although mandated by housing unit policy, daily cell searches rarely occur inside East Block. Excess personal property in a cell is pretty much ignored by the guards. The only exception is if a condemned man broadcasts way too much static-filled 'tude, and fills to overflowing the ears of the guard assigned to his tier. Retaliation usually occurs in the form of a "house-tossing." A tossing consists of dumping the prisoner's personal belongings onto the floor of his cell and trampling on them. The uncertain message is, "Modify your behavior or find another tier to live on!" Most prisoners comply with the message because, next time, the guard might not simply toss the prisoner's property, he or she might tear it up and/or throw it away.

If a tossing doesn't get through to a doltish 'tude-man, a guard can always bring a piece of steel to work, give it to the unit sergeant, and claim he or she found it inside the prisoner's cell. Whether or not the steel has been sharpened, it's metal stock, a potential weapon, the sort of weapon that has been found sticking out of the chests of guards, and that is more than enough to warp-drive a condemned man off an East Block tier into a strip cell deep inside the Adjustment Center—the third death row at San Quentin.

As in North Seg, breakfast is served off a hot cart and yard release follows breakfast. But unlike North Seg, East Block guards don't simply unlock cell doors and let the condemned men saunter onto the tier and out to the exercise yard. In fact, there isn't any tier exercise in East Block, prisoners are only allowed to roam around the yards.

Before leaving their cells, East Block prisoners strip off their clothing and are ordered to strike various nude poses while a guard peeks into the prisoner's body cavities looking for drugs or weapons. Metal detectors and airport-type scanners are employed to search prisoners and their yard clothing for shanks—prison slang for illicitly obtained pieces of steel sharpened on the cement floor of cells and fashioned into stabbing weapons. Handcuffed, the prisoner backs out of his cell onto the tier under the watchful eye of a guard, armed with a mini-14 rifle, manning the catwalk. Venturing out of East Block, the prisoner walks down a guard-lined concrete path heading for the gate of his assigned exercise yard.

There are six exercise yards for prisoners housed with East Block. Each yard is so small and narrow, they seemingly resemble dog runs. Lined up one after another, the yards are separated from each other by sets of two chain-linked fences with a no-man's land between them. Four of the yards are for condemned prisoners. The other two are for non-condemned prisoners who have been yoked out of the general prison population and slammed down inside East Block because they've received a rule violation report from some badge. The rule violation could be as deadly serious as mayhem to totally silly as aggressive eye-contact with a staff-member—whatever that means.

Giving his name and cell number to the guard on the gate, the prisoner's name is checked against the yard list. Stepping through the outer-gate, it's slammed closed. Reaching through a slot in the gate, the guard removes the handcuffs, a switch is thrown, the inner-gate electrically hums open, and the man finally strolls onto the exercise yard. "Free at last, free at last, praise the Lord, I'm free at last!" Well, as free as you can be on a prison yard surrounded by barbed and razor wire strung along the top of the walls and fences. Running halfway around all the exercise yards is an elevated catwalk bolted to the outside wall and manned by guards with rifles. Directly across from the armed guards is a high cinderblock wall, a yellow monolith, that's pitted and scarred from bullets that have banged off its imposing surface.

The condemned yards in East Block have the same exercise equipment as North Seg with the exception of dumbbell weights. A few years ago, an East Block condemned man hammered another one over the head with a dumbbell. The fact that the hammeree survived the hammering clearly demonstrates the physical weakness of the prisoners or the denseness of their skulls—take your pick. Prison officials removed the dumbbells from the yards, but barbell weights are still available for weightlifting or hammering fellow condemned prisoners in their craniums. When you stand on the off-white concrete floor of one of the six exercise yards and gaze up at the yellow wall on one side and the guards with their rifles on the other, you feel as if you've fallen into a kiln that traps in both the heat of the sun's rays and the bodies of society's outcasts. On any given day, forty, fifty, sixty, or more prisoners are crammed onto each yard. All the bodies packed tightly together in concert with the heat radiating from the concrete and cinderblock walls creates a conspiracy to pull the oxygen out of the air, and often a panicky, claustrophobic atmosphere descends to smother and finish killing off any last vestige of humanity still staggering around inside the walls of San Quentin's death row.

Although violence on the East Block yards isn't an everyday occurrence, it's certainly not an unknown stranger, either. Condemned prisoners, who for the most part aren't exactly blessed with an abundance of social toler-ance, fray easily. On a hot summer day when the sun kicks the thermometer into the danger zone, an errant basketball, an unintentional body-to-body contact, a carelessly flicked cigarette can lead to combat.

In these final few years of the twentieth century, guards still try to con-trol prisoners in the same manner they tried and failed with for hundreds of years—bullets. And once let loose from a guard's rifle, a bullet doesn't re-spect the artificial boundaries imposed by the chain-linked fences separating the six yards. If the 223 rounds from the mini-14 rifle doesn't immediately slam into the body of a prisoner, the bullet whacks off the concrete floor or cinderblock wall, fragments, and then scatters, ricocheting around until the pieces come to rest inside someone or something. I've seen many prisoners wounded by bullets or bullet fragments. One prisoner was attacked by an-other prisoner. Instead of shooting the assailant, the guard shot the victim in his elbow. Ripping off his sock, the victim wrapped it around his arm, used his teeth to tug it tight, and the bleeding stopped. The victim's quick action may have saved his life, but did not help his arm—amputated.

In another incident, a fist-fight broke out between two prisoners. A guard on the catwalk fired three shots in rapid succession. One combat-ant dove and the other toppled onto the ground while a red rain showered down. The man who dove was spattered with blood but otherwise escaped the altercation unscathed. The man who toppled over was very still, blood rivered out of a gaping hole in his head to gently lap around the gray brain matter and whole skull fragments now littering the concrete.

Calling from the catwalk down to the guards responding to his whistle, the guard who had done the shooting said, "He had a weapon, it's over there." I stared up at the guard in disbelief because I hadn't seen a weapon. Other prisoners, who also hadn't seen a weapon, started jeering the guard's statement. Searching the yard, the guards didn't find a weapon. The badge on the catwalk with the freshly fired rifle in his hands shrugged, and said, "Well. I saw stabbing motions." There hadn't been any stabbing motions; it was just another typical free-swinging prison fist-fight except that this one resulted in a guard's bullet caving a skull.

In the third incident, a condemned prisoner was shot in the upper-chest and fell into a pool of his own blood when he wasn't fighting, but simply heatedly arguing with another condemned man standing about ten feet away. The shot man was DOA [dead on arrival] at the Marin General Hospital. When an incident occurs, the guards on the catwalk order all the prisoners on the yard, whether they're involved in the fight or not, to get off their feet and plant their bodies onto the concrete floor. Whistles fill the air and more guards come running. When the guards regain some semblance of control over the yard, the sergeant orders any wounded prisoners to come to the yard gate. Any man so damaged that he cannot make it on his own power is picked up by prisoners designated by the sergeant, carried and stuffed in between the gates. Closing the inner-gate, yanking open the outer-gate, the guards lock handcuffs on the wounded or dead before they're loaded onto wheelchairs or bright orange stretchers. Red blood drops trace a crimson trail as they're whisked off to the hospital or to be claimed by next-of-kin. Next, one-by-one the rest of the prisoners are ordered to rise and walk to the gate. Handcuffed, they're taken inside East Block. Caged, they're strip-searched for weapons or any cuts or bruises that might indicate involvement in the "physical altercation."

About five years ago, a condemned man on my assigned East Block exercise yard got it into his head to put his hands on my body and give me a good shove. I, of course, handled the situation with my usual lack of poise and grace. Clenching hands into fists, I bounced them off his skull a couple of times. Hearing the mechanical clack of a rifle bolt slamming home a bullet into a chamber, I flicked my eyes up to the guard on the catwalk: he was aiming his rifle right between my flicking eyes. Instantly, I shoved my antagonist away from me and tossed my hands into the air.

"Get down, RIGHT NOW!" the guard screamed at me.

Only when my butt touched the concrete did the badge rotate his rifle up and away from my cranium. Watching the rifle swing away from its dead-on aim at my head, I realized that I'd been involuntarily holding my breath. Inhaling, I fed oxygen into my wildly pumping, overdriving heart.

Whistles pierced the air, boots pounded pavement, a sergeant joined the scene and ordered me to the yard gate. Handcuffed, my body was yoked out of the gate, and two guards marched me off to the Adjustment Center, the last and the worst of San Quentin's death rows.

## The Adjustment Center

The name "Adjustment Center" evokes an image of a feel-good, "I'm Okay—You're Okay" type of place where condemned men are housed and counseled so that they can learn to cope with the brutal realities of existing day-to-day on death row. That concept couldn't be further from the truth. The Adjustment Center is the deepest, darkest hole at San Quentin. Once upon a time it was the disciplinary housing unit for the entire Department of Corrections, every prison sent its recalcitrant problem prisoners there. Now it mostly deals with death row discipline problems, warehousing a bit over one hundred prisoners on its three floors of which about ninety are condemned.

The Adjustment Center, also called "the AC" or "that other place," is a very clean housing unit, it's antiseptic much like a hospital or a morgue. It's pretty quiet in the AC, but not the tranquil quiet of North Seg, it's like a sullen silence—a wild animal lying low, eyes firmly fixed on its prey, waiting an opportunity to pounce on the unwary. No matter if you're a guard or a prisoner, just about everyone in the AC has buckets of 'tude running through their veins. In fact, the AC's door guard was even kind of nasty to the badges escorting me from East Block.

"Wait here," the AC guard told the East Block badges as he snatched my body and started pulling me inside the maw of the Adjustment Center.

"Need my cuffs back," one of the East Block guards protested and tried to follow me through the door.

"Wait here, I'll bring them to you," the AC guard slammed the door in the face of his fellow green uniform.

Locking me inside a cage, the guard ordered me to remove every piece of clothing from my body. After sending me through a strip search that made East Block searches seem like a casual glance, he gave me a whole different set of state-issue clothing to wear. Nothing you walk into the AC carrying or wearing accompanies you into a cell.

"Excuse me, officer," I said in my most polite manner. "These pants are too large, I wear 32s."

"We've two sizes here," he answered without a hint of sarcasm, humor, or humanity in his voice, "too large and too small. Which size you want?"

I kept the pair he'd already issued me. I thought then and still think now that it was a really good decision.

After a few hours in the cage, an AC escort guard cuffed me up, took me up the stairs to the third floor, and locked me inside another cage.

An hour crept by before the third floor guard appeared and ordered, "Get naked."

"Man, they searched me downstairs already," I casually but not disrespectfully protested, and didn't rise from my seat on the floor of the cage.

Sliding his club out of its ring on his utility belt, the badge firmly banged it against the side of the cage and stated in a bored tone-of-voice, "This is my fourth tour in the AC. I'm here 'cause I like it here. In the AC we get used to dealing with jerks, we kind of specialize in them, and I'm starting to suspect that you're one, Hunter." Listening more to his bored tone than his words, I rose and started pulling clothes off my body, while wondering, why don't they just turn the AC into a nudist colony? Finally, locked inside a strip cell, a cell with nothing much inside it except bedding, air, and me, I started to strongly suspect that compared to the other people roaming around inside the AC in green uniforms and state-issue blue, I wasn't a very tough guy. My thoughts were verified with a vengeance when during my tenure in the AC, a condemned man broke free from his handcuffs while walking down the tier from the shower to his cell. Jumping on the two guards escorting him, the man was smacking both of them around until four or five more badges came running and buried the prisoner in an avalanche of green uniforms. Holding the prisoner down on the floor, the guards took turns booting the body and stomping on his skull until they grew weary, slowed, and finally stopped. As the condemned man was dragged away, another condemned man called from his cell, "How yah doin', man?" The bloody, lumpy, bruised man grinned through swollen lips, and answered lightly, "Not bad, I've been worse."

The guards constantly search AC cells, but the searches don't take too long because San Quentin does not allow AC prisoners to have very much property. In fact, AC prisoners are excluded from almost every aspect of the federal consent decree—no phone calls, they can't use the contact visiting room, no arts or educational programs, and they're only allowed three days a week on their exercise yards. The AC exercise yards are much larger than the East Block's yards, and seem even larger because there's nothing much on them except a basketball, a hoop, and a lot of really angry, dangerous men.

Essentially there's two different ways a prisoner can crash-land inside the AC. One is to receive a serious rule violation such as the one I received for assault and involvement in a physical altercation. The second is to be an identified member of a prison gang. If the condemned prisoner's in the AC for a rule violation report, the classification committee will let him transfer back to East Block or North Seg if he remains disciplinary free for some weeks, months, or years depending on the seriousness of the offense. The only exception is an assault on a staff member. Officially, the term is thirty-six to sixty months in lockup, but in reality, a condemned man charged with assaulting a staff member is never leaving the AC and can only look forward to a pine box parole. If an identified gang member, the condemned man will be released from lockup when he debriefs or dies. My information about debriefing is second-hand from men who have dropped out. The gang member notifies prison authorities of his wish to drop out, he's hooked up to a lie detector machine, and is required to confess to a crime that he committed inside or outside of prison. Once his confession passes the lie detector, he's extensively questioned about every member of the gang. If the dropout isn't forthcoming about his dirty deeds, the debriefing is suspended and the prisoner is not allowed to transfer from the AC. Staff members let the gang know the man started debriefing, gang-bangers start threatening to kill him which tends to put a lot of pressure on the dropout to finish the debriefing and get out of AC. Joining a gang is serious business, dropping out by informing is deadly serious.

Since I was in the AC for an allegation of assault without a weapon on a non-staff member, and no deadly force was used or great bodily injury occurred, my charges weren't considered very serious in the realm of AC offenses. At my disciplinary hearing, my right hand was wrapped in a bandage because banging it off a rock-hard head had fractured it. With a hand still swollen to twice its normal size, it was difficult to deny that I had struck anyone, so I wasn't tempted to use the time-honored alibi which has never, ever worked with any disciplinary hearing lieutenant in the history of corrections, "It wasn't me, man. It was someone who looks like me, and the guard got confused."

I simply pleaded guilty. Dropping the charge to mutual combat, the lieutenant recommended transfer back to East Block after only six weeks in the AC while warning that my next write up for smacking someone would cost me six months to a year in the Adjustment Center. "Won't be a next time," I answered. But as is frequently the case, I was wrong.

About two years later, a guard came to my East Block exercise yard and told me that I had a doctor's appointment. I knew I didn't have an appointment. But the guards have the guns and more importantly the bullets, so I cuffed up and sure enough I was marched to the AC. After a week, I was cuffed and taken in my undershorts (the reason for only undershorts is so the committee can inspect your body for gang tattoos) to the classification committee in order to receive my yard assignment.

At the hearing, I asked the committee why I had been transferred to the AC. Laughing without any mirth at my question, the men-in-suits told me to read my rule violation report. When I told them that I hadn't received a report, they laughed again and placed a report on the table in front of me. Running my eyes over the typed words, it was immediately apparent that another Hunter, one who wasn't on death row, had been written up for "Disrespect of Staff." They'd yoked and beamed the wrong Hunter into the AC. When I brought this to the attention of the committee, the suit running the show became really angry. The man clad in rayon-plaid said I should have told the AC door guard they had the wrong prisoner.

Looking at each member with cynical eyes, I couldn't believe they didn't know a prisoner doesn't tell an AC guard anything unless he's begging for some flashlight therapy administered across the crown of his skull. Smiling, I finally answered, "In that case, I'd like to tell you that you've got the wrong Hunter on death row. Please take me to the East Gate and toss me out of San Quentin." Didn't work, but they all got a chuckle (with a hint of actual levity) out of my wry words, until I added, "Mixing me up with the non-condemned prisoner also named Hunter is no big deal, since you can ship me back to East Block and nab him. But what would you do if you had shoved the other Hunter into the gas chamber instead of me?" Those words stopped the laughter, but I never got an answer to my question. Guess there really isn't one.

Following one of the shootings described by Michael, the warden at San Quentin authorized officers to carry "gas guns" with rubber bullets as an option to standard rifles. In the face of media publicity over the number of shooting deaths throughout the prison system, the Department of Corrections made several changes to its shooting policy to reduce the number of deaths.

Since writing this article, Michael Wayne Hunter has been transferred from Death Row, San Quentin, in California to life imprisonment.

## IT'S TIME FOR ME TO DIE:
## AN INSIDE LOOK AT DEATH ROW

### Michael B. Ross, Death Row, Connecticut

It's time for me to die. I know this because the warden is in front of my cell reading the death warrant to me and several guards are waiting to escort me to the execution chamber. They open my door and walk me into a room less than ten feet away. In the center of that room I see a large, brown, wooden, very uncomfortable-looking chair with several leather straps attached—it's the electric chair. About ten feet in front of the chair is a cinder-block wall. I can't see through to the other side because of a set of Venetian blinds that are closed, but I know that on the other side of that wall are the official witnesses to my imminent execution.

Now things begin to get weird. I notice a large bay window. The side windows are wide open, and they have no bars. Outside it is an absolutely beautiful spring morning. The sunlight is streaming into the room, and I can see and hear the birds chirping outside. The guards walk me to the chair. I'm facing the witness chamber when the blinds are opened. My "official" witnesses are wearing little party hats, have party favors, and are laughing and drinking champagne. Confetti floats through the air.

The guards sit me down and strap me into the chair, but suddenly weightless I rise into the air, leaving my body behind as I float out the window and up over the prison. It's no longer a sunny spring day. It's cold and dark, and the prison lights shine harshly on the ground. It's a bitterly cold winter evening, with no snow on the ground. I float up over the front of the prison and see a crowd of hundreds of people gathered at the front gate. They suddenly start counting down in unison just like it was New Year's Eve: Five . . . four . . . three . . . two . . . one. And they start cheering, shouting and hollering as the lights dim and flicker. There is a pause for thirty seconds, and then they cheer again as the electric chair releases its second discharge of death, causing the prison lights to dim and flicker once more. I now know that I am dead.

My name is Michael Ross, and I am a serial killer responsible for the rape and murder of eight women in Connecticut, New York, and Rhode Island. I have never denied what I did, have fully confessed to my crimes, and was sentenced to death in 1987. Now, however, I am awaiting a new sentencing hearing—ordered by the Connecticut State Supreme Court—that will result either in my being re-sentenced to death or to multiple life sentences without the possibility of release. The crucial issue in my case is, as it has been from the beginning, my mental condition at the time of the crimes—the infamous and much maligned "insanity defense." For years I have been trying to prove that I am suffering from a mental illness that drove me to rape and kill, and that this mental illness made me physically unable to control my actions. I have met with little success.

I used to have that dream on a regular basis when I first came to death row. It wasn't really a dream, but more of a nightmarish daydream or vision. I was pretty depressed and would spend most days on my bunk with the covers pulled up over my head. I had this vision almost daily—while semi-awake. And it seemed as real as anything I have actually experienced. I could almost taste, smell, and feel the sensations. Each time I actually thought it was real until I opened the bay window and told myself, "that's not right." Fortunately I no longer experience the horror of this vision—very seldom anyway. Regular doses of the antidepressant Prozac keep me relatively stable, and the visions tend to stay away.

### What's It Like to Live on Death Row?

Death row here in Connecticut isn't as rough as some death rows elsewhere—especially the ones down South—but it's no "country club" either. Death row in this state is located in a "super-max" prison. I live in a seven-foot by twelve-foot cell—large by prison standards—consisting of a metal bunk, a desk, and a combination toilet/sink. I live alone in this cell and spend twenty-three hours a day here. My only sight of the outside world is through a three-inch by three-foot slot window, which has a wonderful view of the razor-wire fencing and outdoor recreation yard of the prison next door.

I eat all of my meals in my cell—there is no dining hall in this facility.

My meals are delivered to me in a Styrofoam box with a plastic spoon and fork—no plastic knives. Some of the other inmates in this institution eat their meals at tables in the dayrooms like civilized men, but that is a privilege not afforded to death row inmates.

I am allowed one hour of outside recreation five days a week. Our recreation yard is approximately twenty-five feet square with thirty-foot-high concrete walls and chain-link fencing across the top. We are not allowed so much as a handball, and the only activity for exercise is jogging in circles on the concrete floor. Our recreation hour begins at 8 A.M., which means we can see the sun on the walls, but we have to look up before the sun rises high enough that we can actually stand in it. The situation is so poor that only two of us go outside on a regular basis—no one else even bothers. (Michael's note: no longer allowed group recreation. Death row inmates are no longer allowed to socialize together—individual recreation only.)

We are allowed two hours of "out-of-cell" time in our dayroom from 6 P.M. to 8 P.M. daily. At that time we can use the telephone to make collect calls (two fifteen-minute calls per day). Death row inmates have absolutely no contact with other inmates. By far most of my time is spent alone in my cell. When I first came to death row my father bought me a color television set, on which I receive six local broadcast stations. I have a typewriter that I use to type articles that I submit to various publications—mostly anti-death-penalty articles, but more recently I have branched out into more spiritually based articles for religious publications. I also have a small Walkman radio on which I listen to classical music. They say that music soothes the savage soul, and classical music does in fact relax me. I spend many hours with my headphones on listening to this music with my eyes covered—it is how I cope with life here.

Initially I was placed in the "Death Cell," a cell directly adjacent to the execution chamber and usually used only to house the condemned man for the last twenty-four to forty-eight hours before his execution. A guard was posted at a desk directly in front of my cell for twenty-four hours a day, seven days a week. I had absolutely no privacy. I got dressed in front of the guard. I used the toilet in front of the guard. Everything that I did was in front of the guard. And everything was written down in my very own "Death Row Log Book": What time I woke up in the morning. What time I ate my meals and brushed my teeth. Everything. You cannot begin to imagine what that absolute and total lack of privacy does to you. You cannot begin to imagine how it begins to destroy your very sense of humanity—like you are an animal in a cage on display at the zoo. No wonder I spiraled into a clinical depression and had visions of my own execution.

That lasted for almost a year. Then they replaced the guard with a closed-circuit television system that monitored the inside of my cell—for my privacy, they said. In reality, it was because I wasn't a disciplinary problem, and it was cheaper to monitor me by closed circuit television at a desk at the front of the unit than to post a guard on a single inmate for twenty-four hours a day. And it actually gave me less privacy, for at the other end of the camera was a monitor viewed by anyone who happened to pass by, including any female officers. The camera lasted for four more years before I was finally able to convince them that it was an unnecessary invasion of my privacy. The guards make their rounds every half-hour or so, but at least now I know about when to expect him or her so I can time when to use the toilet or get dressed.

When I first came to death row, I was a very high-profile inmate. Everyone knew who Michael Ross was. Everyone knew what I had done. Everyone knew I was sentenced to death, and everyone—so it seemed—agreed with that sentence and hoped it would be carried out as quickly as possible. All of that made me different from any other inmate. At the time, I was the only man under a sentence of death in the State of Connecticut. For two and a half years—until another man was sentenced to death—I was the only man deemed by the state to be unworthy of life itself. And I had received more publicity than any other inmate in the system. Naturally, I stood out—and prison is a bad place to stand out.

Most people here are anonymous. Few prisoners know who the other inmates are or what they did, so they are not judged by their crimes, but rather by what kind of people they are. If they are jerks, they tend to be treated as jerks. If you stay by yourself and don't bother anyone, you tend not to be bothered. But if you stick out, everyone jumps on you. For some people it's a way to deal with their own insecurities—by putting you down they are boosting themselves up. For some people it's a way to divert attention from themselves—I've found that those who yell "tree jumper" the loudest are quite often rapists themselves. Then there are those who join in to be part of the crowd—these are the ones who are friendly when they are alone with you, but suddenly can't stand you when others are criticizing you. And finally, there are those who are just so damn miserable that they can only feel better by trying to make others miserable too.

Not everyone fits into one of these categories. I have made some friends. Most of them are people who don't believe everything they read in the newspaper or hear through the grapevine. They are the ones who tend to approach people with an attitude of "how you treat me is how I will treat you." Unfortunately people like these are few and far between in prison. But at times they can be like a breath of fresh air. When someone simply says, "Hey, Mike, how's it going?" or "Hey, Mike, hang in there," it can mean a lot—especially during the rough times.

And there have been rough times. I received a great deal of harassment from my fellow inmates, and also from the guards. Whenever I went somewhere in the prison—to medical or visiting—there were always the stares, the whispers, and the threats, "Hey, man, do you know who that is?" "He's the one who killed all those girls." "I wish they would let the SOB into population, then we could teach him a lesson." "Ripper!" "Child raper!" "Hey, tree-jumper, we're gonna kill you!" "If it was my sister, you would already be dead." And the ever-present sound mimicking the electric chair, "Bzzzzzzzzzzzzzz."

I have been assaulted on several occasions. I've been hit with bars of soap, doused with cups of urine and feces, and had my food messed with by the guards, who spit on it or put hairs in it. I've had to go to the free-world hospital twice. Once I was stabbed fifteen times by an inmate with a pair of barbershop scissors taped to his hand; I had been set up by the guard, who let the non-death-row inmate out to attack me. The other time I was beaten by an inmate in a stairwell and received several stitches. Fortunately for me, things have settled down considerably since those early years. I still get the stares and the occasional comment, but things are much quieter today.

As you might imagine, I have been examined by a multitude of psychiatric experts over the past fourteen years. All of them—even Dr. Robert B. Miller, the state's own expert psychiatric witness—agree I suffer from a paraphiliac mental disorder called "sexual sadism." This is a mental illness that, according to the testimony of the experts, resulted in my compulsion "to perpetrate violent sexual activity in a repetitive way." The experts also agree that my criminal conduct was a direct result of the uncontrollable aggressive sexual impulses caused by the disorder. The state's only hope of obtaining a conviction and death sentence was to muddy the waters and inflame the jury members' passions so they would ignore any evidence of psychological impairment. In my case, as you might expect, that was quite easy to do, and the state succeeded in obtaining multiple death sentences.

So why was a new sentencing hearing ordered? An *amicus curiae* ("friend of the court") brief was filed by a group of eminent psychiatrists from Connecticut. They were connected to neither the state nor the defense, but they got involved because—as their brief states—of their concern "that the psychiatric issues were distorted at both the guilt and penalty phase of the trial." They summed up our main point of contention perfectly, "By allowing Dr. Miller to testify in a way that led the jury to believe that Mr. Ross could control his behavior—when in fact he and all the other psychiatric experts were of the view that Mr. Ross could not—the court allowed the jury to be effectively misled." The Connecticut State Supreme Court agreed.

What exactly is a paraphiliac mental disorder? It is very difficult to explain, and even more difficult to understand. I'm not even sure that I myself fully understand this disease, and I've been trying to understand what's been going on in my head for a very long time now. Basically, I am plagued by repetitive thoughts, urges, and fantasies of the degradation, rape, and murder of women. I cannot get those thoughts out of my mind.

The best way for the average person to try to understand this is to remember a time when a song played over and over again in your head. Even if you liked the melody, its constant repetition was quite annoying, and the harder you tried to drive it out of your head, the harder it seemed to stick. Now replace that sweet melody with noxious thoughts of degradation, rape, and murder, and you will begin—and only just begin—to understand what was running rampant through my mind uncontrollably. Some people believe that if you think about something day in and day out, you must want to think about it. But that just isn't true when you are discussing mental illness. Most people can't understand because they just can't imagine wanting to commit such horrific acts of unimaginable cruelty. They can't begin to understand this obsession of mine. They think that if you fantasize about something you must want to make the fantasy come true. But it's far more complicated than that. They can't understand how I could fantasize such disgusting imagery, how I could derive such pleasure from that fantasy, and yet be so disgusted later by the exact same thoughts or urges, or at the thought of how much I enjoyed the fantasy just moments before. I could relive the rapes and murders that I committed, and when reliving those despicable acts in my mind I could experience such orgasmic pleasure that it is hard to describe. But afterward I felt such a sense of loathing and self-hatred that I often longed for my execution. I was tired of being tormented by my own sick, demented mind. So unbelievably tired.

And the urge to hurt someone could come over me at any time. Powerful urges welled up for no reason, and with no warning. I remember once when I was being escorted from the Mental Health Unit back to my cell after seeing my psychiatrist. There was a small stairway that led from the Unit to the main corridor. I was being led, without any restraints, by a small, young, female correctional officer. When I got to the stairwell, I was suddenly flooded with an overwhelming desire to hurt her. I knew I had to get out of that stairwell, and I ran up the stairs and out into the hallway. I will never forget how she shouted at me to stop and threatened to write me a disciplinary report—she didn't have a clue as to what was going on. I didn't know this woman; she had done me no harm; yet suddenly I was filled with a powerful desire to hurt her. She never knew just how badly I wanted to hurt her that day. She never knew how close I came to attacking her and maybe even killing her. You would think that after being sentenced to death and living on death row, such urges and thoughts would be curbed. But they weren't, for this illness defies rationality.

I have found some relief, however. About two and a half years after I came to death row, I started to receive weekly injections of a drug called Depo-Provera. Depo-Provera has been used for years as a female contraceptive in Europe and recently was approved for use in America. For sex offenders it is used at a significantly higher dosage than what women take for contraceptive purposes: Women receive 150 milligrams every three months; I received 700 milligrams weekly. In men, Depo-Provera significantly reduces the body's natural production of the male sex hormone, testosterone. For some reason, whether because of some abnormal biological hookup in my brain or some sort of chemical imbalance, testosterone affects my mind differently than it affects the average male's mind.

A few months after I started to receive my weekly injections, my blood serum testosterone levels dropped below prepubescent levels (last month my level was 12 mg/dl, with the normal range being 260–1,250 mg/dl); and as this happened, nothing less than a miracle occurred. My obsessive thoughts, urges, and fantasies began to diminish. Having those thoughts and urges is like living with an obnoxious roommate. You cannot get away from him because he is always there. What Depo-Provera did was to move that roommate down the hall to his own apartment. The problem was still there, but it was a whole lot easier to deal with because it wasn't always in the foreground. He didn't control me anymore—I was in control of him. It was an unbelievable sense of freedom. It made me feel as if I were a human being again, instead of some sort of horrible monster. For three years I had a sort of peace of mind.

Then I developed liver problems, a very rare side effect of the hormonal shots, so I was forced to discontinue the medication. Soon thereafter the noxious thoughts, fantasies, and urges returned. It was horrible. I felt like a blind man who had been given the gift of sight only to have it snatched away again. There was an alternative medication, but it lacked FDA approval as a treatment for sex offenders, so the Department of Corrections refused to approve its use. From my past history we knew what the problem was: testosterone. Get it out of my bloodstream so that it can't reach my mind and I am okay. So I asked to be surgically castrated, with the support and approval of my treating psychiatrist. But the department—which I am sure was afraid of headlines such as "Sex Offender Castrated by State"—refused my request. It took more than a year of fighting by a lot of good people here in the Mental Health Department before I was allowed to receive the alternative medication, a monthly shot of a drug called Depo-Lupron, which I have been receiving to date.

What made the year without medication particularly bad was that I began having thoughts and urges about hurting people here. I remember one young woman in particular, a nurse who had always gone out of her way to help me. She always had a smile, and was always friendly to me, even though she knew who and what I was. I started having thoughts and urges of hurting this woman, and that really tore me up inside. Here was someone whom I liked, who had always helped me, and how did I repay her kindness? By wanting to rape and strangle her. I felt uncomfortable whenever she was around, and I felt so guilty and ashamed that I could hardly look at her. Fortunately nothing ever happened, and she never found out what was going through my mind. That time is past now because I am receiving my medication, but the memories and guilt haven't gone away.

One of my doctors once told me that I am, in a sense, also a victim—a victim of an affliction that no one would want. And sometimes I do feel like a victim, but at the same time I feel guilty and get angry for thinking that way. How dare I consider myself a victim when the real victims are dead? How dare I consider myself a victim when the families of my true victims have to live day by day with the pain of the loss I caused? So what if it is an affliction? So what if I was really sick? Does that really make any difference? Does that absolve me of my responsibility for the deaths of eight totally innocent women? Does it make the women any less dead? Does it ease the pain of their families? No!

I close my eyes and I see the families of the women whom I killed. Even though my trial was over a decade ago, I cannot make the visions go away. I can see Mrs. Shelley on the witness stand testifying about the last time she saw her daughter alive. I can still see the agony in her face and hear the pain in her voice as she described how she and her husband searched for their daughter, and I can vividly recall how I actually saw them searching along the roadway the day after her death. At the time I didn't know who they were, but I knew whom they were searching for. I close my eyes and I am haunted by the vision of Mrs. Stavinsky on the witness stand testifying how on Thanksgiving Day she had to go to the morgue to identify her daughter's body. "She was hurt bad," she testified as she broke down and cried. "She was hurt real bad."

It is hard for me to close my eyes and not see these people as they appeared during the court proceedings. I can still, eleven years later, very clearly see how they looked at me; I can still feel their anger and hatred. I tried very hard to pretend none of this bothered me. I put up a facade of nonchalance to show that nothing was getting to me. I intentionally chatted and joked with my lawyers and with the sheriff's deputies as if I didn't have a care in the world. But although I tried very hard not to show it, I did see the families of my victims. And it is their faces, their pain, that haunt me today.

I wish I knew how to tell them just how sorry I am. But there are no words to describe what I feel. How do you tell someone you are sorry when you have stolen something so very precious from them? How do you tell them you are sorry when those very words sound so inadequate that you are ashamed to even speak them in their presence for fear of making things worse? I cannot even face them, never mind ask for their forgiveness. And while I would really like them to understand what happened and why, I don't expect they will ever truly understand the insanity that drove me to kill their loved ones.

And that is the big question: Was I really insane? The big question that has everyone all riled up is a question that in the end may not matter at all. Whether I was sane or insane can't change the facts of what happened, can't bring anyone back, can't ease the families' pain. And it can't cleanse my guilt, or wash the blood off of my hands. It can't change anything, resolve anything, or absolve anything.

I think that is part of the reason why I volunteered for execution and more recently tried to accept the death penalty and avoid another full-blown penalty hearing. When I first came to death row I was filled with anger at how the prosecutor had twisted and distorted the facts of my case. I was consumed with an intense desire to prove that my mental illness does in fact exist, and that the mental illness did in fact deprive me of my ability to control my actions, and that my mental illness was in fact the cause of my criminal conduct. I wanted so badly for everyone to understand and believe that I really was sick and that it was the sickness within me that did the killing. I wanted to prove that I wasn't the animal the state portrayed me to be. I just wanted the truth to be known.

It took a very long time—years—in fact—for that anger and intense need to exonerate myself to leave me. With the help of my medication, I understand my past much better now, and I am much more at peace with myself now, and not so much concerned with what others might think of me. I would still like to prove the real reasons why I committed such atrocious acts, but it is no longer an overriding concern of mine. And to be completely honest, after years of banging my head against the wall trying to prove my case, I'm tired and no longer certain that I will ever be able to prove my lack of criminal responsibility, and I have come to believe that any such thoughts are simply wishful thinking.

There are times, usually late at night when things finally begin to quiet down around here, that I sit in my cell and wonder, "What the hell am I doing here?" Most people would probably think that this is a pretty silly question; obviously I'm here because I've killed many people and I deserve to be here. And that is okay on one level. But I think of the underlying reasons why I did those terrible things. I believe I am severely mentally ill and that the illness drove me to commit my crimes. I know that I may never be able to prove that in a court of law, but in here, in my cell, I don't have to prove anything to anybody. I know what the truth is. I know that I have an illness and that I'm no more responsible for having that illness than another person is for getting cancer or developing diabetes. But somehow "You're sick, and sometimes people just get sick" doesn't seem to cut it. I feel responsible. I wonder if things in my childhood may have made a difference. My mother was institutionalized twice by our family doctor because of how she was treating, or rather abusing, us kids. Maybe things would have been different if I had run away as my younger brother did. But this is an exercise in futility, because you can't change the past—yet at the same time you can't help but wonder what might have been.

In a way, I guess I am luckier than most inmates, even though I am sitting here on death row. I know and long ago accepted that I can never be freed, that in fact to release me would be to condemn others to their deaths. Regardless of the reasons why I kill—be it premeditated murder, as is generally thought, or the result of insanity—the fact remains that I kill, and there is no reason to believe that will ever change. That's not to say I don't want to get out of this place, for it is very dehumanizing here, and I greatly long for the outside. But I feel a sense of contentment knowing I will never be released. I know that must sound strange coming from a sadistic killer like me, but I do feel as if a huge load has been lifted from my shoulders.

So where do I stand today? The state prosecutor will once again seek the death penalty in the upcoming re-sentencing hearing. The only real issue that needs to be resolved at that hearing is whether or not my "mental capacity was significantly impaired." Under the law that applies in my case, if I am found to be suffering from a "significant mental illness," that will be considered a statutory mitigating factor that by Connecticut law would preclude my being sentenced to death. In that case I would be automatically sentenced to six consecutive life sentences without the possibility of release. The prosecution's strategy will undoubtedly be as it was last time—to inflame the jury's passions into ignoring the evidence of a psychiatric illness. And there is a good chance that he will once again succeed.

Knowing the situation as I do, and wishing to spare all concerned the emotional agony of going through a new trial—especially the families of my victims—I wrote a letter to the prosecutor on September 25, 1994, which said in part:

> There is no need for the penalty hearing to go forward. There is no need and no purpose served in unnecessarily opening old wounds. There is

no need and no purpose served in inflicting further emotional harm or distress on the families of my victims. I do not wish to hurt these people further—it's time for healing. I had volunteered for execution precisely to avoid the situation that we currently find ourselves in. And I am willing to hand you the death penalty "on a silver platter" on the condition that you will work with me to get this over with as quickly and as painlessly as possible. There is no need to drag the families of my victims through more lengthy and disturbing court proceedings. Please allow me to go into the courtroom to admit to my actions; to accept responsibility for my actions; and to accept the death penalty as punishment for those actions. I'm not asking you to do this for me, but for the families involved, who do not deserve to suffer further and who, in some small way, might gain a sense of peace of mind by these actions and my execution.

For almost four years I worked with the state's attorney to fashion an agreement that would allow the death penalty to be imposed without going through a full-blown penalty hearing. We signed that agreement on March 11, 1998. However, on August 1, 1998, a Superior Court judge rejected the agreement because he found it "unsettling" that the prosecutor would work with me on my wish to be executed without a fight. He ruled, "Shortcuts on procedure where an individual's life hangs in the balance cannot be tolerated under our system of criminal justice." This very effectively destroyed four years of hard work. Since I cannot appeal his decision, it appears that I have no choice but to prepare for the long and painful penalty hearing. I very much regret that I have failed the families of my victims. Jury selection and testimony for this new penalty hearing should begin in a few months.

So what can be learned from this sad story? I'm not really sure, because it seems to be pretty tragic all the way around. Maybe it is an indictment of our current medical system and societal attitudes—especially in how we treat the mentally ill. We can begin by treating mental illness as just that: an illness that needs to be recognized and treated instead of stigmatized. Without a doubt there are other Michael Rosses out there in various stages of development. They need places where they can go for help, and they need to know that it is okay for them to go for that help. One of the most difficult and painful things for me to deal with today is to know that had I begun to receive just a one-cc injection of Depo-Lupron once a month fifteen years ago, eight women would be alive today. The problem is real, but the issue of sexual deviancy is a taboo topic in our society. We would much rather turn our backs to the problem and pretend that it doesn't exist.

Am I trying to blame society for my illness? Am I trying to imply that you, as a member of society, are responsible for my turning into a killer? No, of course not. But I am saying that society needs to learn and to make the necessary changes to prevent its recurrence. It's easy for you to point your finger at me, to call me "evil," and to condemn me to death. But if that is all that happens, it will be a terrible waste, for in a sense you will be condemning yourselves to a future filled with Michael Rosses. Future tragic murders such as those I committed can be prevented, but only if society stops turning its back, stops condemning, and begins to squarely acknowledge and treat the problem. Only then will something constructive come out of the events that took the lives of eight women, destroyed the quality of life of their families and friends, resulted in my incarceration, and probable execution, and caused untold shame and anguish to my own family. The past has already happened. It is now up to you to change the future.

*Michael's additional note:* On May 12, 2000, I was re-sentenced to death. My execution has been stayed pending the resolution of the appeals process.

Michael Ross was executed by the State of Connecticut on May 13, 2005.

## DAVE

### Michael Wayne Hunter, Death Row, California

I spoke with Dave Mason the other day, who reiterated his support for the death penalty. This is not an unusual stance. Now that gas chambers, firing squads, gallows, electric chairs, and lethal drugs are all back in business, it is obvious that the death penalty has many supporters. However, for someone like Dave to be in favor of the death penalty is a bit unusual; he is a condemned prisoner on San Quentin's death row.

Dave and I arrived here around the same time, just months apart. We are from different counties and were convicted of different crimes, but we were both sent here for the same reason: to die. After we arrived our convictions and death verdicts were appealed to the California Supreme Court for review. This process isn't discretionary or optional; the review is mandatory for all death sentences. The California Supreme Court must add its stamp of approval before a condemned prisoner can be executed. It's the law.

Dave's and my appeals were heard just months apart, and in both cases a majority of the seven-judge panel affirmed that we should die. This was not an unexpected outcome, since over the past six years the California Supreme Court has voted for death more than ninety percent of the time. Even if the Court upholds a death sentence, a prisoner still has the option for one last review in the federal court. The reason is that the United States Constitution and the California constitution differ, and a court ruling that may conform to California law may not be legal according to federal law. I decided to take this option.

Filing before federal court for judicial review saved my life, at least for now. Assuming that Dave would do the same thing (after all, who wants to die when you can just file a piece of paper?), I was surprised when a mutual friend told me that Dave had refused to file such a petition. He would probably be executed in a couple of months. I decided to send Dave a message telling him that, although I respected his right to do what he thought was best, I wished he would reconsider his decision.

About a week later, returning from the visiting room, Dave and I were locked in adjacent holding cages. I took the opportunity to ask him if it were true that he was waiving his right for federal review.

Dave said, "I'm not going to beg them for my life."

"Dave," I told him, "you're entitled to federal judicial review. The federal courts want to make sure that the State of California is following the law when they kill you."

"Mike, I've always believed in the death penalty. There is no reason for me to change my view just because it's my life that's involved. The people of California think they will be better off with my death. Okay, they can take me out now."

"Okay, Dave, go ahead and pick which way you are going to die, the gas chamber or lethal injection. Write out your last statement for the warden to read; no one but me and a few other people will remember what you wrote. Order and eat your last meal, but when you get dessert and the only thing to do is to walk down the corridor to your death, you will still have the option to file the petition. Don't let pride stop you from having your attorneys file the petition for federal judicial review and save your life. I for one won't think any less of you."

"You don't get it, Mike. I don't want a last meal. I don't want anything from them. It's over."

I thought about telling Dave that his death wouldn't be in a vacuum, and that there were people who would be affected by it. I then realized that this argument had probably been offered repeatedly by Dave's family members and loved ones, who are much closer to him than I. He had already rejected this as a reason to continue his appeals.

Although I don't understand Dave's endorsement of the death penalty, I do understand his embrace of death. The idea of accepting death can be very seductive to a condemned prisoner. The thought of attaining a sense of peace and tranquility after giving up the struggle is very tempting. Also very appealing is the prospect that, by accepting and inviting your greatest fear, death, into your life, you could virtually eliminate the control guards, wardens, judges, and governors have over your fate. At times, resigning myself to the fact that I will die by execution is even attractive to me. It would make everything else seem so trivial and disconnected to my existence, leaving no holds over my mind, my emotions, or my life.

There is also a reverse side to this alluring acceptance of death that I see in some condemned prisoners, however, and that is denial. The prisoner finds some reason, generally only apparent to himself, why other prisoners may be executed but not him. He makes plans for his future once he is released from the grim confines of San Quentin, while managing to ignore that the State of California is using its considerable resources to expedite his demise. I, too, at times, am drawn to such fantasies.

While in the state of denial, I also find myself thinking that others will be executed, but surely someone in authority will see that I'm different and save me. But such thoughts are short-lived. Reality comes crashing in, and I remember I'm only here for one reason, to die, and this will almost surely be my fate. However, "almost surely" is not "definitely," and it is the difference between the absolute of "definitely" and the qualification inherent in "almost surely" that is the source of my determination to resist being seduced by death. In Dave's mind now, the distinction between "almost surely" and "definitely" seems to have blurred and they have become the same.

I will, at least for now, continue the appeals process. While Dave has made his choice and chosen death, I must struggle with my decision from day to day. I still have to decide how many compromises I'm willing to make to try to save my life and if they will make a difference. I may plead for my life over and over in petitions to each level of the federal judiciary from district court to the United States Supreme Court and still die in precisely the same manner as Dave, who will have at least kept a bit of his dignity intact by refusing to beg for his life.

At the end of my discussion with Dave, I could only say to him, "I don't agree with what you're doing, but I understand and respect your decision." Dave looked at me, not unkindly, and said, "Thanks a lot, Mike." Dave was then handcuffed and taken back to his cell on the Old Death Row, and after a few minutes I was returned to my cell in another building, where the death row overflow population is housed.

There are now more than 330 prisoners on San Quentin's death row, with more coming every month. I've lived inside these walls for a long time, and I'm not sure how many people on the outside feel about a guy like Dave. I imagine that most must fear, and therefore hate, him and will be glad when he's dead.

It seems quite certain that the media will be gathering here again, as they did in April, 1992, when they executed Bobby Harris. As with Bobby, I suspect that when they finish with Dave, the media's characterization of him will have little in common with the Dave I know. The Dave I know was never given anything by anyone. He lived his life on his own terms—hard terms, frightening terms for most of society. But I do know that in the end, Dave applied those same hard terms to himself.

David Mason became the second person in California to be executed since the death penalty was reimposed. San Quentin's death row has now grown to house over 400 condemned prisoners.

## A VISIT FROM MOM

### Martin A. Draughton, Death Row, Texas

My mother visited on Tuesday and Wednesday, February 27th and 28th. She was supposed to visit on Monday and Tuesday. Monday I was up in my window all morning till 1 P.M. Then, shortly after 1 P.M. I gave up. Disappointed and a bit worried I just curled up in bed after that.

You see, visitation ends promptly at noon on Wednesdays because the rest of the day is reserved for the media. That means to get our full four hours of this "Special Visit" (because she travels more than 300 miles to visit) I would need to be out there at 8:00 A.M. sharp. And that is impossible. It takes the guards anywhere from twenty minutes to an hour to come get us and escort us to the visiting room. Mom told me that she'd be a little late on Wednesday, 'cause she just can't move that fast first thing in the morning. Okay, I was expecting that. I still was in my window to see her arrive, park the car, and cane-walk the long stretch of sidewalk into the main building. It was 8:44 A.M. when she came in the gate. It was 8:52 A.M. when the picket officer called me over the intercom to tell me I had a visit. I'm already ready. It was 9:24 A.M. when the two escort officers got to my cell. The uncouth woman guard had a large photo album in her hand that she was flipping through when she got to my cell door, with her male co-worker leaning over providing commentary too. I make a comment to them about seeing now why it took them so long to come get me. Didn't receive a response. It was thirty-five minutes by the time I made it to the visiting room a scant hundred yards away.

Because these guards were looking at photos and pussy-footing around instead of taking care of their duties, they were spending BIG DOLLARS that it cost my mother to come all the way from Florida to visit me. Lost time/money that has taken two years to put together. They chewed up/wasted thirty-five minutes of this long awaited visit from my mother. Needless to say I was a little agitated by the time I sat down in front of Mom. I bitched about the whole situation for a moment. She was telling me that she had been out there waiting on me a long time already. I told her it took them thirty-five minutes from the time the picket officer told me I had a visit, to get me out there. And it was right at that moment that [the female officer] was walking back behind my visiting cage and she said, "No it didn't. It took us thirty-six minutes!" in a very sarcastic tone. Mom asked what she said and I told her. This is just a prime example of how little professionalism they have and how little respect these guards have for any citizens who come here to visit anyone on death row. Not all Texas Department of Criminal Justice (TDCJ) ID Correctional Officers are like this, but it seems that the ones who are not are a very small minority.

Back to my Mom. These are the first visits alone with my mother in about ten years, I think. Two years ago she came out with her two sisters who I have not seen since I was eighteen, so Mom and I didn't get much time alone then. I view this time together as possibly our last. Man, she's in bad shape. The way she looks now, I don't know if she will make it another two years till our next visit. In all the years I have been locked up, it's averaged out that she makes it out to visit once every two years. Living on disability income, she just flat out does not have the money to come out. This visit was made possible only because of my dear friend Ursula footing the bill. Visit before this Mom sold some of her furniture to get her share of the money to come out here. When my dear friend heard this news she surprised the hell out of me by informing me she wanted to buy Mom a trip out here to see me. And even despite the wonderful generosity of making the funds available for Mom's trip, it still took me another seventeen MONTHS of planning and preparing for mother, and her having several operations in the interim to heal up from, only to get cheated out of some time by people with no respect and no empathy for anyone else.

I learned that Mom has had surgery on her neck; pins and plates in her neck, pins in her back. She walks with a cane and has little mobility in her right leg. No feeling and grip in her left hand and an imminent surgery on her wrist/hand for carpal tunnel syndrome. She's had angioplasty several times in years past. A pacemaker was almost put in in '95. Man she's really in bad shape. And man when I saw her like that it just really bowled me over and gave me such a heavy heart. I literally came back to my cell each day and exercised hard and long. Then slept the sound sleep of mental and emotional exhaustion. I can't allow myself to get into such decrepit condition. If it takes me until I am eighty years of age before I can ever leave prison, I plan to still be "upwardly mobile."

After our visits on Tuesday and Wednesday, we had Thursday, Friday, Saturday, and Sunday to wait till our next two days of visiting on Monday and Tuesday, March 5th and 6th. I think this helped both of us. Gave us some time to think and resolve to accept "what is."

Mother isn't just physically broken down. Man, she's an emotional wreck too. Many times out there she would spontaneously bust out crying. Not necessarily at anything I said. I remained a stone though. Never once giving in to the emotional outbursts. Usually I just let her go and myself remain stoical and that would bring her back in control. Sometimes I just had to put my foot down and demand that she "stop that crap!" And I tell you, I felt like a really cold hearted bastard for remaining so cold like that. But I can't. Man I just can't go emotional. It's hardly even there anymore.

Instead of emotion now it's anger. Tears don't accomplish anything. But it seems that I learned too early that being pissed off will motivate you.

On our second-to-last day of visiting, Dennis was out there somewhere in the visiting room. He had an execution date approaching in two days. Last time I saw him was back at Ellis Unit. Kathy Cox, of the Salvation Army (Dallas), who visits a number of death row prisoners here was visiting Dennis and picking up his belongings while there in the visiting room. I was in the very first cage this day so that I was right there watching any and all transactions between the visitors and officers, etc. Mom asks me, "What's all these nylon bags of stuff?" I just look at her for a moment while continuing to munch on my M&Ms or whatever it was I had at the moment. I chew and stare at my mother, trying to envision the inner battleground of my mother's tortured soul when I nail this bit of news into her heart. Mom repeats herself more than once but I just munch and stare, trying to formulate my thoughts, and simultaneously trying to find additional inner strength to remain steady while she is crumbling away.

After maybe a full minute I take a swallow of my soda, put everything down and wipe my hands on the counter, still buying myself precious seconds to dredge up more inner resolve. Finally I tell mother that those bags are personal property being picked up by that white-haired woman behind her. And before she can inquire further I tell her that he has an execution date for day after tomorrow and this woman is picking up his stuff. Her eyes get wide, her mouth works up and down but she doesn't say anything. Shock. Just plain shock. After a minute then she breaks down and cries. At least she got to meet Ms. Cox that day, although Ms. Cox really wasn't in the best mood to be meeting people that day.

Ms. Kathy Cox has been involved with prison ministry for more years than I have been on the row. She told me this same day in the visiting room that TDCJ-ID is NOT allowing her to be the spiritual advisor to Dennis Dowthitt on the day of his execution. This woman has been an ordained minister for more than thirty years. I've yet to learn if TDCJ realized they were wrong and allowed this woman in to be this man's spiritual advisor on his last day of life.

My last day of visiting Mom seemed to have been the best one of all. It wasn't the least emotional of all, not by far. Still for some reason it seemed to be the best one. And when it came time for us to say goodbyes to one another, surprisingly there weren't a lot of waterworks from Mom—maybe because she still planned to see the warden and give him an earful before she left for good and knew she needed to have some wits about her. And I've heard from both sisters already that indeed she did speak to the warden and gave him a piece of her mind about how she was treated here, about how [one officer] hung up on her when attempting to pre-arrange these special visits, and many other things.

At one point during our last day we were talking seriously and I told Mom that she would more than likely be "long gone" before I ever walked the streets again as a free man, if ever. She sobbed and nodded her head. But while I had her full attention I also pointed out to her that I was one of the fortunate ones in here, insofar as I have an out-of-state law firm representing me who are leaving no stone unturned in their efforts to do everything to be successful in my appeals and get this death sentence off my back. I told Mom that if she didn't take anything else away from these visits that I wanted her to take with her the belief and knowledge that I am a fighter and a survivor and that I am doing everything possible to secure a future for myself.

Another very poignant moment during our last day was when a fellow by the name of Michael was out into the visiting booth opposite of mine so that I could just move my eyes and observe his visit, and vice-versa. Soon as Michael was put into the booth we made eye contact and immediately I was struck with pangs of guilt. I'd thought about him often during the past couple years since I saw him last. Eventually my Mom commented about my distraction so I ran it all down to her.

"Yeah, I know I'm distracted Mom. It's that dude over there visiting with the guy with the goatee and long hair and the blonde woman. You see I'd been wanting to apologize to this guy since summer '98 when I last saw him, when we lived on the same wing together back at Ellis . . . ."

There was a situation you see, a prison soap opera (but dangerous just the same) that really escalated out of hand and the end result is my cellie ends up knocking this man out cold. Dropped him face down in a puddle of water out on the rec yard so that he had to be flipped over so he didn't drown! Looked like about a third of his lip was knocked off too. Gashed open very badly. Well, even though I didn't do this, I still could have done something to facilitate a much different outcome of the whole situation.

Michael ended up holding his mud and not snitching on anyone so he has that to his character. But still the whole situation was wrong and shouldn't have happened and by my proximity to the whole scene and the principal players in the situation, I feel bad about not doing something. And there he sits right across from me now. And I am aware that he has an execution date coming up March 28. (Today, as I write this.)

Michael's visitors leave and I mouth to him if he's doing okay. He signs to me that he has a date for the 28th. I hang my head and slowly shake it from side to side. Mom is tripping now, wanting to know what's going on. I'd already told Mom the whole sordid story about why I feel the need to apologize to this man and now I just relayed the news to her that he has an execution date for the end of this month. So Mom sneaks to the booth behind her and picks up the phone and speaks to Michael for a minute. I cannot hear what is being said. Michael looks over Mom's shoulder at me and nods his head and says "it's okay" and something else. Mom comes back and tells me that he forgives me completely and then slips into a really bad state for a few moments. I motion to Michael that I will be praying for him. Mom is sobbing bad. On the verge of wailing. Choking out the question, "How in the hell do you deal with this shit like this? And for so long? And still manage to . . . ." At this point, I too, have tears in my eyes. I look over at Michael again, lower my head, wipe my eyes, vigorously whip my head back and forth a couple of times to stifle my own sobs and I tell Mom, "All right, that's enough of that! These are our last hours, so can the crying." Mom knows I won't tolerate much of that so she gets herself together within the next few minutes. And then I tell her that she has just gotten a small taste of my world. Only a small taste. As for how I handle it, that is still a mystery. Makes me look towards God, truly. And a belief in myself that I never had before this whole ordeal. I've lost more friends to this Texas killing machine than I can recall from memory. I would have to consult my older death row lists.

This was the really emotional point of our last visit. Then our time was up and we said our goodbyes, and Mom says that this is probably her last visit out here. And I admitted that I had this thought all along. Told her that it hasn't really been a barrel of laughs but that it was "needed" by both of us. And we kissed the glass and I told her to leave before she got in trouble for sticking around so long after we were told our time is up.

After a good twenty-five minutes I am escorted back to my building and locked up in a legal visit booth in the hall and strip searched there. Then I'm taken back to my cell. I get out of my hot, stuffy clothes, down to my boxers again and then climb up in the window. After about twenty minutes I see Mom walk out of the main building. "So, she did get to speak to the warden after all" I mused to myself. Before we ended our visit, I made Mom write a note and put it in her pocket that read; "Felicia, if these bastards give me a heart attack and kill me while I'm here, I want you to do everything possible to sue their asses off!" I made Mom write that and show it to me and put it in her pocket. But I saw Mother leave that day. And other than missing her flight back in Houston, all was well. I will steadily be wondering if this is indeed my mother's last visit.

*Update.* Learned from my neighbor while I was writing this that Michael got a stay of execution from the Texas Court of Criminal Appeals.

## SKIRTING THE RULES

Richard Rossi, Death Row, Arizona

I have an amusing anecdote to share. I have a friend who lives in Tucson and he tries to visit me whenever possible. I don't get many visits so they are really important to me. Jack had been meaning to drive up for the last four months, without success. Finally he found himself free to visit. The prison has a dress code for visitors. One item that cannot be worn by visitors is blue jeans, the reason being that we used to wear blue jeans when we were at Cell Block Six. Most other prison units still wear blue jeans, whilst here at Eyman we now wear bright orange jump suits. So if a prisoner makes an escape he can easily be located.

So on Sunday morning I was in the visitation room waiting to see Jack. All the visitors came in and there was no Jack. The visitation officer came to my window and told me that Jack would be a few minutes late. She did not say why. A few minutes later I noticed Jack at the entrance door. Since there is a large visitation desk in the center of the room, all I could see was that Jack was wearing what appeared to be 1970s-style polyester pants with very large and loud plaid designs. When he walked around the desk that was obstructing my view, I could see that his pants had no legs! It looked as if he was wearing a long Scottish kilt or dress.

As I was checking what Jack was wearing, my eyes looked past him only to notice that every visitor as well as convict in the room was staring intently at Jack and me. Although it was only a few seconds during which everyone's attention was focused on the two of us, it seemed as if an eternity had passed. Not a sound could be heard. It was so very surreal. When one talks about shock and embarrassment, nothing could top this experience.

After the moment passed I asked Jack what was going on. He explained that since the prisoners were now wearing bright orange jump suits, then he assumed that nobody could confuse a visitor wearing blue jeans with a prisoner making an escape. However, the visitation officer refused to let Jack visit in blue jeans. A supervisor was summoned and Jack asked him if the rules prohibited him from wearing a dress? After careful consideration they said he could wear a dress. I guess no one thought about cross-dressing when they formulated the rules! So Jack made his exit and went back to his car. In the trunk he had a large plaid table cloth he and his family used for picnics. He wrapped it around himself and made a small hole at his waist through which to pass his belt so that the dress would not fall down. European dress designers beware. The rest of the visit went well.

After all of the visitors left I was inundated with questions from all the convicts. Such as "What's up with that? . . . Who was that guy? . . . Why was he wearing a dress?" It took half an hour to begin to calm matters down. Today, a week later, I did not have a visit, but when one of the men from this pod who was out there last week came back from his visit today he told me that all the guys were still talking and laughing about Jack's wardrobe choice of a week ago. I am sure it will be discussed for years to come. No one ever remembers having seen or heard of a similar situation at visitation. I have to admit that this had to have been the funniest event inside these cold hard walls in the fifteen years I have been here. A touch of much-needed comic relief goes a long way in this place.

## SCARS

### Jarvis Masters, Death Row, California

I remember the first time my eyes really witnessed the scars on the bodies of almost every one of my fellow prisoners. I was outside on a maximum custody exercise yard. I stood along a fence, praising the air that the yard gave to my lungs that my death row prison cell didn't. I wasn't in a rush to pick up a basketball or do anything. I just stood in my own silence.

I looked at the other prisoners on the yard playing basketball, handball, showering, and talking to one another. I saw the prisoners I felt closest to, John and Pete and David, lifting weights out on the yard. I noticed the unbelievable similarity of the whip-like scars on their bare skin, shining with sweat from pumping iron in the hot sun. A deep sense of sadness came over me as I watched these strong and powerful men lift hundreds of pounds of weights over their heads. I looked around the yard to see if the prisoners besides John, Pete, and David had the same type of scars. Sadly enough, they did. There were men on the handball and basketball courts, in the shower, and elsewhere that seemed to have whip marks and deep gashes all over their bodies. It shocked me silent to look behind their legs, on their backs, all over their ribs and see the gruesome discovery of this entire yard of men with the evidence of the violence in their lives. Here, hidden, were America's lost children—surviving in rage and in refuge from society. Most of us were born in the fifties and sixties when there were few laws protecting us from the child abuse that victimized us.

Then, as sudden as a shock, a terrible sense of sadness came over me. I thought of my mother, who had died within that year. "Wow," I thought, "I still wish I had been there when she died." Suddenly, all of the acts of abuse that had taken place in my childhood just came to the surface. I remembered being beaten and whipped by my stepfather and all the silent and lonely nights and days of abandonment by my mother, who was a heroin addict. Only recently, in the '80s, has this society come to know and realize with some understanding the alarming rate of child abuse in this country.

Yet, what is lost and given up on by society are the men who walk the prison exercise yards throughout the nation for crimes often related to the horrible violence done to them as children. No such connection is seen by either the adult in prison who was abused as a child or by American society at large. A prisoner will not use the term "child abuse" as his/her own.

But because our histories were so connected, it was as if we had all had the same parents. I made up my mind that sometime that day, I would bring John, Pete, and David together. I wanted to talk about the scars I had noticed and see if I could open them up to think about their abuse as children. I was a trusted comrade to most of these men, and to a few of them I was their only family. But even so, to dare myself to go into their remembered pain and to convince them that they, like me, had been physically abused by our parents was something out of the ordinary for me.

"Am I crazy?" I wondered, to have this idea of wanting to open up these men who probably had never spoken openly of their horrible experiences of child abuse. "None of these men will ever say that their parents have physically or sexually abused them," I thought.

They looked hardened to the core as they stood around a weightlifting bench, proud of their bodies and the images they projected standing there. It occurred to me, as I was approaching them, that such a posture of pride symbolized the battle wounds that they had "made their bones" with. This is prison talk for "prove your manhood." Yet my own denials had at one time been similar in kind, when I had been hardened and never wanted to see my parents as the cause and source of the mental and physical scars I wore. The difficulty in speaking with these men would be to somehow interpret the usual prison language of all of us in sharing our histories. Shucking and jiving is the usual way to talk to cover up sensitive matters with prison humor.

This was how John, a twenty-eight-year old, bulky, six-foot-three-inch tall convicted murderer, started when I asked him, while others listened, about the scars on his face: John explained that his father had loved him enough to have taught him how to fight when he was only five years old. In a sense, he said, he grew up with a loving fear of his father. He pointed out to me a very noticeable and nasty scar on his upper shoulder. He laughingly went on to say that his father had hit him with a steel rod when John tried to protect his mother from being beaten by his father. I realized, as I should have known, that these experiences in John's childhood haunted him, as many abused memories do. His detailed accounts somehow told us what he must have really suffered as a child. This was especially when he showed us all a gash on his back that was hidden by a tattoo of a dragon. It was a very ugly scar—like I imagined those of a slave who had been whipped. As John directed me closer to see it, he said, "Rub your finger down the dragon's spine." As I did so, I felt what I thought was a thick tight string that moved nastily like a worm beneath the layer of his skin. "DAMN, John, what in the hell happened to you!?" I asked. John explained that when he was nine or ten his father chased him with a cord. John ran and tried to hide under a bed. He grabbed the springs under the bed and held on as his father pulled him by the legs and hit his back repeatedly with the cord until he fell unconscious and woke up later with a deep flesh wound. John, again with a cold smile on his face, admitted jokingly that that was the last time he ever ran from his father. I first met John when we were both in youth homes in Southern California. We were only eleven years old. Throughout the years we traveled together through the juvenile systems until the penitentiary became our final stop. David and Pete told very similar stories of beatings which occurred at early ages. All of their stories of how they had been abused as children spoke of a life that had a very telling side of how we all came to be in one of the worst prisons in the country.

It scares me to realize that some prisoners will eventually re-enter society and father children and repeat on their own children what has happened to them. With no programs in most prisons to speak to child abuse, a high percentage of the prisoners abused as children will ultimately do this. Thus the cycle of abuse and crime will continue. I believe that institutionalization is a kind of refuge for many of the men from the devastation of child abuse in their lives. Most children who were abused as children were taken from the custody of their natural parents at very early ages. The authority figures placed them in foster homes, youth homes, or juvenile halls to protect the children from further abuse. These settings in most cases were adopted by the children, becoming their protective shield that kept them safe. For most prisoners abused as children, prisons are a continuation of this same process of living in a state of painful refuge. Not until I read a series of books on adults who had been abused as children, and about healing the shame that binds persons to their past, did I truly become committed to the self-examination of my own childhood abuse. I began to unfold and unravel all the hidden causes behind why I just expected to go from one youth institution to the next. I really never tried to stay out of these places and neither did my friends.

I spoke to John, Pete, and David very openly about my parents physically and mentally abusing me. I told how I had been neglected and abandoned by them when I was only five years old. I shared some of the horrors of my past—telling how my mother had left me and my sisters alone for days with our newborn twin brother and sister when I was only four years old. The baby boy died from a crib death which I always believed was my own fault, since I had been made responsible for him. I spoke to them of the pain and hurt that I carried through more than a dozen institutions I had been in. And I told how it was that all of these events ultimately entrapped me in a cycle of lashing out against everything. I never wanted to look inward to face the fact that I was hurting—crying out for help long after the abuse, neglect, and abandonment by my parents. Hearing me express my own pain and hurt, they all seemed to avoid linking my experiences with theirs. The term "abuse" spoke of a hidden truth: we had all been victims of child abuse. This was something that hurt them to agree with, and sadly, they never did. Instead, we all just fell silent around the weightlifting bench as each one of us squatted down and thought. We all stared across the yard at the other men exercising. The feeling I had was that we were all looking and seeing something that was clear and sad to us all. John and I spoke again privately later that day, walking together along the fence. Surprisingly, he said to me, "You know something, the day I got used to getting beaten up by my father and by counselors in all those group homes was the day that I knew nothing would ever hurt me again. Everything that I thought could hurt me, I saw as a game. I had nothing to lose and just about everything to gain. A prison cell to me is something that will always be here for me." I looked at John as he said all this to me, and I didn't know what to say. Then it occurred to me that John was speaking for most of the men I had met in prison.

Secretly, we all like it here. This place welcomes a man who is full of rage and violence. Here, he is not abnormal, not different. Here, his rage is nothing new. Prison lifestyle is an extension of his inner life. "Look around," I told him. "Look at all these men. Don't we all say that we are men out here on this exercise yard? This prison defines us as such. But there would be much greater power in what you and I can see out here if we could all see ourselves as human beings first. I bet if you truly thought of yourself as one human being, and of me as another, and others out here as more human beings, you would gradually begin to wonder freely and openly about the nature of your life. Try to replace your false manhood impressions," I said to John, "with your human existence and all those old experiences you had as a child will seek to come out. Human beings cry," I said to John, "and don't be surprised that you will cry when confronting your past with your human love."

Jarvis Masters has recently been transferred from Death Row, San Quentin, California, to life imprisonment.

## TRANSCENDING

### Martin A. Draughton, Death Row, Texas

I had a blessing a few days ago when it was my day to go to the outside rec yard (but still within the building). It rained on me and the other guy out there with me. He was in the adjacent yard. After a little while he had me pound on the inch-thick glass window and get them to come get him and take him in. I stayed outside. My recreation hour came and went, but I was part of the last change, therefore I ended up getting about forty-five extra minutes. After being out there only about twenty minutes it started raining. So I stayed out and played in the rain by myself for the next hour. A simple act like just being in the rain was really cool, therapeutic even. I was alone out there. It was quiet. Only me and the sound of the rain falling on concrete; oh yeah, and the sporadic buzzers and sirens signaling begin or end of count, or the occasional blast of some female voice over the loudspeaker aiming down into the yard. But really these things have become almost white noise for me already. Almost. But I think the peaceful rain helped me simply tune it out altogether that day. It was a soft, soothing, gentle rain.

Falling straight down, I played, sliding back and forth across the smooth concrete. (Had to sew up my gym shorts afterwards! Even a sewing needle is contraband in this place! So I was breaking institution rules by just sewing up my shorts. Sad.) Anyway after a while the sun was shining on my small parcel of concrete and the rain was still softly falling. I sat down cross-legged with my eyes closed for a few moments. Then I laid back . . . arms and legs thrown wide, facing upwards into the rain. I remember my recollections of those moments . . .

A time eight to nine years ago, a cellmate I shared a cell with for one and a half years. This was the one and only Ted Cole, the other half of our poetry-writing partnership and joint pen-name Trovatore Poetaster. I remembered walking and playing in the rain back in the recreation yard at Ellis Unit and how we used to stop up the drain and grab a broom and sweep up as much as we could before it got too soaked. And the concrete-filled horseshoe pit would fill up with water. We'd hope and pray for a long rain and no lightning. First crack of thunder and we'd be rounded up off the yard. The horseshoe pit would fill with water and it'd keep getting deeper. The concrete basketball court was really slick to start with, but with just a little water added we had an instant "SLIP-n-SLIDE." I suppose it does take a healthy body to play like this, 'cause man, concrete does not give! But you shoulda seen me. I would take a few good strong strides and get sufficient momentum and go down into a slide and slide right into that pit of about twelve inches of water. I'd slide on my butt. On my back. On my stomach. Of course I was not the only one immensely enjoying this type of play. I think those moments were the purest moments in these men's life that they had ever known during their lives of incarceration, a simple joy. It didn't matter that we were getting bruised up.

It didn't matter that our clothes were getting ripped up, it didn't matter that we didn't have dry clothes to put on the next morning when we filed out to go to work in the garment factory . . . All that mattered was that this liquid joy/blessing keep falling on us, that we might forget our sorrows for a spell. These wonderful moments in the rain were something special, be sure. For myself it was also something from "outside" and something that my captors could not control, turn on or off, something from heaven even. In a certain sense I guess I'd say it was a baptism of sorts, for indeed I can count a number of men who I believe truly transcended their predicament, at least for an afternoon.

So I laid there in the rain and I thought back on these times I shared with other friends and acquaintances in here. And then without seeing it coming and being able to stop myself, I reminded myself that all these men are dead now. My rain stopped falling shortly after that and I was taken back to my cage.

# 3

## EXECUTION

*An execution is not simply death. It is just as different from the privation of life as a concentration camp is from prison. It adds to death a rule, a public premeditation known to the future victim, an organization which is itself a source of moral sufferings more terrible than death. Capital punishment is the most premeditated of murders, to which no criminal's deed, however calculated can be compared. For there to be an equivalency, the death penalty would have to punish a criminal who had warned his victim of the date at which he would inflict a horrible death on him and who, from that moment onward, had confined him at his mercy for months. Such a monster is not encountered in private life.*

—Albert Camus

## CHANGING THE PROTOCOL
### Richard Rossi, Death Row, Arizona

In the gruesome business of executing people, there are specific rules that are followed step by step according to an official Execution Protocol. The policy is restricted and secret. Prisoners cannot know how they are going to be executed. Nothing is to be added or deleted from the official protocol. At least that is the way it is supposed to be. There are certain procedures that go into effect almost immediately after the condemned person receives his execution warrant. The warrants are usually dated thirty-five days before the event. The first thing that occurs is that you receive a copy of the execution warrant from the warden or his designee. Then you are given various other forms to fill out. These include: Last Meal Request; Execution Witness List; Application to the Board of Executive Clemency; Method of Execution; Disposal of Property; Disposal of Remains; Last Will & Testament.

When the condemned person reaches fourteen days before the execution date he or she is moved to a death watch cell for observation. Practically no property is allowed while you are on death watch. When we were at CB6 (before the move to Eyman in 1997) an officer was posted outside your cell twenty-four hours a day. Your every move is recorded on a clipboard. The object of this is to prevent you from committing suicide and thus cheat the state out of its ritual of execution. When your time runs down to forty-eight hours before the event, you are moved to the holding cell of the death house at the Central Unit.

In September 1997 all of death row was moved from CB6 to the Special Management Unit II at Eyman complex. The protocol remained the same. At the fourteen day point, you were still transported back to CB6 to the observation cell. This procedure continued until last month. One morning we were awakened by the sound of inmates being moved. All ten prisoners in pod number 2 were being moved. Before you knew it, all ten were gone and the pod was completely empty. A few mornings later heavy construction was going on. Sparks were flying, drills were whining and hammers were banging. This racket went on for days. No one could figure out what was happening. Curiosity can drive you mad around here. One can compare this situation to that of animals in a zoo. The animals are always very anxious about any changes in their cages and surrounding environment, especially when it is not possible to see what is occurring. It was not until fourteen days before a scheduled execution that we figured out what was taking place. They moved the condemned man into the empty pod number 2, which was now going to be used as the death watch cell instead of transporting the prisoner back to CB6. Video cameras had been installed—one outside the cells and another in the exercise room. A TV monitor and VCR were installed in the guard tower. Now every move could be observed and simultaneously recorded on videotape. Twenty-four hours a day.

When you are in the observation cell you have no property. Each morning you are given an orange jump suit and your bed linens are collected. Your cell is searched and you begin your day. In the evening, you surrender your jump suit and you are given new bed linens. All this is done so that you do not hang yourself. You are allowed one sheet of paper to write on and a three-inch pencil. To get another sheet of paper you must surrender the sheet of paper you have. This is bizarre. I know of no method of committing suicide with a piece of paper. It is futile to try to make sense out of these rituals. Needless to say it is difficult to write farewell letters under such circumstances.

It was curious to watch the officers turn into predators as they participated in these activities. It started when construction work was under way to transform pod number 2 into the observation pod. The officers were running around like busy bees tending the hive. They were so happy to be able to contribute toward the preparations to kill another human being. They were humming and singing. Actually falling over themselves in the process. I asked one of the officers how they could afford to leave ten cells empty with the remaining 110 cells filled to capacity and at least four new men were on their way to the row from recent death sentences. He smiled at me and in a boastful manner said that there was no problem. That "a new day had dawned because they were going to be dispatching a whole lot of us old timers to the death house shortly." I see all of this as a sickness. There is such perverse pleasure derived on the part of these officers in the anticipation of executing us. Nothing will ever change in their eyes. We will forever be considered scum by our keepers. Life on the row is difficult and depressing enough without being confronted by the undercurrent of such hostility. The ritual itself takes its toll on you. It is designed to be a constant reminder that the state does not forget and it will have all of the suffering and pain it can get out of us before killing us.

It appears as if the Eighth Amendment against "cruel and unusual" punishment does not apply anymore. When a person is allowed to suffer two sentences for a crime, one must wonder. Most murderers who do not get the death penalty are given sentences of twenty-five years to life. Usually after the twenty-five years in prison the gates are opened and they go free. Whereas a death row inmate's sentence can be delayed for twenty to twenty-five years whereupon execution still follows. No consideration is given to the additional life sentence that may have been served. Instead of taking this additional punishment into consideration at an executive clemency hearing, the state and the victim's family cry foul, arguing that it is the prisoner who is responsible for any delay after manipulating and cheating the public in order to stay alive. In reality it is the public's own state courts that cause these long delays in the process of trying to undo their faulty rulings and unjust sentences.

This is not to say that the victims are not entitled to procure punishment of an offender for a murder, but to mete out double punishment must be considered "cruel and unusual." What legitimate penological purpose is served by executing an individual after he or she has already served a life sentence? Where is the written rule of law permitting such suffering? When a person serves a life sentence in general population the life style is completely different. You have many liberties and privileges. You can have a structured life, being out of your cell for most of the time. You can walk around, have contact visits, you have more personal property. You can have a job. All of these are not allowed for death row. We are in solitary confinement, locked in our cages for 23 ½ hours a day. This is the hardest time to do. It is long and cruel. A life sentence served on death row equals two to three life sentences in general population.

Although delaying executions for decades is not written in the law, nor considered by the clemency board or the public as being a legitimate mitigating factor at the clemency hearing prior to execution, the suffering involved cannot be denied. It certainly is part of an unwritten execution protocol that imposes as much pain, suffering, and revenge as possible on the condemned prisoner. Regardless of the fact that the judge never imposed this additional punishment, we are certainly made to endure it. I guess the proverbial "pound of flesh" is no longer sufficient payment for one's atonement. All we have left to give is our life. What more can we give? What more do they want? The protocol needs to be changed and the madness must stop.

## CAPITAL ACCOUNTABILITY
### Roger W. Murray II, Death Row, Arizona

Executions have essentially become a moot subject. They happen with such frequency that most Americans never give them a second thought. It's almost like the public no longer perceives executions as putting a human being to death, but a process in which they aren't involved. Death is a fact of life we all eventually face. Knowing the exact moment and method when I will die has given me an opportunity to contemplate life and death. I am after all an inmate on Arizona's death row. It is said I am to be killed off as punishment for crimes for which I was convicted. There isn't anything wrong with society holding people accountable for their actions. Without this objective the world would certainly be a chaotic environment. However, there are occasions when society gets it wrong. It will not matter, if I don't have my wrongful convictions overturned—I will die.

In 1992 the State of Arizona passed a law that gave all inmates sentenced before November of that year a choice between lethal injection or the gas chamber. Myself and brother "Robert" were some of the last inmates who still have this choice (we were sentenced on October 27th, 1992). Like most other inmates I will likely choose lethal injection. But, the method of execution really doesn't matter, it's over in a few minutes and I'm just as dead. What really matters is the thirty-six days leading up to the execution. Most of the public doesn't consider these days as part of the process. But, in reality, it is a major part that no one ever seems to talk about.

Most inmates already know what the outcome of their case will be long before the courts make their decisions. But, it's still a shock when the process actually begins. There is little, if any, amount of preparations physical or mental that can prepare one for this day. Most are not informed they will be receiving a death warrant until it's officially issued, sometimes an inmate will be warned by his attorney first, but this is a rare occasion. Most are caught unsuspecting when it happens. It varies from inmate to inmate, but usually there will be three or four officers come to the cell under false pretenses. Their usual spiel is something like, "we were just told to come get you." Or "you're wanted up at disciplinary." After the routine strip search you're handcuffed behind the back and off you go to one of the front offices. Once inside the office you are politely guided to a chair sitting across a desk. The desk surface is littered with papers, files, and a little cassette recorder. The room as business-like as the local insurance dealer's, has been crowded with department officers, staff, and others there to observe a man receive his death warrant. It's got to be a curiosity to witness how a man will react being informed he only has thirty-six days left to live. For some it's a once in a lifetime opportunity . . . to others, a mournful assignment.

Sitting behind the desk per regulation is the inmate's counselor. He'll turn on the tape recorder to have proof the inmate received his death warrant. This stems from an incident where an inmate was within days of his execution and hadn't been told. The counselor will read the entire death warrant. It contains the date and time for said execution to be carried out. The counselor will ask if you have any questions. By this point your brain is pretty much distracted, so, you have few questions. The prominent thought going through one's mind is "How will I get a stay?" Or, "What will my mother feel?" or, "This is not real." You are given a montage of forms to fill out over the next few weeks, such as: method of execution, last meal, who you want to witness the execution, religious advisors, disposition of property left behind, disposition of remains, and a few other non-descript forms. Then you are escorted back to the cell to contemplate your impending death.

As you pass by other cells inmates can sense what has happened. Just as I've done with other inmates, it's their expression, a certain pallor of mortality realized. Finally someone will knowingly ask, "so, what did they want" or, "you'll get a stay." But, deep in the back of your mind the question looms. Even if a stay is there for the asking, knowing you have a stay coming, the question hangs thickly within the recesses of the mind. "Am I going to die?"

An inmate will remain in his regular cell until two weeks prior to his execution, at this appointed time he's moved into a specially designed "Death Watch" cell. Once there, he'll be monitored around the clock by two officers stationed outside the cell. Also staring into the cell 24/7 is a closed-circuit TV camera allowing a third officer to watch from a control room and record cell activity. Once an inmate is on "death watch" you are not allowed to talk or associate with other inmates. You are completely deprived of conversation. Most of the officers stationed on death watch try and avoid talking with the inmate. I have been told by different officers it is a measure taken to remain detached from the situation as they wouldn't want to begin to regard the condemned as anything beyond a mere number.

Inside the cell you are only allowed the basic amenities: toothbrush, toothpaste, small bar of soap, wash cloth, towel. No TVs or radio for those who may have had a disruptive or suicidal past. There really is no reason for ADC [Arizona Department of Corrections] to isolate an inmate in this manner for two very long weeks except, maybe to force him to withdraw inside himself, from isolation, from lack of communication. There is no privacy. Being constantly observed twenty-four-hours a day by three officers and your every move recorded is quite intimidating. Everything around you is choreographed by ADC officials, right down to when you get out of bed. Eat, shower, use the telephone, legal visits, read mail, go to bed. Any feelings you may have harbored about controlling your life are systematically reduced to zero. You have absolutely no control.

Humiliation and reducing an inmate's self-esteem and will to live is the name of the game at this point. Every piece of mail received from family and friends will be opened by officers. Some say they read it, others claim only to scan the contents. One is no longer trusted to shave himself, instead you are handcuffed behind your back and the officers do it with an electric shaver. (I'm a grown man, I don't need someone else to shave me.)

You are not allowed a brush or comb, but they will give you a plastic palm brush without a handle—just a loop for your finger. Same type used to rub down dogs and cats. Thirty-two hours prior to the execution the inmate is transported to the "Death House" located a couple of miles away with another high-security cell waiting his arrival. The Death House is a block building housing both the gas chamber and lethal injection room. This building is meticulously maintained and sanitized, it is cold and bland, some say it reeks with the smell and feel of death. Very few have been to this cell and returned to talk about it. Mr. Paris Carringer is one of the lucky few, he was within hours of execution. Today, he's at home with his family and friends . . .

Sitting in a cell only feet from the execution chamber must be quite an experience. No one really wants to die, even people who commit suicide don't want to die, they just don't want to go on living their life. Can't face up to what's in the future so they check out. The public mostly perceives lethal injection as simply "falling asleep." I strongly disagree, though it may seem a fast and painless "humane" death, this is not always the case.

Consider the cases of John Brewer and James Clark, both executed in 1993 by lethal injection in Arizona. Their deaths appeared to be nothing beyond the typical injection. They were given a dose of Sodium Pentothal [the brand name of sodium thiopental] first to render them unconscious. This to eliminate the suffocating sensation of the Pavulon [also known as pancuronium bromide] which is secondly injected to shut down the respiratory system. The third and final injection is potassium chloride, which induces cardiac arrest. Without the full effects of the Sodium Pentothal, the body would flail around like a fish out of water under the effects of the second two drugs—without the first to subdue the body and mind.

During an autopsy by the county medical examiner it was determined that both Clark and Brewer had received a dosage of Sodium Pentothal below therapeutic levels. It is the opinion of many professionals [that] because the level of Sodium Pentothal was inadequate, both inmates lay upon the execution table paralyzed, yet conscious of their surroundings. Under this chilling supposition both would have died a slow painful death, unable to move or scream out their agony. Paralyzed, asphyxiation, cardiac arrest. Nobody knows how these men felt as they lay there, unable to move until death finally overcame them. I do wonder if this is the kind of accountability society has in mind?

When I think of lethal injection I don't see it as "falling asleep." I see it as a process that is going to take my life. Most of the public doesn't consider the feelings and emotions an inmate has prior to execution. Maybe that's because they can't relate to the inmate as anything beyond a number getting what he has coming? Consider this: To myself, there is no difference between lethal injection and being tossed head first into a wood chipping machine. Both are fast and seemingly painless. Only this chipper leaves behind a big mess, not unlike the mess left behind in the hearts of those who cared for the inmate. Just the thought of dying this way is enough to send chills down the spine of the most hardened individual. It appears a horrible, terrible way to die. Facing the injection chamber is very much like facing that wood chipper. My emotions are no different. Quick, easy, painless, hassle-free death, the wood chipper is actually a quicker death than injection.

What happens? Approximately thirty minutes prior to the execution the inmate is ready, the IVs are in place and he's left alone on the table. What words are there to describe what's going through his mind as he lays there? Horror? Terror? Hope for a stay? Panic? Fright? Relief that it's over? All of these words seem to come up wholly short as an explanation. This has got to be the most intense feeling imaginable, knowing that he is going to die in minutes and there's nothing he can do to stop it . . . Laying on this injection table the inmate may as well be on a conveyor belt inching along toward a wood chipping machine. He knows at the end of the line absolute death will occur. He knows it should be relatively painless and rather quick, but the thought of dying is suddenly a terrifying reality. As the curtains are drawn back the witnesses get their first and only look at the condemned. He's lying on this table draped with a sheet pulled up to his chin, a pillow under his head. For the most part he looks like its time for bed. This is the only picture the American public ever sees of the Execution Protocol. What they don't see is a human being who's tied down by thirteen leather straps, needles in both arms. An incision into the body might have been preformed to connect with a vein, or dissection into the leg or neck. The sanitary smell of the room, they can't feel his fear of death, his desire to live, can't see his bloodshot eyes, sense his high blood pressure. They don't see if an angelic spirit carries an innocent soul to Heaven, but rather assume it's the deserving being cast into Hell. They only see a small part of the Execution Protocol that has been carefully scripted by the government so as to avoid offending anyone's sensibilities.

Most people don't relate lethal injection to death in a wood chipper. We see the chipper as a horrible death, and it is. But it's little different from injection. Both have a stark reality to them. Dead is dead, no matter how you get there. An inmate would die just as fast either way. But, knowing how and when you'll die gives ample time to think, time to feel the full range of emotions, time for the reality of the situation to set in.

# SURVIVING AN EXECUTION DATE

## Dominique Malon with Sam Hawkins, Death Row, Texas

It sounds senseless that a civilized state, in the name of Justice, can nowadays be so barbaric toward some of its citizens, driving them along a slow, well-organized route of sadistic torture to finally exterminate them as a solution to cure criminality. No words will ever express what it is like to go through an execution date, what follows endeavors to bring a testimony.

### Tuesday, February 9, 1993. 8:15 A.M.

I cannot remember what the weather was like on this day. I was cold, I had not slept much. My body and my mind were under an intense pressure. I was trying hard to get rid of it; this day looked to be a long one and I could not fail in what I expected from myself: to give Sam [Hawkins] the support and the comfort he needed on the very strenuous way of his sixth execution date.

### The Last Visit

Fifteen years on death row, a serious date, indeed, one minute after midnight, tonight. I am sitting alone in the waiting room of Ellis 1 Unit, next to the visiting room. I know what I have to do: push the fear, the anguish to the side so my usual inner peace will be the only owner of the place. Easier to say than to do. But reminding myself of the courage, the dignity, and the wisdom that Sam showed when we met the days before blows my stress out. He needs me strong and smiling, not weak and sad. I get up and I walk straight to the place I was assigned, attracting the compassionate attention of the few other visitors who know what I have to deal with. Sam appears, his hands cuffed behind his back, he enters the cage, the guard locks it, removes the cuffs through a small window. Sam can then sit down and we are face to face, a thick wired-glass partition between us. We smile and look deeply at each other to make sure that our hope is well alive and that we have the situation under control. We both admit that we did not sleep much. The day before, at about 12:30 A.M., he was moved to the death watch cell after all his property had been taken from him. He told me, "The guards came every fifteen minutes to write down all I did, all I drank, ate, used the toilet stool, pee, or fell asleep, whatever I did was written down.

This also continued all night long. At 2:45 A.M. on the 9th, I was awakened for breakfast, I ate little, and the guards watched what I ate and wrote it down."

Sam's life is now in the hands of the U.S. Supreme Court for the second time in little more than four years. On December 12, 1988, he already made the trip to the Death House, to be executed at the first minute of the next day and a stay was granted one hour and twenty minutes before the limit. Sam and I do not lie to each other; we share fully how we feel: tired, stressed, painful but still hopeful, and ready to go through those dark hours knowing that the decision of the Supreme Court will come late for the best or for the worst. We both have the will to stay strong whatever it takes, well aware that it will be a constant struggle and that, as the time goes by, the pressure will intensify. Some of his family flew from Georgia and Florida. They have not seen Sam for years. They join us some twenty minutes later. I listen to the moving words Sam has for his children, back to him very recently, telling them that if he was to die in the coming hours, he expects them to be good, honest, to always have the right behavior, to love people and to have no place for hatred in their heart. All day long, he has words of wisdom and of love for all of us. But as the time is going by, I can see how hard he is struggling; so much suffering appears on his face from time to time. The glass partition is more oppressive than it has ever been and I feel so powerless in comforting him. No one to reach out a helping hand; no shoulder to lean on, no hug, a total deprivation of physical contact for years. This is never permitted, not even at the last minute.

### The Trip to the Death House

At 3:00 P.M., much earlier than expected, the guards come to take Sam for the dreadful trip to the Walls, the old prison where the executions are carried out, downtown Huntsville. Sam says, "On the way to the Death House, my hands and feet are shackled; the warden and another [prison official] drive behind the van with high powered shotguns. The guards in the van have high powered shotguns." Before leaving Ellis 1, somebody tells us that we can go to the Walls Unit and visit Sam until 5:00 P.M. but upon reaching the place, our request is denied, and the countdown of the most terrible hours I ever had in my life starts.

## The Countdown

Sam is now in the hands of the executioners that want so badly to kill him. He is their prey and I am well aware that they will spare him no detail of the deadly protocol of revenge. On January 7, at about 1:00 A.M., he was taken from the cell for a 535–mile trip to Lubbock, the place he was sentenced to die fifteen years ago. The sheriff told him, "This will be your last trip to Lubbock; you will be executed on February 10th." The captain laughed and asked Sam, "How long are you here?" Sam reluctantly said, "Fifteen years." He then asked the sheriff, "Who told you I would die?" The sheriff said, "Both the attorney general's office and the prosecution office." Sam said no more but was moved by [the sheriff's] expectation that he would die. When they reached Lubbock, Sam went in the courtroom and was given the execution date. Immediately he was driven back to Ellis 1 where he arrived about 10:00 P.M.

Sam is strong, he believes in God, he even lives in God; also, Sam is realistic and he knows that the date is serious. He is ready to die. I am ready to see him dying, despite my pain and the terrible loss I shall have to cope with. We do not fear death, we both believe that it is surely sweeter than the daily life on death row he is so tired of, a real mad house that requests a daily struggle to try to keep a balance. But the rite of execution is such a torture that the strongest person in the world cannot go through it without being scared.

## The Questions to Deal with in the Final Hours

I drive the family back to the Hospitality House, the place they are housed and where more than accommodation is provided to those visiting the prisoners, a warm comforting atmosphere that is truly priceless in such circumstances. At that time, Sam is going through the steps of the deadly rite. This is how he described it:

> They told me to shower, so I did. They gave me a blue shirt and pants. I refused the meal. They fingerprinted me. I was placed in a yellow holding cell with a wire screen. Two guards sat in chairs directly in front of the cell facing me non-stop. There was no privacy and when I sat on the toilet stool they remain looking even when I wipe my ass. The guard told me where and when I would be buried. From that point I waited and waited and hoped for a stay while the prison minister told me how

I would die. The warden came and told me in a demanding way how I would die and what they expected from me in a way of participation. Same words as four years ago. The warden told me I would be killed and when, and how. He said, "Participate and die easily or resist and suffer more." He said, "We shall strap you to a gurney, eight straps, put needles in both arms in your veins. Solutions shall flow through your veins until you are dead. You shall be permitted to have very brief last words."

Do you understand what will happen to you?
Do you have any questions?
What do you want for a last meal?
Do you plan to make a last statement?
What do you want us to do with your body?
What do you want to do with your property?
Who do you want to have your money?
Who will witness your execution?
Do you know what we expect you to do?
Are you comfortable?
If not, what can we do?
If your stay is denied, who do you want to call?
What color clothes do you want to die in?

Those are the questions all death row prisoners have to answer in the final hours.

### The Death Chaplain

Sam is alone, two blocks away from us. The family and I talk of him, of the wonderful man they discovered today, of the true love he radiates. We talk of the past events that drove him on death row, we read the newspapers describing him as a monster, forgetting to release the explanations, the mitigating evidence of his case that could help people to understand why he came to do wrong. But it is easier to execute when you make people believe that society gets rid of a man who is not a human being. I am lost in my thoughts. Somebody rings at the door. A prison minister comes in. He introduces himself as "the death chaplain." He has no compassion, no comforting words. He wants to talk to the three of us who will witness the execution. He takes us in the next room and tells us that he does not like this situation, that he is not responsible for the death sentence but he has to give us some details. He says that Sam had his last shower, his last meal, and has been told how he will be executed and what is expected from him in way of participation; then he takes out a writing pad and he starts to make a drawing of the death watch cell Sam is locked in, just in front of the death chamber. He draws him strapped on the gurney, escaping not one of the sadistic details such as the numbers of straps he will be tied with, and the place of the hole in the wall through which the tube containing the poison will flow. Then he explains how Sam will be killed: first he will be put to sleep and this is not painful, he said, then his breathing will be blocked, then his heart will be stopped. All this will take a few minutes. "Some men die easily, some others die hard," he says. Then he adds some more details to his drawing: the place where we shall stand, behind bars, first row; second row, the authorities; third row, the press, bars, no wired-glass partition. For the first time, almost nothing will separate us, but we are told that the distance between the gurney and the bars forbids all physical contacts. "When you will hear the door slamming, it will be the sign that the execution is starting."

My heart is beating too fast, I feel dizzy. I just cannot believe it. It is about 7:00 P.M., five hours before the time, and the way this man, a minister, is talking to us of Sam's death with such an assertive tone makes our hope fade. Do we really have to know so much, so long in advance? But he is not finished, we have to know about Sam's last will, who will have his property, who will have the few dollars remaining on his inmate account, and most of all, the details of his funerals. "Sam will be buried tomorrow morning, 8:30, at the prison cemetery. He has been asked which color he wants to wear, he has not expressed any." God, how long will this man speak to us of Sam's death, Sam's funeral, while he is still well alive, struggling hard? But he has not said yet the only thing we really need to know: we are expected at the death house by 11:15 P.M. Then he asks if we have any questions. What could be left? We had more than expected, more than needed. So he gets up, puts his folder and writing pad back in his attaché case and leaves just like a businessman would do after his last meeting of the day.

### Keeping My Hope Alive

It is now time for me to go back to the hotel for interviews. I reluctantly leave the family, we need each other so badly. But I am more than ever determined to speak out. I owe it to Sam and to all the men sharing the same fate. On my way back to the Hospitality House, I am telling myself that I must not let myself be intimidated by the staging of Sam's killing. I must struggle as hard as he is doing, and not give in to fear. It is about 9:00 P.M., now. We are all sitting on the sofa, not far from the telephone. We can hardly speak. Every second brings more pressure, more torture. I have the feeling that my back is against a wall and a monstrous, infernal engine is slowing coming toward me. But no way out and it will crush me. No, I shall not kneel, I shall not cry, I shall not faint. I am not alone, we are not alone. So many people we never heard of before, and friends from many countries have sent messages of support, and they are now praying with us. Thinking of their love so freely given makes me smile in gratitude. Love is the key. If only the whole world could realize that only true love can heal all wounds. I am with Sam in my mind, the pain is huge, from time to time a dagger sticks deeper in the wound, I am scared but I am still capable of pulling myself together. I muster all my courage, and regain some peace. I cannot believe that Sam will die tonight. Why kill a man like him? He has nothing to do with the mentally ill man he was sixteen years ago. Taking his life, imposing on us this terrible suffering, is of no comfort to the family and friends of the victims; it will not make the world safer and it will not prevent another sick man from doing what he did. Sam is healed and his only will is to love people, to help them, to share with them the wisdom he gained over the years. Killing him makes no sense.

*The Phone Call*

9:55 P.M. The phone rings. The Supreme Court has taken a decision. The pressure at this very moment is incredible. We are paralyzed. Sam is speaking. "The Supreme Court has granted a stay. I love you all." This time we have no reason to keep control on our emotions! We cry, hug and kiss each other. Our happiness is as intense as the pressure was a few seconds earlier. We do not know what will be next. Another execution date? Another trial? But for a few seconds, our joy is not mixed with fear. We would like to rush to the prison, to hug Sam, to talk with him, but this is not permitted and it will take a full week until I can visit him again.

10:30 P.M. I drive back to the hotel to call my family. Though it is 5:30 A.M. in France, I know they are not sleeping. I[t] was so painful those last days thinking that I may have to announce to them that Sam was no longer with us. My younger daughter takes the call, she cries for joy and I cry with her. I talk to my other daughter, to my mother.

### Back to Ellis 1 Unit

Sam is taken back to death row, exhausted. He sums up his feelings, "It was a cruel and tense, stressful and painful ordeal. There was much torture, intense and severe stress, much psychological and physical strain. We were stressed and pressured beyond limits. For those who believe in Heaven and Hell, and we do believe there is a better place God has prepared for all who love him, Dominique and I have already been to Hell." For the second time in four years, Sam makes the trip back from the Death House. "I was placed in an empty cell, no mattress, nothing. But at 1:00 A.M. I received a mattress, sheets, pillow, and blankets. No, no, I could not sleep at all. I was drained and exhausted."

On Tuesday, February 16, one week after the ordeal, the prison permitted me at last to visit Sam. We shared our happiness but also we both realized that we are no longer the same people we were before this terrible experience. You can never get used to it, no matter how many dates a man is given. Each on our side, not even permitted to stay together in the last hours, we reached the pit of the sadistic cold terror that too many people have to endure. In the final hours, it drove me crazy that there was nobody to call on to have it stopped. Who is really responsible for it? All those who take part in it carefully hide one behind the other. The killing is anonymous. It makes it easier.

On February 21, 1995, Sam Hawkins was executed by the state of Texas.

## THE DOG AND PONY SHOW

### Richard Rossi, Death Row, Arizona

In the past week, two brothers—Karl and Walter LaGrand—were executed by the state of Arizona. They were friends of mine. It took seventeen years to put on this little "dog and pony show" for the world to see. After all, the state deserved to get all of its entertainment value in exchange for the room and board they provided Karl and Walter. Karl and Walter could not refuse, but they did not go easy.

They both elected to die as they were sentenced, by the gas chamber. The last time the gas chamber was used was for Donald Harding in 1992. Harding died such a gruesome death in the gas chamber that the state promptly changed the law from cyanide gas to lethal injection. Those sentenced before 1992 could choose gas or lethal injection, but all new candidates must be injected. It looks more humane, like putting down an unwanted animal.

By choosing gas as his method of execution, Karl knew that the Ninth Circuit Court of Appeals would issue a stay of execution because they had previously declared the gas chamber to be "cruel and unusual" punishment. Once the stay was granted, the state appealed to the U.S. Supreme Court in order to get the stay lifted. The Supreme Court, our guardians of morality and law, quickly lifted the stay. The execution would proceed. Uncharacteristically, the state allowed Karl to change from gas to lethal injection. At a certain point the condemned cannot change execution methods. It was not so much that the state was being kind, rather that they understood the negative implications of gassing a German citizen with the German government's representatives here watching. The world was watching. It hearkens one back to the days of the Holocaust when millions were gassed to death. Civilization has evolved to abhor such barbarism. How embarrassing and ironic to gas a German citizen! When all of the last minute "gang plank" appeals failed, the poisons flowed into Karl's veins putting him into the big sleep.

Just seven days later, his brother Walter was scheduled to be executed by cyanide gas. During Walter's clemency hearing he apologized numerous times to all the victims' families. The German government raised the issue that the LaGrand brothers were not allowed to contact their German consular officials when they were arrested. The issue was also brought to the International Court of Justice in The Hague, Netherlands. Also at the clemency hearing, the state admitted that they knew the brothers were German and should have been allowed to make the phone call. The denial of the phone call violated international treaties. In an unexpected move, the clemency board voted 2–1 to recommend to Governor Jane Hull that a sixty-day stay of execution be allowed so that this issue could be properly addressed. This was the first time the clemency board recommended anything less than death. However, the governor was quick to deny this request and proceed with the execution. The dilemma Hull faced was that if she allowed the sixty-day stay and at some point relief was granted to Walter and he could not be executed, then how would she deal with having killed Karl LaGrand the week before? So she had to see to it that Walter's execution proceeded. The loose ends had to be "tidied" up.

Walter was executed at 9:30 P.M. and it took an excruciating eighteen minutes for him to die. Witnesses claimed that Walter died hard. It was a painful death. Can you imagine watching as a man goes into spasms and endless involuntary convulsions for eighteen minutes? What kind of society does this to its own citizens? It belies the wisdom of the U.S. Supreme Court to allow executions in the gas chamber. After all, they have said cyanide gas was not "cruel and unusual." Regretfully, none of the Supreme Court justices has actually experienced being strapped inside of a gas chamber and made to suck in cyanide vapors to test their beliefs. They say that justice is blind for a reason.

It seems our society has not learned from history. For the past fifty years the world has condemned the method of gassing other human beings. Does the "Holocaust" and the "final solution" mean anything? We must have forgotten that lesson. The German people have struggled all of these years to overcome the evils of past mistakes. How cruel and hypocritical then to be helpless to stop the death of one of their own in a gas chamber! How insensitive!

It is unconscionable to allow people to be put to death with cyanide gas. Why does the world community allow this? We do it in private; we only allow victims' families, the prisoner's family, and a few reporters to watch the event. No matter how many times witnesses relate the horrors of these spectacles, the executions continue. The executions are not even newsworthy and rarely get mentioned.

Is society safer each time we execute another human being? Not really. We on the row die a little each day for as long as twenty to twenty-five years. We die on the "installment plan." This punishment is worse than execution. We live and breathe death every day. Never knowing when our number will be called. It's like living the same bad dream day after day for eternity. This is where no tomorrows exist, only endless todays. The state of Arizona was able to put on another exhibition for the world. To haul out some broken down souls and parade them around in the time-honored tradition of the "Dog and Pony Show."

Walter could have changed the method from gas to lethal injection, but he chose to take gas in the hope that some public consciousness would be raised. The jury is still out on that. Take care, Walter. I'll see you in another lifetime, hopefully a lifetime with more compassion and a lot less pain and suffering

## THE LONG WALK

### Don Hawkins, Death Row, Oklahoma

What are the right words for expressing one's feelings at a time like this? How can I spell out the tears that roll down my cheeks, the tightness in my jaws, the lump in my throat? I'm lying here on my bunk in my cell listening to the radio and watching a TV program called "The Ultimate Debt."

This morning I was awakened by the sound of shuffling feet outside my cell door. As I remember them there, I see the wardens, major, captain, and the goon squad made up of fifteen of the biggest prison guards wearing black jumpsuits, helmets with face shields, and carrying long night sticks. Each man is ready to take control of any trouble there may be. The lead man of the group is holding in front of him a 2' x 4' Plexiglas electronic shield. I've heard it is charged with 10,000 volts and if hit with it a person will forget who he is for a while.

They are standing in front of my friend Chuck Coleman's cell, talking to him. He is dressed in new prison blues and looks to be ready to go with them. This time they won't handcuff him to move him outside of his cell. The warden decided to let him be a man today and not treat him like an animal when moving him. This is called "letting him keep his dignity."

Chuck has made this same walk several times before, but this time he just looks different. There's a sense of nervousness showing on his pale colored face. In his hand is a fairly large Bible. The door is opening now, and Chuck steps out with his arms raised. The warden pats him down, being sure to check every area of his outer body form. A woman viewing this with a video camera is ready to get every detail. If there's an incident, they'll have it on tape as they restrain him with whatever force is necessary.

The warden and Chuck exchange a few words about the property in his cell and then they move on down the run to the security gate. I watch them as they move as a group through the sally port doors and out into the rotunda where they disappear from my view. I lay my mirror down and feel an anger rise up in me. For a moment I seemed to be searching for a reasonable thought to give meaning to this experience.

The pretty black assistant warden has stayed behind and is standing here in front of my cell by Chuck's door. After about fifteen minutes, one of the other wardens from the group that led Chuck out comes back and joins her to pack up Chuck's property. After a minute or two they are joined by the unit case manager.

I go back into the back of my cell and lie down. I wonder just what these people must be feeling as they handle Chuck's personal things, putting them into boxes. This is the first time these prison heads have had to pack up a man's property. Finally I drift off to sleep.

It's about noon as I wake up. It had been a long night. Chuck, my good brother Randle, and I had been talking most of the night about the sovereign will of God. Several times, I'd have to pull back from the conversation and dry my eyes. All three of us were having a hard time being strong. After eating my lunch I go out on the yard to get out of this building. It is just too quiet all of a sudden. For once in over twenty years the men were facing a paper tiger coming alive and putting fear into the air. Other than an occasional shout of victory from one of the men who has just beat another in a handball game, no one seems to be willing to talk on the yard either. It's a long hour of silent yard time.

Once back inside, I catch myself wanting to holler over at Chuck to pass the time of day, only to see the empty cell peering at me. Every so often there is a news special on T.V. giving an update on Chuck's situation. I am hoping for good news so I can look for the goon squad bringing him back, this time in handcuffs as they had done the previous time he took the long walk. Nothing I try to do throughout this long, quiet day seems to be important enough to calm my racing thoughts of Chuck's date. Now here it is 10:42 P.M., and there's this special program coming on that is called, "The Ultimate Debt." The news cameras are set up out in front of the prison here. The news personality has just said that Chuck's lawyers say they have given up filing any more pleas for his life. The program ends at 10:50.

It is heartwarming to hear that Chuck is holding up strongly. He had a hamburger, candy bar, and two cokes for lunch. He refused a last meal, because he said it wouldn't be his last. His wife, kids, and grandkids were here to see him earlier in the day. They said everyone was smiling as he spoke with the kids about school and the crafts he'd been sending them. In forty-five minutes they'll move him from his death watch cell into the death chamber. I'm sure his thinking is going from the joy of his family visits to what waits for him in that other room. He has to be an emotional yo-yo.

The prison staff were shown on the TV with sad, almost hollow, expressions. None wants to see Chuck die. They have dealt with him personally for twelve years and have known the man and his emotions. No longer is his mind clouded by drugs, alcohol, and a certain order of life's events. His emotions surfaced and he now can feel pain and remorse. The Warden wouldn't even face the camera.

I don't think I'd want visitors when it's my date with the executioner. I won't play the tough guy. I love my family and friends. I'd feel my very heart being torn out to know I'd be leaving them behind. The reason I can wake up each new morning on death row, thanking God for another day of life, is because I can feel their love for me. But here I am thinking about me while my friend is going to die in about forty minutes. I was talking to him last night, but tonight I can remember all the things I really wanted to say, and what I could have said but didn't. I want to think he's praying with his heart now. No time for "what ifs?"—time only for genuine prayer as honest as he can feel to pray.

Thirty-seven minutes now—about twenty minutes until they move him into the death chamber and strap him down to the death bed. There's a live coverage show on the radio now. I can hear the people in the background singing songs. The man says they have candles lit and are wearing T-shirts that say, "Don't kill for me." Thirty-two minutes now until midnight. The execution is scheduled for 12:01. If carried out, it will be Oklahoma's first in over twenty-five years. I can think of many reprobates who are much more the candidates for execution than this repented man of God that I know who were given life or less for the same crime as Chuck's. On paper he's still the man who was sentenced to die, and that's the man the courts who decide his appeal see.

It's not easy to keep my mind on this pen and paper as I hear the mixed feelings of people being interviewed. Those who know Chuck speak of him as a friend. Those who only read the papers speak of him as an enemy. Which is he? Who would know best?

11:38 P.M. In five minutes he'll be moved into the death chamber.

11:40 P.M. I would think they are telling him to get ready, without really having to say for what he should be getting ready. These are novel events for all who are involved, so I'm sure nerves are on pins and needles. Even though the prison staff has rehearsed the killing of a man several times so they'll be good at it when the time comes, it's different now that it is actually happening for real.

I can only imagine what's going on inside of Chuck's mind. Is there still a feeling of hope inside this man as he sees everyone doing the opposite of what would support his hope? Does every unannounced sound stir a nervous response within him as he hears the sound of a clock's tick pounding inside his head? Can he even relax to think clearly enough to truly understand all that is going on around him? I wonder if the new prison blues he's wearing will bear witness for the next man what energies have moved through them? Is the only hope now being kept alive in the heart of his wife as she stands, feeling her place as the "silent" prisoner? Does "please" mean anything now as he, we, wait for any change in events?

11:47 P.M. I feel that by now he has been moved and strapped down to the deathbed. Fourteen minutes until the plunger is pushed by the executioner. The twelve witnesses are sure to be watching his every movement, listening for whatever sounds a condemned man would make. Seven minutes now. Time goes by so fast when it is most precious. What thoughts could he possibly be exercising to escape from such excruciating torment as so many work together to see him dead? Of course, "excruciating" comes from a word relating to the Cross.

There will be three drugs administered at once. I'm not sure how they work, but one is supposed to put him to sleep while the others collapse the heart and lung muscles. It takes about ten to fifteen minutes to execute a man from start to finish. Fifteen minutes is a long time to be feeling the clutches of death pulling on you.

12:00 Midnight. He must know it's over for him, because there's a clock for him to see. Time is in slow motion; yet the clock is moving in fast gear. What can I say? It wasn't God's will for him to live?

12:01 A.M. I'd presume the executioner has pushed the plunger, and Chuck can now taste the drugs and feel them burn away at his life. He must be scared and praying as intelligibly as he can. I know I would be.

12:02; 12:03; 12:04; 12:05; 12:06; 12:07; 12:08; 12:09 A.M. They are saying they'll interview the twelve witnesses after it's over.

12:10 A.M. I'll say more as I hear something. The phone just rang in the media center. False alarm. It was for a media personality.

12:17 A.M. The phone rings again. "The execution is running behind schedule," says Mr. Massey. Something else for Chuck to wonder about as he watches those people stumble over each other in the process of taking what God gave him. A few moments of tears for me.

12:39 A.M. The phone rings again. Mr. Massey is nodding his head, "Yes." Charles Troy Coleman was pronounced dead at 12:35 A.M. They had trouble getting the needle in his right arm; so after several attempts they stuck it in his left arm. It took fourteen seconds to kill him once the drugs were administered. One witness said Charles' body went limp about fourteen to fifteen seconds after the warden looked at the executioner and instructed him to let it begin.

Just shortly after midnight, during the execution process, Chuck asked the warden to read a Bible text to him. Then he asked the chaplain to do the same reading, Psalm 23, as he was dying. The warden asked him if he had any final words. Chuck said, "Just tell everybody I love them, and I have peace in my heart." During the reading of the Bible text, Chuck would say, "Thank you, Jesus." Once during the execution he looked at Mandy Welch, his lawyer, and smiled. He told her that he loved her.

At 12:28 he took a heavy breath, and gurgling sounds were coming from him as his chest stopped moving. One witness said he took two to three breaths, lost color in his face, and then stopped moving. They all say it was such a somber peaceful event. He just left the prison for the last time, and this empty cell is calling for its next body to store away until the date of "the long walk."

The death row guard who works the row just came to me with tears in his eyes. Every canteen day Chuck would buy an insane man some canteen items and put them in his cell as Chuck went to shower. Sonny would wake up and they'd be there for him. Sonny just woke up and didn't find anything. He asked the guard to go check with Chuck and see if he had something for him. Forgive me if I stop here and cry.

Don Hawkins was executed by the state of Oklahoma on August 8, 2003.

## INSIDE THE DEATH CHAMBER

Transcript of a radio broadcast entitled "Witness to an Execution" produced by Stacy Abramson and David Isay

JIM BRAZZIL: My name is Jim Brazzil. I am a chaplain with the Texas Department of Criminal Justice. Part of my responsibility is being in the death chamber at the time of execution. I have been with 114 people at the time of their execution.

KENNETH DEAN: My name is Kenneth Dean. I'm the Major at the Huntsville Unit. I've participated in and witnessed approximately 120 executions.

MICHAEL GRACZYK: I'm Michael Graczyk and I'm the correspondent in charge of the Houston bureau of the Associated Press. I've witnessed approximately 170 executions.

TERRY GREEN: I have been a participant in 31 executions.

LEIGHANNE GIDEON: I witnessed 52 executions.

LARRY FITZGERALD: Probably somewhere in the neighborhood of 115 executions.

LONNIE JOHNSON: Approximately 105, 110 executions.

KATHY WALT: 36 or 37 executions.

FRED ALLEN: 130 executions.

WAYNE SORGE: I've witnessed 162 executions by lethal injection in the state of Texas.

JIM WILLETT: I'm Jim Willett. I've overseen about 75 executions at the Walls Unit in Huntsville, Texas.

*(Music fades to sound of the Walls Unit.)*

I started as a guard here twenty-nine years ago and have been warden since May of 1998. The Walls takes up almost two city blocks right in the middle of town. We're a maximum-security facility, home to 1500 inmates.

*(Walls Unit fades to sounds of the death house.)*

We also house the state's death house. Since 1924 all executions in Texas have taken place right here. We've carried out a lot of executions here lately, and with all the debate about the death penalty I thought this might be a good time to let you hear exactly how we do these things. Sometimes I wonder whether people really understand what goes on down here and the effect it has on us.

The death house sits in a corner of the prison. It's a small brick building with eight cells and a death chamber. Most days it's empty and quiet. Death row is actually located about forty miles east of the Walls. But on execution day the condemned prisoner is transported here.

The inmate arrives at the death house early in the afternoon on the day of his execution and gets placed in a cell. He spends the afternoon with the death house chaplain . . . waiting. At 2:00 he's allowed a phone call, at 3:00 a visit with his attorney and his spiritual advisor, at 4:30 he's given his last meal.

But I'm gonna start our story where the execution process really begins. At five minutes to six, I'm sitting in my office. I get up from my chair, put on my jacket, and walk back to the death house. At this time the inmate is in his cell, talking with the prison's chaplain, Jim Brazzil.

BRAZZIL: I've had 'em where they wanted to sing. I had one offender tell lawyer jokes. That was his time during that five minutes right before he was executed—wanted to tell lawyer jokes. And I've had 'em want to do exercises, do calisthenics sitting in there, you know, because it's such a nervous time. Because at that time reality has truly set in that in a few moments he's going to be dead.

WILLETT: One of my supervisors will get a call at 6:00 from the governor's office, and one from the attorney general's office, telling us that it's okay to go ahead with this execution. The inmate'll be in the second cell and I usually go down there and I call his name and tell him it's time to come with me to the next room.

BRAZZIL: He'll walk up to the cell where we are and he'll say, "It's time." And so they will unlock the cell and he's not handcuffed or chained. He's just sitting there. And he and I will walk into the chamber.

WILLETT: When he gets into the chamber, I'll tell him to sit down on the gurney and then lay down with his head on [the] pillow. At that time when he gets in there, all of the straps are undone. And within probably thirty, forty-five seconds the officers have him completely strapped in.

DEAN: My name is Kenneth Dean and I've participated in approximately over a hundred executions as a member of the tie down team. Each supervisor is assigned a different portion—like we have a head person, a right arm, left arm, right leg, left leg. And the right leg man will tell him, "I need you to hop up onto the gurney. Lay your head on this end, put your feet on this end." Simultaneously while he's laying down the straps are being put across him.

GREEN: I'm Captain Terry Green. I'm a member of the tie down team in the execution process. What I do, I will strap the offender's left wrist. And then there are two belts—one that comes across the top of his left shoulder—and then another goes right straight across his abdominal area.

DEAN: Some of them are very calm. Some of them are upset. Some of them are crying.

GREEN: Some of them have been sweating. Some of them will have the smell of anxiety, if you will. Of fear.

DEAN: Usually within about twenty seconds he's completely strapped down. Twenty to thirty seconds. I mean, it's down to a fine art.

GREEN: It's basically a situation where we just make sure he is secure. That he won't be jumping up, that he won't be able to squirm out of the restraints themselves, and that the job can be done—the job being the execution itself.

DEAN: After all the straps are done they will look at you and they'll say, "Thank you." And here you've just strapped them into the table. And they look at you in the eye and tell you, "Thank you for everything that you've done." And, you know, that's kind of a weird feeling.

*(Music fades in.)*

DEAN: It's kind of hard to explain what you actually feel, you know, when you talk to a man and you kind of get to know that person, and then you walk him out of a cell and you take him in there to the chamber and tie him down. And then a few minutes later he's . . . he's gone.

GREEN: Just another part of doing what I do as a correctional officer. It's something that the vast majority of the people want done. And so I am one of the few people in the state that is able to play a part in the process.

DEAN: It's a very unique job. Very unique. Not many people are willing to do this or can do this. I . . . I do believe in what I do. If I didn't and I felt that it was morally wrong or ethically wrong, then I wouldn't participate in it. And that's something we are not required to do—is participate in it. But I do this voluntarily.

GREEN: One thing I am glad of is that we're not using electric chair. I don't think I would want to be part of that. This process here, it's clinical. The inmate, other than the fact that he's expired, you don't know anything has happened to him. And, you know, that's good.

DEAN: You know, it's something that everybody has to deal with it in their own way. You know, some people they might like to drink and forget about it. I can take my mind off things when I go fishing. I like the outdoors and that's just how I cope with it.

*(Music fades out.)*

WILLETT: At 6:05 the medical team inserts the needles and hooks up the IVs.

BRAZZIL: After they are strapped down then all the officers will leave. And then it's the warden and myself in the chamber with him, and there'll be a medical team come in and they will establish an IV into each arm.

WILLETT: I have been somewhat surprised. It never crossed my mind that some of these people are just like the rest of us and are scared to death of a needle. Usually, if it goes right, and normally it does, usually in about three minutes they've got this guy hooked up to the lines. And at that time the inmate's lying on the gurney and myself and Chaplain Brazzil are in the execution chamber with the inmate.

BRAZZIL: I usually put my hand on their leg right below their knee, you know, and I usually give 'em a squeeze, let 'em know I'm right there. You can feel the trembling, the fear that's there, the anxiety that's there. You can feel the heart surging, you know. You can see it pounding through their shirt.

WILLETT: I've seen them so nervous they get one of these twitches in their leg or something and can't stop it. And I've seen the opposite. I've seen people lay up there, hooked up and waiting for the witnesses to come in. I believe I could say they were more calm than I am with you right now.

WILLETT: At 6:09 my staff escorts the witnesses into two small rooms adjacent to the death chamber. They push up real close to the windows to get a view. Larry Fitzgerald is our public relations officer. He's witnessed about 120 executions.

FITZGERALD: Once the IVs are established, then we bring the witnesses in, and in Texas the inmate is allowed five witnesses plus a spiritual advisor. The victims are allowed five witnesses. Plus there are five media witnesses.

SORGE: I'm Wayne Sorge, news director of KSAM in Huntsville, Texas. Well when we're brought into the room, the inmate is already strapped to the gurney and the tubes are inserted in each wrist.

GIDEON: My name is Leighanne Gideon. I am a former reporter for the *Hunts-*

*ville Item*. The gurney—I mean it takes up almost the entire room. And it's just sitting there right in the middle: a big silver gurney with white pads and the big brown leather straps with huge silver buckles.

GRACZYK: I'm Michael Graczyk from the Associated Press. When they're on the gurney they're stretched out. His arms are extended. I've often compared it to almost a crucifixion kind of activity. Only as opposed to having the person upright, he is lying down.

JOHN MORITZ: I'm John Moritz. I'm a reporter with the *Fort Worth Star Telegram*. The warden will stand at the head of the condemned man and the chaplain will generally be standing with his hand on the condemned person's knee. The warden will ask if the condemned man has any last words he'd like to say. A boom mike will come down from the ceiling and sometimes you can see the man who's strapped in with probably eight to ten straps across his body—he'll struggle to get his voice close to the mike. It's not necessary, but he does it anyway.

GRACZYK: And the inmate either declines to speak or says nothing or says a lot or sings or prays or does any number of things.

MORITZ: Generally the voice is emotional, nervous, cracks a little bit.

GIDEON: A lot of inmates apologize. A lot of inmates will say that you're executing an innocent man. And then there have been some men who have been executed that I knew, and I've had them tell me goodbye.

WILLETT: I will have talked to him at least once and somewhere in there found out how I'm gonna know when he's through with his statement. And most of them will tell me "This will be my last line." Or some of them just say, "Warden, I'll tell you," and they will literally just turn to me and say, "Warden that's all."

MORITZ: The warden will remove his glasses, which is the signal to the executioners behind a mirrored glass window. And when the glasses come off, the lethal injection begins to flow.

*(Music fades in.)*

GIDEON: I was twenty-six years old when I witnessed my first execution. After the execution was over, I felt numb. And that's a good way to explain it. And a lot of people will tell you that, that it's just a very numb feeling afterwards.

MORITZ: The first execution I did, I was wondering how I'd react to it. But it's like any other unpleasant situation a reporter is asked to cover. At som'

point there's a detachment. You realize that it's not about you; it's about the guy who's about ready to be put to death.

GIDEON: I've walked out of [the] death chamber numb and my legs feeling like rubber sometimes, my head maybe not really feeling like it's attached to my shoulders. I've been told that it's perfectly normal, everyone feels it, and that after a while that numb feeling goes away. And indeed it does.

SORGE: I wrestle with myself about the fact that it's easier now, and was I right to make part of my income from watching people die? And I have to recognize the fact that what I do for a living is hold up a mirror to people of what their world is. Capital punishment is part of that, and if you are in the city where more capital punishment occurs than any place else in the civilized world, that's got to be part of the job.

*(Music ends.)*

WILLETT: At 6:12 the executioner—a member of my staff whose identity is kept secret—begins to administer the chemicals. This is public relations officer Larry Fitzgerald again.

FITZGERALD: Texas doesn't use a machine. Some states use an actual injection machine. We use a syringe that is administered through an IV tube from another room.

BRAZZIL: This is Chaplain Brazzil again. The first chemical that's used is a drug called Sodium Pentothal, okay, and Sodium Pentothal is the same chemical that they use on you whenever you are going to have surgery, and it works very quick.

WILLETT: I know that at times they know when it's happening to 'em. One in particular I can remember, he said, "I can taste it."

BRAZZIL: Had one man who wanted to sing "Silent Night." He made his final statement and then after the warden gave the signal he started singing "Silent Night," and he got to the point "Round yon virgin mother and child" and just as he got "child" out was the last word.

MORITZ: The people inside the room watching it are invariably silent. Sometimes you find people holding hands, maybe a mother and father of a murder victim or friends of the condemned man.

GIDEON: It's very quiet. It's extremely quiet. You can hear every breath everyone takes around you. You can hear the cries, the weeping, the praying.

FITZGERALD: The second chemical is panchromium bromide, which is a muscle relaxant. It causes the diaphragm and the lungs to collapse.

WILLETT: It's usually a real . . . real deep breath. Just seems like they draw in all the air they can.

GIDEON: And then whenever that breath goes, it's like a snore. I mean it's like *[makes sound]*—kind of like taking a balloon and squishing that balloon and the sound that a balloon makes when you're squishing the air out of it.

MORITZ: Generally there is some erratic movement on the part of the inmate, some coughing, sputtering, occasionally a gasp. Then there's quiet.

BRAZZIL: I've had several of them where watching their last breath go from their bodies and their eyes never unfix from mine. I mean actually lock together. And I can close my eyes now and see those eyes. My feelings and my emotions are extremely intense at that time. I've never . . . I've never really been able to describe it. And I guess in a way I'm kind of afraid to describe it. I've never really delved into that part of my feelings yet.

FITZGERALD: The third chemical actually stops the heart.

WILLETT: At that point, and it's just something out of tradition—and I certainly haven't messed with it because it's worked—I was told to wait three minutes from that point and I have kept it to a tee, three minutes.

GIDEON: You see no more breathing, you hear no more sounds. It's just waiting.

GRACZYK: I had a mother collapse right in front of me. We were standing virtually shoulder to shoulder. She collapsed, hit the floor, went into hyperventilation, almost convulsions.

GIDEON: I've seen family members collapse in there. I've seen them scream and wail. I've seen them beat the glass.

SORGE: I've seen them fall into the floor, totally lose control. And yet how do you tell a mother that she can't be there in the last moments of her son's life?

GIDEON: You'll never hear another sound like a mother wailing whenever she is watching her son be executed. There's no other sound like it. It is just this horrendous wail. You can't get away from it. That wail surrounds the room. It's definitely something you won't ever forget.

(*Music fades in.*)

PICKETT: My name is Reverend Carroll Pickett. I'm a Presbyterian minister. I'm retired from the Walls Unit where I was chaplain for the death house. And I walked with and stood by and witnessed the execution of ninety-five inmates, from the first one that was done in 1982 until the end of August, 1995.

In the beginning days of executions in Texas we were faced with something that nobody had ever done before. Nobody had ever been executed by lethal injection. It was a brand new concept of humane execution. And we were to do the very first one. It was a new—almost a new world. In the beginning everybody was a name, but as it got on they just started doing it bam bam bam. You do three a year is one thing. You do thirty-five a year, that's a lot.

I've had guards—lots of guards quit. Even those tough guards you talk about. A lot of those quit. Some of them couldn't take it. Some of them couldn't take it.

After they're strapped down and the needles are flowing and you've got probably forty-five seconds where you and he are together for the last time, and nobody—nobody—can hear what goes on there. And the conversations that took place in there were, well, basically indescribable. It was always something different. A guy would say, "I want you to pray this prayer." One of 'em would say, "I just want to tell you thank you." One of them would say, "Don't forget to mail my letters." Another one would say, "Just tell me again, is it gonna hurt?" One of them would say, "What do I say when I see God?" You've got forty-five seconds and you're trying to tell the guy what to say to God?

*(Music fades out.)*

WILLETT: At 6:20 I call in a doctor to examine the inmate and pronounce death.

GRACZYK: This is Mike Graczyk from the Associated Press. The physician will take a stethoscope, look for a heartbeat or a pulse, shine a light in their eyes, and look at his watch and decide what time it is, and pronounce the time of death. And the warden repeats the time of death. We turn around, the guard opens the door, and we file out.

BRAZZIL: At that point all of the witnesses are escorted out immediately and the medical team will then come in and take the IVs out.

GREEN: And then we, the team members including myself, go in and unstrap him and then assist in putting him on the funeral home gurney until such time as he's wheeled out and that's the end of the process.

WILLETT: The procedure is almost always over by 6:25, and we're free to go. The executions seem to affect all of us differently. Some get quiet and reflective after, others less so, but I have no doubt that it's disturbing for all of us. It always bothers you. It does me.

*Fred Allen, who used to be part of the tie-down team, participated in about 120 executions before he had to stop. This is the first time Fred has ever talked about his experience publicly.*

FRED ALLEN: I was just working in the shop and all of a sudden something just triggered in me and I started shaking. And then I walked back into the house and my wife asked "What's the matter?" and I said "I don't feel good." And tears—uncontrollable tears—was coming out of my eyes. And she said, "What's the matter?" And I said, "I just thought about that execution that I did two days ago, and everybody else's that I was involved with." And what it was, was something triggered within and it just—everybody—all of these executions all of a sudden all sprung forward.

WILLETT: Three years later, Fred can still see the eyes of the men he helped tie down.

ALLEN: Just like taking slides in a film projector and having a button and just pushing a button and just watching, over and over: him, him, him. I don't know if it's mental breakdown, I don't know if . . . probably would be classified more as a traumatic stress, similar to what individuals in war had. You know, they'd come back from war, it might be three months, it might be two years, it might be five years, all of a sudden they relive it again, and all that has to come out. You see I can barely even talk because I'm thinking more and more of it. You know, there was just so many of 'em.

WILLETT: After sixteen years in the prison system, Fred resigned. He now works as a carpenter.

ALLEN: My main concern right now is these other individuals. I hope that this doesn't happen to them—the ones that participate, the ones that go through this procedure now. And I will say honestly—and I believe very sincerely— somewhere down the line something is going to trigger. Everybody has a stopping point. Everybody has a certain level. That's all there is to it.

WILLETT: I don't believe the rest of my officers are going to break like Fred did, but I do worry about my staff. I can see it in their eyes sometimes, particularly when we do a lot of executions in a short period of time. So far this year we've done thirty-three, and I'm guessing we'll get some place close to fifty by the end of 2000. That'll be a record.

I'll be retiring next year and to tell you the truth this is something I won't miss a bit. There are times when I'm standing there, watching those fluids start to flow, and wonder whether what we're doing here is right. It's something I'll be thinking about for the rest of my life.

*(Music fades in.)*

## THE STRUGGLE FOR A SPIRITUALITY: NICHOLAS INGRAM'S LIFE, FINAL DAYS, AND EXECUTION

### Sister Ruth Evans, member, Life Lines

The State of Georgia in the U.S.A. is one of four Southern "Death Belt" states, so described because of the frequency with which they sentence defendants to death. In June 1996, Amnesty International published a thirty-page document, *The Death Penalty in Georgia: Racist, Arbitrary and Unfair.* According to Amnesty, the death penalty developed in Georgia in the early twentieth century as a socially acceptable alternative to lynching. Prosecutors still continue to be more likely to seek the death penalty if the victim is white or the defendant black. In common with many of the states which have a death penalty, Georgia often fails to provide adequate legal assistance for those facing a capital trial. Before July 1988, it was one of the states without legislation to protect the mentally retarded from execution. Even so, a mentally retarded man, William Hance, was executed on March 31, 1994, despite the new legislation that had been passed. Georgia is one of the states which allow people to be sentenced to death for crimes committed under eighteen years of age. Christopher Burger was executed on December 7, 1993, for a crime committed when he was seventeen. The death penalty in Georgia is politically motivated: like many American states, Georgia elects officials in the judicial process. The Clinton administration was aware of Amnesty's conclusions but has refused to accept them.

Nicholas Lee Ingram was a white inmate of American-British nationality on Georgia's death row. He was arrested late on June 3, 1983. A white middle-aged couple had been tied to a tree behind their house in Cobb County and shot in the head. John Sawyer was dead. His wife, Mary, survived her tragic and horrifying ordeal. Ingram and a friend had spent the afternoon drinking, taking drugs, and breaking into houses. Nicholas Ingram was an alcoholic and a drug addict. His alcoholism dated back to his step-mother's practice of plying him with alcohol, to the point of unconsciousness, from his early teens. He had a medically recorded condition of alcoholic blackouts and alcoholic automatism. Due to an alcoholic blackout, Ingram had no recollection of what had happened at the Sawyers' house and whether he had shot them.

Ingram was sedated with Thorazine, a powerful anti-psychotic drug, during his trial, and the jury, which was kept ignorant of this, took his drug-induced impassivity for impenitence. It is not uncommon for a mentally ill person to be sentenced to death in the United States. Ingram's accomplice testified for the prosecution and told the court that Ingram had broken into the Sawyers' home alone. The accomplice was not prosecuted. Ingram was sentenced to death on his twentieth birthday and sent to death row in a mental state which medical opinion later agreed had been psychotic. He lived there for nearly twelve years before his execution.

*Life on Death Row*

Contrary to what they were led to believe, Nicholas Ingram was deeply sorry for the suffering of the Sawyer family. On Georgia's death row, he inhabited a seven- by eight-foot cell. He was locked up for most of the day. Three times a week he was allowed into a yard to exercise. The window in his cell was high but he could just manage to glimpse the natural world. In the intense heat of summer he used to lie down on the cement floor to feel cooler. These are typical death row conditions in the United States. The most important person to Ingram within this enclosed world was his friend, Tom Stephens, who lived in the cell next door.

On death row, Ingram became a client of the lawyer Clive Stafford Smith. Both men happened to have been born in the same Cambridge maternity ward. When his school days at Radley College ended, Stafford Smith turned down a place at Clare College, Cambridge, choosing instead to study in the United States with a view to working against the death penalty. He became a capital defense attorney and has been enormously successful in saving death row inmates from execution. In 1993, he founded the Louisiana Crisis Assistance Center in New Orleans. Here, dedicated lawyers work on death row cases for a fraction of the salary that would be available to them in other areas of the law. Stafford Smith argues that according to the standards of a European court, Ingram's conviction was invalid, because his state of alcohol-induced psychosis meant that he was not capable of intending to cause the torment to which the Sawyers were subjected.

On death row, according to Stafford Smith, Ingram recovered from his psychotic mental state, but he was severely depressed, more so even than most death row inmates. The prison did not offer him medication. In between sentencing and execution, an inmate's appeal for life is denied again and again. This takes an immense toll and drives some people insane. For Ingram, Stafford Smith says, the cycle of expectation and despair was an unbearable torture. Ingram's horror of the appeal process was intensified by his desire to protect his family and friends from suffering. He corresponded with a pen pal in Britain for five years. She writes, "He came across to me as a very caring person. Nicky rarely spoke about the appeal process, he always seemed to want to shield family and friends from worry. When everything became public towards the end he told me that he had always tried to shield me from the press."

Stafford Smith and Ingram met when they were twenty-six and twenty-two respectively. Ingram was on the point of dropping his appeals in order to avoid subjecting his family to the appeal process. Stafford Smith, however, "struck a bargain with him," obtaining permission from Ingram to do one set of appeals. Ingram gave in for Stafford Smith, rather than for himself. Stafford Smith describes how their relationship developed. "Nicky found it difficult to trust people after what he had experienced. Once I got through to him, which was not easy, he was one of the most loyal clients I have had. Before we were close it was difficult, because he kept trying to stop me doing things on his behalf. He was trying to protect his family. Once we became close he knew what it meant to me [to save his life], and he didn't get in my way." According to Stafford Smith, Ingram was "very loyal" to his family and "always" put them before himself.

On one occasion, Ingram's pen pal suggested that she travel to the States to visit him. Visits on death row are conducted in a degrading way for both the visitor and inmate. Ingram was sensitive and proud. He could not accept her offer, despite the high value he placed upon their friendship. She reflected, "I said that it would be nice if I could visit him but he wrote back and said that although it would be nice for us to meet he would not want me to see him in a place like that."

There is no present on death row, no "reality of now," Ingram wrote in a poem, because there is no "fairness." The poem describes the moral tensions on death row. Ingram was twenty-seven when he wrote it and had seen fifteen of his peers go to the electric chair.

> When trust is gone you no longer believe in
> words because words are so easily spoken they'll
> blind one to the truth.
>
> When hope is gone you no longer believe in
> dreams because the unobtainable dreams are seen
> as the fire that burns with hope . . .
>
> When love is gone you no longer believe in
> people because people are the ones who speak the
> words of love.
>
> When all this is gone then the only thing left to
> believe in is the truth . . .

According to Stafford Smith, Ingram was by nature, "an outdoor man." An important influence on the spirituality Ingram developed on death row was his love for the natural world and the suffering caused by his separation from it. Stafford Smith describes Ingram's spirituality like this:

> Nicky reacted against what he saw as the mean-spiritedness of the prison chaplains. He leaned in favor of people who he felt were being oppressed worldwide. Consequently, he felt most comfortable with the animist faith of the Australian Aborigines. This gave him a sense of community and empathy with a natural order from which he felt excluded by being locked up in a concrete cell all day. He experienced an empathy for people and things victimized by societal abuse. Nicky was a very spiritual person. He didn't reject Christianity but he couldn't accept the messengers of Christianity on death row. Nicky never felt there was any effort on the part of the official Christian ministers to relieve his suffering.

Death row chaplains are employees of the state, and Ingram's view of them is shared by most death row inmates. Ingram had a spiritual advisor, Randy Loney, who encouraged him in his spirituality and was a friend. Unlike many death row inmates, Ingram was realistic about the future.

He believed that he was going to be executed. On June 29, 1993, his best friend, Tom Stephens, went to the chair. Ingram was distraught. His pen pal comments, "The death hit Nicky very hard. He told me that they were like brothers." In an interview before his own execution, which Stafford Smith made available to the press, Ingram reflected on the experience, "You have to live with death all the time. When you see friends die, you either become afraid, or you accept that death is a change. I have come to believe that a spiritual part of me will continue after death."[1] For Ingram death had become a way of entering into the experience of life. He regarded death as an entry into "his future." In the same interview he commented, "Life on Death Row is not life." His pen pal writes, "We never really discussed religion. He did express his views from time to time with the odd remark such as, 'death is but a passing season for a man or a woman,' he held no fear of death and did not want me to fear it for him."

Days before Ingram died, Stafford Smith was quoted saying, "Nicky wanted to go in to the execution chamber for [Tom Stephens]."[2] Stafford Smith confirms that Ingram meant what he said but adds that he did not speak out of conscious heroism. "Nicky didn't care very much about his own life. It was all you could do to keep him wanting to stay alive."

*The Execution*

The American media tends to portray death row inmates as subhuman. Whether or not an inmate has a chance to express anything of his true self to the public in the run-up to his execution is determined by factors outside his control. In January 1998, Karla Faye Tucker approached her death by lethal injection in Texas. Fifteen years earlier, under the influence of drugs, she killed a former boyfriend and his girlfriend with a pickaxe as they slept. On death row she converted to Christianity and became an exemplary inmate. Before she died on February 3, Karla Tucker appeared on television, radiant in Christ for all to see. Even execution-hardened Texas was shocked.

Nicholas Ingram did not have the opportunity to give a television interview, nor did his plight win the sympathy in America that is sometimes accorded to a beautiful woman. And Ingram was not a Christian. In the U.S.A. his execution was a non-event, significant only because it was interesting to the British. Stafford Smith received hate mail.

Ingram was scheduled to die on April 6, 1995. The run-up generated extensive media coverage and intense curiosity in Britain. Ingram received letters of support from his homeland and this meant a great deal to him. The British Government argued throughout that it had no responsibility to intervene until the American appeal system, which it claimed to respect, had run its course. The fallacy of this argument, Stafford Smith points out, is that "appeals never run out until twenty minutes before they kill you." John Major happened to be in Washington days before Ingram was due to die. Ingram's mother, Anne Ingram, begged him to use his meeting with President Clinton to intercede for her son. She failed. Stafford Smith has reasons for believing that if Major had intervened for Ingram, his life would have been spared.

On the afternoon of April 5, Judge Hal Craig ordered Ingram to appear in court against his wishes. Ingram wanted to spend the time with his family. At the appeal hearing, Ingram's defense argued that death in the electric chair was "cruel and unusual punishment," which was prohibited by the Eighth Amendment of the American Constitution. Commenting on Ingram's presence, Stafford Smith says, "We tried to do it [present the terrifying facts about electrocution] in a way he wouldn't have to hear more than he had to." British journalists described Ingram as struggling for composure. Craig denied the appeal. He had in fact never ruled in favor of the defense.

On the evening of April 5, Wayne Garner, Chairman of the Georgia Board of Pardons and Paroles, raised hopes of a commutation by initiating a private interview with the condemned man. The gesture was unprecedented. Stafford Smith comments, "It gave us hope. It is not easy to execute someone you have met. The conversation went well. Nicky and I were very excited about it." For the first night in days, Ingram slept soundly. Tragically, the next morning these hopes were dashed. Amnesty International comments, "Having interviewed Ingram for his very life, the Board denied clemency." According to Amnesty, the clemency policy of the Board is "random in the extreme."

Ingram's personal belongings were appropriated by the state and he was issued a few necessary items on loan. He spent April 6 receiving visits from his family. He told them, "When your time comes, your time comes." To his mother he said, "I love you, Mum. I love you."[3] He expected to die at 7 P.M. At 5:55 P.M., he was granted a twenty-four hour stay of execution which according to Stafford Smith was "rare" at this stage. Ingram was not informed and the prison began to prepare him for execution. Ingram described what happened in a sworn affidavit that is quoted by Amnesty in its Georgia document under the heading "The cruelty of executions." Ingram had been denied the support of his spiritual adviser by a federal court and two official chaplains were imposed upon him.

> Apparently, at 5:55 P.M. my case was stayed but nobody told me. Indeed, at 6:20 P.M.—the time I know because the guards told me—they began to seriously prepare me for execution. It was devoid of humanity, a bunch of sick people who apparently volunteered for the job, acting like I was a lamb for the slaughter. They shaved my head with electric shears . . . They treated me like an animal, and said it was just a job. They had put on [me] some pants with a cut up leg for where they would attach the electrodes. They asked me what I wanted for a last meal. I said I did not want food, but I did want some cigarettes. They said the new policies forbid smoking. The chaplains were there most of the time—even before, when they put a finger up my anus in the strip naked "physical" exam . . . They told me it all starts again at 4 P.M. today with the "physical" once more, and I am to die tonight.

The greatest physical intrusion during the preparation for electrocution, Stafford Smith says, is the shaving of head and shin. Later, Ingram told Stafford Smith that the guards mocked him as he was shaved and that the Christian chaplains mocked him too. According to Ingram, the guards and chaplains were joking together about whether he would make a good conductor of electricity. The chaplains also tried to convert Ingram to Christianity. Ingram perceived this as an attempt to appropriate what belonged to him, his spirituality. In the affidavit Ingram commented, "They would not do anything about all this, but were trying to get me to accept their beliefs. I have my own strong religious feelings and did not want a philosophical debate with them."

When Stafford Smith finally spoke to Ingram on the phone, he was astounded to discover that Ingram believed he was going to die in twenty minutes time. This exploitation of Ingram's helplessness was illegal. Stafford Smith Says, "It was gratuitous torture. I said this at the time repeatedly in an attempt to put pressure on the British Government."[4]

Ingram had always been pessimistic about his chances of escaping execution. On April 7, because of the stay and the level of support from Britain, he experienced real optimism. Stafford Smith describes seeing him with a shaved head as a "physical shock." Ingram was unable to eat but he wanted cigarettes. The prison refused. Stafford Smith comments, "We had a huge argument about whether it really made any sense for them to try and preserve his health." The prison also refused Ingram a bandanna to cover his shaved head when receiving visits from his family. Ingram could not face his relatives without one. Again Stafford Smith was obliged to enter into a dispute. Vicki Gavalas, press officer for the Georgia Department of Corrections, kept the assembled press informed about what was happening to Ingram in a tone which, according to *The (London) Times,* would have been appropriate for "the weather report."[5]

That afternoon Ingram was granted a second stay, this time a seventy-two hour one. Stafford Smith comments, "I thought we had two or three days to work with." But the stay was overturned, allowing the execution to proceed that night. Ingram was alone as he waited. He was stripped, dressed, shaved and his head smeared with conducting jelly for a second time.

Stafford Smith had a final phone call with his close friend and client between 8:32 P.M. and 8:46 P.M., minutes before Ingram was led to the chair. Ingram expressed anxiety about the effect that witnessing the execution would have on Stafford Smith. He asked his lawyer to go on fighting for other death row inmates and to tell his mother that he loved her. Ingram found it difficult to speak in public. Earlier, he had told Stafford Smith that he would not be able to make a final statement in the execution chamber and intended to spit upon the warden. Stafford Smith was concerned about the effect the gesture would have on the way Ingram was remembered. However, he understands Ingram's reasons for making this decision: "Nicky never wanted to be part of their execution charade. Nicky didn't understand why he was meant to have a final meal when he wasn't hungry and they were going to kill him anyway. He didn't understand why he had to have a final prayer with some Christian chaplain who had laughed about his death. And he didn't understand why, dry-mouthed with terror, he should give a closing speech, just to fulfill their stereotype of how his death should happen. He wasn't willing to take part in their choreography of his own death."

Subsequent press quotations are taken from April 9 coverage. *The Sunday Express* had a journalist present at the execution. The paper boasted, "I Watch Him Die" and "Spitting killer goes to electric chair." Inevitably, Stafford Smith comments, Ingram's gesture fulfilled the stereotype of some journalists. Unlike the American press, he found most members of the British press sympathetic to his fight, a fact which obviously heartened him at the time. The British press drew heavily on Stafford Smith and their coverage was frequently critical of Georgia's legal process and its representatives.

However, the British press had no personal knowledge of Ingram. *The Observer* reported that his "short, ugly life" had ended in "stony unrepentence." Assuming Ingram had been killed instantly, *The Independent* began its coverage with the words, "The first four seconds were surely enough." According to *The Independent,* Ingram departed this life much as he had lived it—"angry, defiant and contemptuous of all around him." On March 22, *The Daily Telegraph* had given detailed coverage to Ingram's interview and to the extenuating circumstances and doubts surrounding his alleged crime. But *The Sunday Telegraph's* coverage of the execution had a very different tone. The paper announced Ingram's death with a headline that expressed more outrage over Ingram's spitting than his electrocution, "Spitting with rage, Ingram goes to his Maker."

Alone among journalists, prosecutors, and guards, Stafford Smith wept as Ingram died. He says that despite the terror Ingram experienced in his anticipation of death, he died with "remarkable courage." He continues, "Nicky was put to death methodically and barbarically. Members of the press were gullible who believed Nicky's death was painless, as the prison said."

The Attorney General of Georgia, Michael Bowers, chose to watch Ingram die. *The Independent* quoted him as he left the prison, "You can't turn an execution into a surgical procedure." The paper also quoted Stafford Smith, who had been entrusted with Ingram's final statement. "Mr. Stafford Smith was distraught, choking back tears. 'Nicky wasn't very good at speaking. He asked me to make a statement for him. He asked me to say he wasn't the one getting hurt, but his family and the family of the Sawyers. He told me he hoped for something better now, because what had happened in this life had been so sad.'"

On April 12, 1995, *The Guardian* printed an article by Clive Stafford Smith which described Nicholas Ingram's barbaric death.[6] In the summer of 1996, the state of Georgia hosted the Olympic games in Atlanta.

Sister Ruth Evans is a member of the Poor Clare Community, an enclosed order of nuns.

**Notes**

1. *The Daily Telegraph* (March 22, 1995).
2. *The Times* (London) (April 1, 1995).
3. *The Times* (London) (April 7, 1995).
4. An Amnesty document, *USA: The Death Penalty in Texas: Lethal Injustice* (March 1999) states, "For the authorities to subject a prisoner to the gratuitous extreme mental suffering of being put through the preparations for an execution which they know will not take place, can amount to a form of torture as defined by the United Nations Convention against Torture and Other Cruel, Inhuman or Degrading Treatment or Punishment, ratified by the USA on 21 October 1994," 12–13.
5. *The Times* (London) (April 8, 1905).
6. "My Private View of a Ritual Death."

## WITNESSING AN EXECUTION

Erika Trueman, member, Human Writes

Do not be fooled into believing that lethal injection is humane. It is nothing of the sort.

Today is Wednesday, November 10, 1999. As I write this I look at the clock. It is 2:04 P.M., and I think back to the exact time two weeks ago when I sat in the waiting room of Arizona State Prison, and thought of my friend who had just fifty-six minutes left to live. For eight years we had been pen pals and during that time we have laughed together, cried together, shared thoughts, views, memories, dreams of the future, and generally did what friends do—we talked and we listened to each other. Two weeks ago at this time I sat with his mother, who was desperately trying to do anything but think of her son being prepared to be killed.

In May this year, Ignacio Ortiz's appeal was denied and his death sentence was reaffirmed by the Ninth Circuit Court of Appeals. The Supreme Court subsequently refused to review his case again. For twenty years and ten months Ignacio and his various attorneys have tried to get his sentence overturned, and now it looked as though their efforts were in vain.

I phoned the attorney in May and asked him what hope there was for Ignacio. His answer was short: None. But as he had protested the re-sentencing to death and the Supreme Court was now on summer vacation, Ignacio would have at least until September before a warrant would be signed. Four months of waiting was to come, twelve weeks of respite, hope, and fear and hope again, recurring in nightmares and tears. We both acknowledged the reality of what might happen, yet neither of us talked much about it in letters. Ignacio's letters were still full of hope for his eventual freedom and I did not have the heart to repeat what his attorney had told me. As it got to August the frequency of our letters increased. There was much to be said before it was too late. The Supreme Court had returned the protest of his attorney without comment and an execution date was set for October 27th, 1999.

I read the words, but they didn't seem to register. If you live with the possibility or even certainty of an event for long it is easy to just accept it when it happens. I sometimes think the waiting was even harder than the knowledge of the warrant being finally signed. As I read it I felt numb at first, aware of the pain Ignacio might be going through now, followed by an outcry of "Why," and the inner silence that follows the empty feeling of inevitability. To kill is wrong. Period. To kill to show that killing is wrong, however, makes no logical sense. It is nothing but society's attempt to ignore their failings in helping those who commit crimes or even to ask why crimes are committed.

A week before my flight I finally received an e-mail from Ignacio's attorney in which he told me that I would not be allowed to visit Ignacio as the dates I had booked for my flight were too close to the execution date. I panicked and phoned the prison. It was confirmed that for the last two weeks before an execution only the immediate family members, the attorneys, and the spiritual advisor is allowed to see the condemned. I spent the next few days on the telephone, speaking for hours with various officials in Arizona, going as high as I possibly could. I told them of the wrongly given information that my visit would be guaranteed if Ignacio applies for a special permit, I begged, I pleaded. But the decision was final. I was not going to see my friend, though two days before my flight was due I was told by a prison administrator that Ignacio had requested me to witness his execution. So I flew out with a mixture of fear and dread, hope and terror.

I traveled overnight to Gatwick airport, London, for my flight at noon the following day. It took a total of thirty-two hours to get to Phoenix. I arrived exhausted, hot, and anxious. A friend of Ignacio and his wife (both ministers) picked me up from the airport.

The following day I received my "invitation" (as the prison called it) to witness Ignacio's death with detailed instructions for witnesses. As I read the invitation I noticed that "contact with family members of the condemned is not permitted on prison property" . . . and I thought of Ignacio's eighty-year-old mother who would be the only member of his family to attend. I felt outraged at the insensitivity and callousness of prohibiting contact with her on prison ground.

I received another letter in Phoenix from Ignacio, and he indicated that I might get a visit on the morning of the execution. Ignacio wanted me and a friend, who was also going to be a witness, to be at the prison at 7:30 A.M. He said, if we go to the prison chaplain, he would then call the office. Someone in the office would go to Ignacio and ask him if he wanted to see us and he would then say, "Yes." We would be driven to his cell and could say good-bye. Surely I thought no one could be so inhumane to deny him this little act of kindness on the day of his death.

The minister and I were outside the prison gates at 6:30 A.M. The execution was scheduled for 3:00 P.M. and I just wanted to be there; I had no peace in the hotel and wanted to go the prison as early as possible. I had not slept for two nights. How can I sleep if I look at the clock and think of Ignacio, having just twenty-seven hours left to live, then twenty-six, twenty-five, twenty. I watched the seconds move, and every second took an eternity, yet the hours flew by, indicating an end that I so wanted to escape. With every moment I thought of what might be his "last." His last evening meal, his last shower, his last breakfast, his last shave, his last . . . what? What was he doing at this moment? How I wished I could help him cope with facing his death at the hands of those who have known him for many years. They have known him change and find a purpose in life, and still they failed to see his humanity. I needed to be close to the prison, not cooped up in some hotel, with an irrational fear that the car would break down on the journey to the little town of Florence, or that the clocks would be slow or that I might oversleep, or any of the other fears that haunt us when we blur the line between reality and illusion. I wanted to say good-bye and yet had an indescribable fear of doing so. I also thought of Ignacio's mother who was going to be at the prison for her last visit that morning. How would Ignacio cope? For nearly twenty-one years he had not felt a loving touch, nothing but brutal hands that hurt and are at best careless or indifferent of his person. I felt the pain of condemnation and I felt something of the incredible loneliness and wrongness Ignacio felt. How much pain can a man endure and how much strength does it take not to break? And how is it possible that we can inflict such pain on our fellow humans?

We arrived at the prison, it was now 6:45 A.M. We entered and were taken to the office of the prison chaplain. But we were too early, it was still locked. He had not yet arrived. We were taken somewhere else to wait. I watched some inmates clean the yard. They watched us while continuing with their work. Certainly they would not be death row prisoners, but I wondered what they thought of capital punishment. Did they have the same feeling that it is wrong? Maybe they just felt relief that they were not on death row. Did they even care?

Finally, we were taken back to the prison chaplain's office. He was in, eating his breakfast. We introduced ourselves and mentioned Ignacio's assurance that we can visit, if he, the prison chaplain, arranges it with the death watch office. His reaction was dismissive; it had nothing whatsoever to do with him. "Why are you coming to me?" I appealed to his humanity for help and told him that I had been promised a visit by this very prison before I flew out. "Sorry," he said, "that has nothing to do with me." The telephone rang and for the next ten minutes or so he spoke to someone who inquired about the body of the deceased . . . We did not hear the questions, but we heard the answers of the chaplain. "There will be a post-mortem . . . just a routine thing . . . no, it takes about thirty days before his personal belongings are released . . . yeah, she can pick it up or we can send it out . . . about thirty dollars . . . I heard she wanted cremation . . . or if she wants she can sort out something else, but that's really up to her . . . no, we wouldn't pay for that . . . he can always be buried here, if she can't afford it . . ." The conversation went on and on. The minister and I looked at each other, we didn't speak but our thoughts must have been the same. They are talking of Ignacio, as if he is already dead. And it wasn't just the words I heard, I also heard the tone in his voice, it was very cold, very impassive, and very hard. He, the man of God, did not care. He simply did not care.

When he had finished the conversation I asked him whether he had talked of Ignacio and he denied this. "No, someone else died here." I did

not believe him. We asked the chaplain to take us to the warden. I wanted
to ask him, beg him, to allow us to say good-bye. The chaplain took us to
a waiting area in the main building and told us to wait. We sat and waited,
quietly talking of the telephone conversation we had listened to and in the
silences of our conversation thought of our friend and what he might feel
now. We waited for over an hour, prison officers walked past us, got drinks
from the vending machine close by, talking and laughing as if this was just
a normal day for them.

It was nearly 9:00 when a female officer asked us who we were and why
we sat there. We told her that the prison chaplain had gone to get the warden and asked us to wait. Taking our letters of invitation and checking our
identifications she left us, and returned some minutes later. "The warden
will see you shortly," she said and left. The warden did come a few minutes
later but his face was cold and his eyes hard. "You can't visit." I explained
that I had been promised a visit, but he was not to be moved. "You have
been given the wrong information, and I will not make an exception." He
told us to go away and come back later. Then he left us, empty and disappointed. I had asked for just ten minutes to say good-bye, yet even that was
more than he was willing to give to a man facing imminent death.

We left the prison and drove around for an hour; anything to pass the
time. Our thoughts were not at the beauty of the desert, but at the inevitability of time passing. Could we stop time, or should we even wish to? Is not
any time that is prolonged before the execution time that is spent in fear and
terror? We got back to the prison at 10:30 A.M. We were checked and taken
to the waiting room for the witnesses Ignacio had requested. The room we
entered had a large table in the middle, with a dozen or so chairs around it.
Some people were already present and we were introduced. I shook hands
but didn't hear or understand the words said. I felt totally empty inside.
There were two other witnesses for Ignacio, both ministers and pen pals. A
female guard in uniform checked us for contraband and/or weapons with
a metal detector before we sat down. Two other guards in civilian clothes
sat at the table, with quick eyes that did not miss a thing, silently watching
us. One of them had a list of names, and ticked off that we had arrived.
Ignacio's mother was not yet there, neither was his attorney who had told
me that he planned to come on the day of the execution. I hoped that Ignacio was at peace, but I had no way to find out. The feelings of emptiness

had left me and all I felt was anger. Anger at the system that takes a man and decides he does not deserve to live, and anger at our failings to see that he is human, just like us.

About half an hour after we got into the waiting room Ignacio's mother returned from her last visit to see her son. I had not seen her before, but when the door opened and an old woman stood there, looked at me and opened her arms, and said, "Erika," I decided to ignore point two of the invitation of what I was and was not allowed to do, and stood up to embrace her. Nobody stopped me. Isabel and I sat together and talked of Ignacio, of the son she loved and of the friend I loved, while the three ministers talked about their faith and about their belief in the everlasting afterlife Ignacio was going to have.

Shortly afterwards Ignacio's spiritual advisor arrived. He also recognized me as Ignacio had shown him my photo and my letters. Father Nacho told me of Ignacio's last visit with his mother. They spoke to each other through a glass window, but in the room where Isabel sat the guards had the radio on and, being hard of hearing, Ignacio had to shout so his mother could understand him. He was very upset about this and at first refused to shout, it was only when the minister told him that this was the only way for his mother to understand, that he felt able to do so. I remember Ignacio from our visit five years ago and he was a soft-spoken man. How hard it must have been for him to see his mother under such circumstances! And what a small act of compassion it would have been for the guards to turn off the radio. But compassion does not rate very highly on death row. Father Nacho told me that Ignacio was very upset at not seeing me. And so we both used his minister as a messenger to relay last words to each other. He left to see my friend again.

The time of waiting was hard. These were the longest hours of my life. There was a clock on the wall and I kept looking at it, yet the minutes seemed to go so slow that what seemed like an hour only moved the hands of the clock a few minutes further to the inevitable. Ignacio's Christian friends were still talking of their faith, the guards still silently watched us, Isabel and I were sitting close together. I felt like being stranded on an island, with no boat to leave. The others had their purpose, their belief or their conviction that what was going to happen was right, yet Ignacio's mother and I had nothing like this. Could we swim or would we drown? All we had was the knowledge that the man we cared for was going to be killed. It was only 11 o'clock, a full four hours before the execution took place, but what does one talk about in those hours? Isabel was desperate to talk, but she did not seem to understand me well. Her English was not too good. She is Mexican and started to teach me Spanish. We were both eager to find something to pass the time. She must have felt it much stronger than I.

Back in the waiting room with the untouched buffet the time went slowly, I kept looking at the clock and thought of what Ignacio must be doing and thinking now. Would he now have his last meal? Were they already taking him, strapping him onto the gurney? What did he think? Was he at peace? Father Nacho came back and told me that Ignacio knew I was there. "How is he?" I asked. "He is excited as if he is going on a trip, thinking of whether he has done everything . . . wondering whether he has forgotten something . . . ," he replied. "He is OK, he is at peace. He will be united with our Lord soon, he knows that." Father Nacho stayed with Isabel and me and the three of us talked quietly, my eyes straying towards the clock on the wall, its hands moving ever so slowly.

It was now 2:50 P.M. when the door opened and we were told it was time to go. As we left the air-conditioned building the desert heat hit me. Florence is in what they call "the valley of the sun" and it was ninety-five degrees, even though it was the end of October. As we walked I looked up and saw the blue sky, the blazing sun, and, as I watched a bird flying above me, the scene seemed surreal. There was life all around me, yet I was to watch a man being killed. How can life and death be so close? In a few minutes the sun would still shine, the bird would still fly, yet the man now lying on the gurney would no longer breathe, his body slowly decomposing; he would continue to live only in our memories, traces fading over time.

I do not know how far we walked. The pastor later talked of a quarter of a mile to walk. The only thing I was aware of was the life-giving heat of the sun, the bird flying above, Isabel's hand in mine, occasionally squeezing it and me putting one foot in front of the other. I took one step at a time, not knowing, nor caring where we walked. Fear rose in me and replaced the anger. It gnawed at my stomach, burned into my soul like acid. This could not be real, this was not happening. Yet every step took me closer. Panic welled in me and the feeling I had earlier of being stranded on an island with no boat to leave increased. Yet now I was not only stranded, the water was lapping at my feet, rising and rising ever more. I needed to run away and escape, to hide. Panic overwhelmed me that I would drown. And yet my feet moved slowly forward, one step at a time. I was holding Isabel's hand, Father Nacho holding her other hand. He prayed quietly, speaking words of comfort to Isabel, I heard myself saying things like, "It will be over soon, his suffering will be over. He will not hurt anymore," fully aware that the platitudes I spoke to Isabel were wholly inadequate. Yet I had nothing else to offer her. I walked on automatic pilot, spoke words that seemed empty and without meaning while my soul was drowning in a sea of fear and terror, wondering what is reality, what is illusion.

There were to be forty-two witnesses (twenty-nine had arrived), most of them official, but also two children of the victim. The witness room was separated in steps so that those in the second, third, and fourth row stood higher than others and could see equally well. We were the first to arrive and stood in the front row. As we walked towards the open door Father Nacho whispered to us, "Don't go in first, his head is near the door." I nodded and held Isabel back. She didn't understand and wanted to go in. I repeated the words, "His head is near the door." I don't know whether she understood, but she slowed and let Ignacio's other witnesses go in first, we followed. I was determined to hold on to Isabel, and equally determined to allow her to be as close to her son as she could.

The room was only dimly lit. There was a large dark blue curtain in front of us, which covered the whole wall. I had both my arms around Isabel and Father Nacho had his arm around the both of us, quietly speaking to Isabel, praying now with urgency in his voice. Slowly the other witnesses arrived. There was total silence. Nobody spoke. We did not look round to see who was behind us. We heard footsteps, but they did not exist for us. All that existed in our thoughts was the dark blue curtain and the man who was behind it. Once everybody was inside, a guard who stood by the door locked it and spoke something into the mobile phone he held. "Everybody is inside," I heard.

It seemed a long time, but was probably only a minute or so when the curtain opened and we saw Ignacio. He was already strapped onto the gurney, with a white sheet covering him up to his neck. We could not see the straps that held him, nor could we see the needles they had inserted ready for the poison to flow. Ignacio lay still, his eyes shut and head towards the ceiling.

After a short while someone came in, stood by Ignacio's feet and we heard a click as the microphone was switched on. The officer announced that there was no stay. The microphone was switched off and the officer walked out again, without looking at the man about to die. Then, after a short while, someone else came in to read the warrant, and while doing so looked only at the witnesses. I noticed that Ignacio started to shake. His face was set, but his hands and particularly his feet were shaking violently. Keeping his eyes fixed on the witnesses, the officer who read the warrant asked if Ignacio had any last words, without ever looking at him. In a loud and clear voice Ignacio said, "Yes." "Jesus Christ is the Lord" (repeating the words in Spanish), "Heavenly Father, into your hands I commend my spirit" (and again repeating his words in Spanish). As he was saying "into your hands" his voice broke and he had difficulty in speaking the last words. He said, "Thank you" and was silent after that. His eyes remained shut, his face set. The loudspeakers were switched off and I saw a tear run down the side of Ignacio's face. He was so close to me that I felt I could touch him if I reached out my hands if it had not been for the glass between us.

At the wall behind him was an opening, which had been covered with some curtain material. There was movement of the curtain, as if there was a draft. I knew that the tubes stiffened as the poison began to flow; the first injection took place. I watched Ignacio's face. I so much wanted to instill some kind of comfort or friendship or love in him to ease these final moments. I had planned so many things that I hoped would help him, show him he was cared for. I had rehearsed this moment in hours of fear and anger and disbelief. I had wanted to reach out to him, smile, put all my expressions of friendship and love and respect for him into my face, anything at all that would make it just a little easier for him. But he did not open his eyes, he could not if he wanted to keep his composure. Clinging to Isabel I watched for anything in his face to change, any reaction. I saw his head and chest heave up once as if he was choking. He breathed twice more and then lay still, his eyes and mouth now slightly open. We stood and waited. I knew he was dead, but I expected him to turn around and look at me, I willed him to live, to get up and walk away. An officer came in and announced, "Death at 3:05 P.M. Please take note. Death at 3:05 P.M. Please take note," and he never looked at the man in whose death he had just taken part. It was as if for all those who spoke to the witnesses, this man on the gurney did not exist, as if he had already gone, left his humanity behind like an old coat that one can just take off or put on as one pleases.

The doors opened and we (Ignacio's witnesses) were taken out and taken immediately in a van to the car park. Nobody spoke. I felt numb and empty. Isabel was picked up by friends and they left immediately, his attorney left with a short good-bye. Father Nacho hastily wrote his address down for me, and left to see some other prisoners, and only the minister and I stood in the empty car park. I saw nobody else. There was no media, no protestors, nobody but us. The road had been blocked off earlier, but still I thought someone must have been there. Did nobody know what went on? Did nobody care? Was it real? And what happened to life now. Would it go on as normal, TV news reporting traffic accidents and scandals, the citizens of Arizona reading about the execution with their morning coffee, grateful that they can now sleep safer as another "animal" has been killed? Was society really safer now? I left the following day.

Ignacio Ortiz was executed on October 27th, 1999, aged 58. His last wish was for his remains to be cremated and the ashes scattered over his grandmother's grave on his birthday, December 21st. He had been brought up by his grandmother and wanted to be reunited with her in death. Yet in the weeks and months that followed his death, I became aware that his wish had not been granted. I was informed that permission for cremation had been denied by members of his family and his body was moved from the prison to the county of his birth. But it was not accepted there either, as he had died in a different county. The prison refused to take him back as he had already left their premises. Finally, I received a copy from the Holy Hope Cemetery in Tucson. Ignacio's remains were laid to rest on Thursday, August 3rd, 2000—9 ½ months after he was executed by the state of Arizona.

# LOVE ME NOW

Ignacio Ortiz

If you are ever going to love me,
Love me now, while I can know
The sweet and tender feelings
Which from true affection flow.
Love me now while I am living,
Do not wait until I'm gone
And then have it chiseled in marble
Sweet words on ice-cold stone.
If you have tender thoughts of me
Please tell me now.
If you wait until I'm sleeping never to awaken
There will be death between us
And I won't hear you then.
So, if you love me, even a little bit,
Let me know it while I am living
So I can treasure it.

 **POEMS**

*May the bad not kill the good,*
*Nor the good kill the bad*
*I am a poet, without any bias,*
*I say without doubt or hesitation*
*There are no good assassins.*
　　—Pablo Neruda

## RECIPE FOR PRISON PRUNO

Jarvis Masters, Death Row, California

Take ten peeled oranges,
Jarvis Masters, it is the judgment and
    sentence of this court,
One 8 oz. bowl of fruit cocktail,
That the charged information was true,
Squeeze the fruit into a small plastic bag,
And the jury having previously, on said
    date,
And put the juice along with the mash
    inside,
Found that the penalty shall be death,
Add 16 oz. of water and seal the bag tightly.

And this court having, on August 20, 1991
Place the bag into your sink,
Denied your motion for a new trial,
And heat it with hot running water for 15
    minutes.
It is the order of this Court that you
    suffer death,
Wrap towels around the bag to keep it warm
    for fermentation.
Said penalty to be inflicted within the
    walls of San Quentin,

Stash the bag in your cell undisturbed for
    48 hours.
At which place you shall be put to death,
When the time has elapsed,
In the manner prescribed by law,
Add 40 to 60 cubes of white sugar,
The date later to be fixed by the Court in
    warrant of execution.
Six teaspoons of ketchup,
You are remanded to the custody of the
    warden of San Quentin,
Then heat again for thirty minutes,
To be held by him pending final
Secure the bag as done before,
Determination of your appeal.
Then stash the bag undisturbed again for 72
    hours.
It is so ordered.
Re-heat daily for 15 minutes.
In witness whereof,
After 72 hours,
I have hereon set my hands as Judge of this
    Superior Court,
With a spoon, skim off the mash,
And I have caused the seal of this Court to
    Be affixed thereto.
Pour the remaining portion into two 16 oz.
    cups.
May God have mercy on your soul,
Guzzle down quickly!
Mr. Jarvis Masters.
Gulp Gulp Gulp Gulp!

## SO MANY TIMES

Mark Robertson, Death Row, Texas

So many times
I'd see her up
    upon that stand,
It ripped through my soul.
I'd see her sit
    with a tear in her eye,
Demolished the stone in me.
So many times,
So many times?
I'd hurt her and
Bring her to a place
She wants not to be;
To break down and cry.
I see the pain inside;
It lashed at me, like
Razors oh so sharp
And shred me to ribbons;
A million tearful parts.
So many times. . . .
Still many months later,
I feel that pain inside,
And I do love you Mother;
This pain shall go away,
As it seeps back down
Into my heart.
So many times,
So many times?

## TO BE SEEN, TO BE DONE

Benjamin Zephaniah, member, Life Lines

If you are to be seen
Why hide
Behind curtains, robes
Order and law,
If you are so true
Why lie
To the mouths that speak
Of you,
Why bite
The hand
That's feeding you.

If you are to live with us
Why not
Protect us,
We need you now
And always,
For ever
And ever
Be good,
If you want respect
Just be
As equal as we,
What do you mean
Without we?

You came to save our madness
But madness turned you on,
We have one question
Justice,
That is,
Where have you gone??

## DEATH ROW LAMENT

### James Heard, Death Row, California

What's wrong with this picture?
Let me describe it, so you will see.
There is a man, sitting in a small cell.
His head is in his hands, looks like he's
    going through hell!
He sits there motionless, with hardly any
    light.

One could only imagine, what could be this
    man's plight.
He looks very depressed, but there is no
    sadness on his face.
He just sits there—quietly staring at
    empty space.
I wonder what this man's crime might be?
Hey! Wait a minute!! That poor man is me.

## YOU ARE IN

### Karl Louis Guillen, Arizona State Prison

The cold grey cement rips your ear,
    and
As you hit the not-so-clean floor,
Cruel voices now mock your new fate,
Even as you don't want to care anymore.
Your one blanket smells like piss,
Your background thoughts have never been
    louder.
A voice screams in terror,
It's your own, you realize too late.

As cruel voices mock your new fate,
Behind the black bars watch things pass by,
Look through the cheese grater, your
    window to the sky.
Tears falling silently, for no one can know,
You might get punked or become the new
    show.

## CAPITAL EXISTENCE

James Heard, Death Row, California

I am sitting here . . .
Every now and then I sigh.
I am lying here . . .
Once in a while I moan.
I hardly smile . . .
Except to hide my pain.
It's getting harder to think . . .
What if I am going insane?
I can see the stress in the faces around
    me,
Fear the sadness in their voices,
Feel the depression surrounding me,
Smell the fear . . .
I am on Death Row.

## MY GOD

Karl Louis Guillen, Arizona State Prison

My pain dawns like a teardrop falling
Like a locomotive's distant calling
Forever standing, here at this ledge.
"*My Lord,*" I cry as dry winds take me to the
    edge . . .

And Death crosses towards me
Yet stops, staring from across the street.
I hear its putrid breath, in and out,
Rattling, like the pitter-patter of little feet.

Yet beyond where lies the circus of pain
Within my head, my dread, my dreams
You await, with such spirit and love
Very brave, while I live amongst these screams.

*"Hath Thou forsaken me?" I ask,*
*"My innocence has been purposely concealed.*
*Why now these bars PROVE my wickedness*
*That before yesterday had never revealed?"*

*"My God? My God . . ."*

## LIVING DEATH

Kevin Brian Dowling, Death Row, Pennsylvania

Your whole life can change in a second, and you
Never even see it coming.
Life doesn't always turn out the way it was
     supposed to.
It seems we live two lives—the life you learn
With and the life you live with.
What once was, is no longer.
What was to be, will never be!
The road is life you chose has been closed.
The road now given to you is unfamiliar,
Your distance and destination unknown.
The darkness of the night is profoundly different
From the darkness of closed spaces,

The night has no boundaries, and it offers
  endless
Mysteries, discoveries, wonders, and opportunities for
  joy.
The isolation of a death row cell redefines the night and
  compels introspection.
Most of us are murky ponds, containing infinite layers of
Suspended participles, stirred by strange currents in their
  greatest depths.
Sometimes there is no darker place than our own
  thoughts,
A moonless midnight of the mind.

## OBLIQUE SOJOURN

Leroy D. Cropper, Death Row, Arizona

Dark thoughts glittering like a ghetto
Solidify my world beyond infliction.
Traveling beside the endless winds,
Searching and cursing, my shoes worn thin.
Lacerating dreams, cradle my sleep.
Sarcastic laughter comforts my day.
Couldn't share the pain, unable to forgive,
Dark thoughts welcome me home.

## THE DUNGEON

Karl Louis Guillen, Arizona State Prison

Pristine grey walls, eight by ten
And darker grey doors of steel and cold.
I watch and listen to the lifeless sounds
  of bodies this darkness doth enfold . . .
Light of sun or moon does not exist
In here, my dungeon home
Where only cockroaches and mice may live

Beyond the circle of cement I roam.
Night sounds invade my sleep,
Tortured screams from souls of pain.
I wrap the cloth around my ears
Only to hear their cries within.
Through the nights my mind wanders
While sleep comes in tosses and turns
To dreams of love, peace, a brief respite
From this wilderness where anger burns.
Constant buzzing of voices shake me from my
    drift,
It is the everlasting bulb, glaring dull white
Behind the Plexiglas barrier, scratch-marked,
They do not break without a fight.
I feel this sickness of spirit invading,
My heart feels the sun rising beyond the door,
I battle against my fears and fantasies,
Shut my eyes, watch the memories of before . . .


## RED MAN

Shoz Dijiji, Death Row, Texas


With whom can I talk,
Where do I fit,
With whom will I walk,
Where am I to sit?
I stand looking around,
As my heart slowly sinks to the ground;
The Black, are playing basket-ball,
Or sitting along the fence,
Talking their jive;
The White, sit in a corner rapping,
Or doing their drugs,
In search of another life;

The Brown (Mexicans) are sitting,
In another little corner, as if,
They were in a world all their own;
Red man,
Where will you sit,
With whom can you walk,
Where do you fit,
With whom will you talk?

## COME BACK TO ME

Keith B. Taylor, Death Row, Georgia

Today I thought to myself
Today I fought with myself
Come back to me, come back to me
My love I once had
Come back to me, come back to me
My peace I'll be glad
Today I cry by myself
Someday I'll die by myself
Come back to me, come back to me
My spirit I'm sad
Come back to me, come back to me
My life I'll be glad
Today I must say to myself
Today I must pray for myself
Oh God! my love from heaven above
Oh God! my peace, which never cease
Oh God! my spirit, I pray you hear it
Oh God! my life, my life, my life

## JOURNEY TO NOWHERE

Ramon Rogers, Death Row, California

I pace back and forth in a straight line, thinking of nothing,
 trying to do time.
The soles of my shoes grow thinner each day, black hairs on my
 head are turning to grey.
My sight starts to blur, my eyes are quite sore, pacing
 repeatedly across this hard floor.
A thousand miles have already been paved, but there's no
 destination this side of the grave.

Lungs fill with stagnant, polluted burnt air, the smell of death is
 everywhere.
The heart beats weak with question and fear, maintaining a life
 that is going nowhere.
A stomach twisted in a thousand knots, lives are discarded and
 easily forgot.
The flood can boil just under the skin, when things go wrong
 'cuz you never can win.

There is this spinning inside my head. Without my freedom, life
 is now dead.
The darkness cloaks the brightest of days, the chills in the
 bones are here to stay.
The laughter, the love, the pleasure, the pain, everything is
 numb and all feelings retrained.
The pains of today will be gone tomorrow. After due time
 there'll be no more sorrow.

My paces slow with each passing day. My strides grow short
    and will power frays.
The distance traveled is less than before, will God ever help to
    open this door?
Hours are now endless and years have no end, lost in the
    wastelands without any friends,
The flight is not over even when won, 'cuz when least
    expected, another has begun.

I pace back and forth in a straight line, thinking of nothing,
    trying to do time.

## BEYOND THE CEILING

Karl Louis Guillen, Arizona State Prison

Blocks of cement,
Tons of cover on my hear,
I scream to breathe,
I think I'm dead,
I think I'm dead.

On the other side, where you can't see,
Rumors of some great blue.
A force, they say, watching over me, and
Rumor HE's watching you.

Stars and sun and love and life
Behind the rocks upon my head.
A baton awaits to further my strife,
Unless I'm already dead.

Comfort is found under the weight,
My soul thrives though deprived of air,
Or am I trapped dying while I wait?
Everything an illusion, nothing really there?

## THIS HORROR

Karl Louis Guillen, Arizona State Prison

I write this horror.
My hair has long since turned gray,
My walls are different shades
Of the same color, of the same day.
I sleep in my corner
Where my dreams appear at night,
I stare out from my four walls,
I know there is a sun, but I see no light.
In the corner of my eye
Blurry spiders dance beyond my reach,
During the boredom I talk to them,
Sometimes they to me in their odd little speech.

This corner of the world becomes to none
For this horror is only for the few.
Do not look inside or become attracted to the gist
Or my horror will come upon you too . . .

## A "NOT SO BAD" MAN

Karl Louis Guillen, Arizona State Prison

Back in '98 I thought I knew everything.
Those were days I'd listen to nobody at all.
Heard the county jail pigeons sing,
Damned if I wasn't 21
Thought I had seen it all!
But there was a *"not so bad"* man.
I looked into his dying eyes,
He hurt no one, only talked some shit,
But still he had to die.
Someone screamed: *"Oh, my God,"*
A spray so hot it burned my skin.

Looked down at this newly painted canvas,
In those blood black eyes was a whirlwind,
The fires and storms in his faded windows,
No one but I saw the lightening flash,
Or covered the long 10–inch gash.
Blood spilled into my brain that day,
The "not so bad" man died and fell.
Storm clouds passed somewhere along the way,
Another *"not so bad"* man gone to hell.
Those were the days I knew nothing at all,
Just a fool beyond another brick wall.
Took a "not so bad" man's death to knock me
    down,
Back in '98, in the silence, on the bloody ground.


## FALLING IN

Karl Louis Guillen, Arizona State Prison

He peers out the gray bars.
It seems his gaze is trapped behind a thousand
    steel stripes,
His soul is stifled with longing,
His will paralyzed by stagnancy.
Each footstep slapping cement with force,
Naked toes bruised from testing the edges of the
    cage.
Something in his crazy grin,
Arched brows like wicked mountain peeks,
Around and around he goes,
There's subtle dignity in circles,
He never stops, never gives in.
The world beyond has forgotten him
He has tripped and stumbled
Over the brink he has fallen in.

## WHEN IT'S AT YOUR DOOR

Mark Allen Robertson, Death Row, Texas

You sit, lay the tax
And wait another damp night
Within the yellow light of cheap bulbs,
Within the gray walls and near
The plight
Of struggling men,
Men,
Who struggle for their lives.

You will be laid into the earth,
Be laid by men wearing linen clothes
With linen heat, for
The state does not buy wool.
You sleep at dawn, dusk,
Or night and day,
Doesn't really matter.
It doesn't matter at all.
For you have responsibilities
Of a rock.

Just sit and wait
Till some force comes and
Holds you sway . . .
And makes you lie down
Like the cold, hard men,
Whom I have seen
With tears in their eyes.

Why should I be surprised?
It drives you mad.
I've seen it come and pass.
It comes and goes;
It drives you crazy,
But you cannot go insane,
Because the insanity
Keeps
You
Going,
When darkness surrounds your day.

When sleep does not arrive,
You just lie there,
Staring,
Wearily.
Wondering when you will fly
Out of your body and
Into the night.
And you wonder if
There really is a hell;
A place where you'll burn
For pleasures procured,
So you count the tickets of sin,
You count the receipts
Of your deeds, but,
You are always in the red.

You hear the voices too.
Voices prattling all the time,
Some of God,
Some of money,
Some
Of love gone by,
And you think:

"How stupid their conversation is!"
They argue and screech,
Making constant fuss,
Because if they are silent,
Mute and still,
Then perhaps,
Just perhaps,
They become just like you.

But do you really fear?
Yes,
A Little,
Like the child once feared the dark room
With the open closet door,
Yet just as with all trips,
With all years through time,
You learn to learn
What's to be feared and
What's trite,
And you care for neither,
For neither care for you,
So over you roll.
And slap your pillow.
Looking at the time,
Hoping,
That your neighbor does not hear,
Cannot hear,
The thoughts within your mind.

## I DREW A CHESSBOARD ON MY BED

James Heard, Death Row, California

I drew a chessboard on my bed,
To help keep the demons out of my head.

Everyday I struggled against depression and sadness,
Is there anything that can defeat this madness?

I drew that chessboard on my bed,
Because of my situation . . . which I deeply dread!

I've been confined many years behind bars,
   and the state wants my life,
I drew that chessboard to help me get rid of the strife.

I try not to think about time . . .
I mean the short time I've got left,
But I can't shake the ugly specter of death!

The state has armed guards to keep me here,
So they can carry out the death penalty which they think I fear.

I watch the armed guards walk by each hour of every day,
And I wonder why they smile as they point their weapons my way?

I drew a chessboard on my bed,
And I'm ready to play,
But I fall to my knees and begin to pray . . .
For some damn chess pieces!

## FIND OUT WHAT YOU SEEK

Tracy A. Hansen, Death Row, Mississippi

One searching,
For a beautiful path of life.
One searching,
For a dreadful path of death.
And one,
Just living,
Or just dying,
Finding nothing.

## A MENTAL MIRAGE

Marion Wilson, Death Row, Georgia

The candle light flickers,
My guiding light,
My beacon of hope . . .
A mental mirage
That I follow faithfully.
Drawn to its dance,
Shadows on the walls
    Of my mind . . .
An effortless rhythm
That I struggle
To keep pace with.
Life's misery,
Like a strong wind
It's a threat
Unto the flame
But this candle light
Is extraordinary . . .
It stands firm.
The wind blows harder

But the flame
Burns brighter . . .
Defeat is not its destiny.
A mental mirage
That I follow faithfully,
My guiding light,
My beacon of hope
The candle light flickers.


## A SPECIAL FRIEND

Tracy A. Hansen, Death Row, Mississippi

There
    When I wanted.
There
    When I needed.
And though I cursed you
    A million times,
    You never left me.

When I cried and cried
    On account of you,
I came back smiling
    On account of you.

You taught me and showed me
    Why no tear is born
    Without the warmth of a smile.

You taught me and showed me
    A smile once felt
    Is a smile forever.

Sometimes it's hard to live with you,
 But I could never live without you.

I love you,
 My precious memory.

## FOR YOU

Joan Warren, member, Human Writes

I will climb a tree for you
And in a cave of verdant green
From which sweet, secret, forked retreat
Smell sweet air of the free for you
As my heart beats for you.

I will walk in the rain for you
Wet warm will soothe, as nature's balm
Re-fragrances the earth with dew,
Soothing, seeping through each space—
And I will thirst for you.

I will feed the birds for you
And watch, as roses blush and bloom,
Each blade of grass shoot green towards the blue.
While I can taste the green upon the tongue—
I'll taste for you—and photosynthesize while I am
 young.

While I can watch the seasons come and go
And snow can show the robins to and fro,
As winter puts a hush upon the earth—
For what it's worth—I'll watch for you
And see the evening star shine through the midnight
 blue.

And I can feel the wind for you
And keenly cold, I will grow old raw nosed, red
    eared, I'll brave the east,
The piercing east which strikes right through, for
    you.
And tears which run on ruddy cheeks,
I'll weep for you, I'll weep for you.

I will bed and board for you
And spend for you and hoard for you,
And taste and touch and see and such,
And much, much more for you.
I'll bite and chew
And hack and hew
At life, for life? for you.

## I THINK I'LL CALL IT MORNING

James Heard, Death Row, California

I'm gonna take myself a piece of sunshine
And paint it all over my sky.
Be no rain. Be no rain.
I'm gonna take the song from every bird
And make them sing it just for me.
Be no rain.
And I think I'll call it morning from now on.
Why should I survive on sadness!
Convince myself I've got to be alone?
Why should I subscribe to this world's madness

Knowing that I've got to live on?
I think I'll call it morning from now on.
I'm gonna take myself a piece of sunshine
And paint it all over my sky.
Be no rain. Be no rain.

I'm gonna take the song from every bird.
And make them sing it just for me.
Why should I hang my head?
Why should I let tears fall from my eyes.
When I seen everything that there is to see.
And I know that there ain't no sense in crying!
I know that there ain't no sense in crying!
I think I'll call it morning from now on.


## LOOK INTO THE DARKNESS
William (Bill) Clark, Death Row, California

When I look into the darkness,
I don't see what you see.
I don't see the negative, self-destructive or frightening image . . .
That paralyzes you.
I don't see the frantic, desperate or diabolical image . . .
That confounds you.
I don't see the crude, violent or immoral image . . .
That repulses you.

When I look into the darkness,
I see a positive, pure and enchanting image . . .
That inspires me.
I see a strong, purposeful yet compassionate image . . .
That encourages me.
I see a kind, tranquil and honorable image . . .
That relaxes me.

When I look into the darkness,
I don't see what you see.
When I look into the darkness,
The image I see is me.
Because all this time I've spent looking into the darkness . . .
I've been looking into a mirror.

## TRYING TO DESCRIBE

Martin A. Draughon, Death Row, Texas

The joy that I have . . .
The peace that I feel . . .
The love that I share . . .
It's all very new, but Oh, it is so real!
It fills my heart, soul and mind—
    every fiber of my being.
It overwhelms me at times
    and is often hard to describe.
It keeps me intoxicated
    with a clean, pure, "perfect high."
I'm changed into another person,
    someone I never knew;
A better, kinder, more loving one
    that I want to share with you.


## BEFORE I FORGET

Karl Louis Guillen, Arizona State Prison

Words are like blood flowing,
They tell of a pain suffered
A blow received, a knife taken.
Even when black boots stomp
Or strike soft flesh kept close to death,
Words come like subtle memories.
Old bells from the distant past
Ring again and again, but are they
Boots to the head, or some vision of a past
These walls have stolen.
But the mind remains
To accept the day after day,
To receive the brutality and the pains
To wretched cells and mini-hells.

Here comes the boots,
Here comes the bells . . . I give you this poem, freedom yet,
Tomorrow more words will flow and the walls
Steal these poems I forget.

## MY POEM

Karl Louis Guillen, Arizona State Prison

My poem
Is the lost ship
That shall never again see the waves
Or feel the splashes against its hull.
Never more to hear the cannon shot,
Feel the puncturing of oaken flesh
And the compression of air and sea
As all hands fall below.
For upon this barbed rock
I'm ground.
The tide leaves me gently, like a razor's slice.
The sea bleeding away
Surrendering my hull to the sky,
Yonder blue becoming . . .
To another sea, another home.

## DEATH ROW POETS

U. A. Fanthorpe

(FOR MARIE MULVEY-ROBERTS)

To wait, to watch. Vocation
Of the prisoner and the poet.

Not those who choose not to watch,
Chess-players, crossword-puzzlers, those who
    flinch

From the blazing face of Time, and focus
On small exacting things. But the poets,

The prisoners, whose stretch is finite,
Look straight in Time's face, and see

The unrepeatable marvel of each second.
Consider these prisoners, these poets.

Consider also those who are taught not to see,
To blanket violence by conditioning;

Decent men, kind to wives, who must not know
Which of them pressed the button;

Who must learn to see the dummy, not the person;
Who must be helped, by rectal plug and catheter,

Not to smell the body's final protest.
Consider these men also. And those who give them
     their orders.

## EXECUTIONER

James Armando Card Sr., Death Row, Florida

The shadow of death may walk on feet of air
     but his name I know;

It is so much his custom to steal in the night,
Or creep thru' day's shadows
Disguised as a thief;
     but his name I know.

One may ponder the ages
How this shadow of death may introduce himself,
And never expect the obvious;
    because his name you know!

We have shaken hands, death's shadow and I,
Twice in as many years?
But never an ubiquitous clinch
    for I truly know his name.

With a deep, faint gleam of yearning
In the dark recesses of my eyes
I laughed!
For not only do I know his name,
I have learned his mode as well;
And when he comes, that third and final time
I will embrace him.
The surprise will be his,
    for then he will surely know my name!

## THE WUORNOS PROTOCOL— THE FINAL SOLUTION

### John Huggins, Death Row, Florida

In the darkness of a concrete cell, lit briefly by the cigarette ember, the passing sands of time mark well her death watch, I'll remember. The wind outside invades my walls and swirls about my room, I lay here thinking about her and how she'll go to her tomb. Man is created of dust, and his end is in the dust. He is like a broken potsherd, a fading flower, like a floating note, a passing shadow, and like a dream that flies away. So is woman. Really believing that one is about to die is hard. Hospital patients rotted through with cancer. Convicts walking to the death house for execution. Sailors on a ship going down in a storm. All cling to a secret hope that it is all a mistake, that some relieving word will come to lift the strangling nightmare. Yet another twenty-four hours in her funeral march of time, she lies awake half listening, to a prison filled with men's songs. As her cigarette grows shorter, she remembers all the wrongs. It is said she hated men, and killed not just a few. All around her tonight men lift her high in prayer, if only she knew. The Russian roulette of madness, the life we've all abused. She crushes out her cigarette, and from the depths of a softened heart, lets go of all regrets. Oh Lord, please help me find my way into your light. Take my hand and guide me from my soul's dark night.

Aileen Wuornos was executed on October 9, 2002, in Florida. No men were allowed near her.

## NICKY

### Sister Ruth Evans, member, Life Lines

IN MEMORY OF NICHOLAS INGRAM, A BRITISH CITIZEN
WHO WAS EXECUTED IN GEORGIA ON APRIL 7, 1995

There were few to watch with you,
Throughout your long Gethsemane.
So long, so long America.

You were much too thin,
All of your hair was gone.
Your eyes were spent and much too old
And yet you were still young.

Why could you not rest that night?
And why could you not eat?
They made you sit upon a chair,
Put thongs around your feet.

Nothing brings to rest in me
The memory of your pain.
I know that you will not come back.
You will not come again.

## KNOWING THE DAY

Rogelio Reyes Cannady, Death Row, Texas

The sun has not yet risen on the prison of Ellis Unit and its death row.
All is calm, the prisoners are sleeping.

Even so,
Voices can be heard in two cells,
A quiet conversation between two men.
Then suddenly,
From the back of one of those long cages of 1.5m x 2.7m
A man burst into tears,
The desperate sobs of an anguished man.

In the next-door cell,
A man is sitting,
Listening to his friend near the heating ventilation.

He is opening his heart to the infinite wave of emotions
which overwhelms his companion of suffering.

Their cells are disposed in such a way that they cannot see each other,
One way of communicating is the heating ventilation system.

So, after years of silence, of withdrawal into oneself
For fear of critical judgments,
One of these men got overwhelmed by a wave of emotions he cannot
control.
He must talk to someone.
He cries his anguish,
He tells his deepest fears:
The days go by and slowly the 10th of February inches closer:
This day is his date.*

Distressing, cruel and intolerable vision
Of two men whose lives run at a parallel at times.
Both know what suffering is about.

Yet, walls and bars isolate them
Preventing the little human contact they could wish to have
In those terrible moments of reprieve between
Life (life, really?) and death,

Their death planned in cold-blood,
Legalized by
    An archaic and inhuman system.

* Jorge Cordova was executed on February 10, 1999.

## OUR DISGRACE . . .

Karl Louis Guillen, Arizona State Prison

A man fell today,
He left with a sudden grace.
Unplug your TV, put down your phone,
Listen up all! I saw his face!
Tubes dangled from his arms,
Knives were stabbing his veins.
The plunger fell,
Maybe he went to hell.
Has the whole world gone insane?
Government sponsored murder,
Politicians hiding behind chromium doors,
Feeling the need to speed up the pace,
To lock away us all behind a fence,
But today I saw a man fall,
I was assured of his innocence . . .
Humanity exchanged for greed and face.
Put down your book, look away from the screen!
Listen up all! I saw our disgrace . . .

## YOU HIDE WHERE YOU CAN'T
Tracy A. Hansen, Death Row, Mississippi

You,
    With your mysterious embrace,
    Your echoing infinity
    And your mocking face.
Don't think you've fooled me.

Fear you?
    Not I, know you too well.
    You will not possess me,
    Nor threaten me with hell.
Though, forth comes the horizon we must share.

Find you?
    Yes, find you I will.
    Though your discovery is a must,
    It's of my choice still.
I will walk upon your ground and kiss you.

Love you?
    No, love for you can't be.
    You will caress me with chills,
    But I will break free.
I laugh last, at you, the one called death.


## WORDS THAT I HEAR
Edwin Smith, former Chaplain, Death Row, Texas

And now I slip into the darkness of time,
Unknown to a world so cruel and unkind,
No peace I find in this tormented mind,
Words of judgment are all that I hear.

I took a life, sorrow I've reaped,
Innocent victims, I have caused to weep,
A date with death is mine to keep,
Words of judgment are all that I hear.

I live in a cage that's six by ten,
Lonely and cold and unfit for men,
I wish I had done things differently then,
Words of judgment are all that I hear.

A Chaplain came by and spoke of God's love,
He spoke of a heaven, a home up above,
He said God's spirit was gentle as a dove,
Words of judgment are all that I hear,

I stare out my window, a slit for a view,
Hoping to catch just a quick glimpse of you,
My time is soon, my date is not due,
Words of judgment are all that I hear.

As I wait for the guards to come,
I think of my words and the things I have done.
I hope my passing is remembered by some,
Words of judgment are all that I hear.

I lie on the gurney, my heart racing fast,
Asking forgiveness to my vile, rotten past,
Over me death, its shadow doth cast,
Words of judgment are all that I hear.

What's this I see! With outstretched wings,
Could it be one of those Angelic beings?
Beautiful music, I hear its sweet ring,
Welcome home, are the words I now hear.

## MY FINAL PRAYER

Ray "Running Bear" Allen, Oklahoma Cherokee
on Death Row, California

I am thankful to you, Grandfather
Take me from the West, where the sun sets,
Where my mind sinks into its depths,
To your home in the North;
Cold northern winds that test my strength
And to the East, a place of new light.
May I have the courage to journey South,
To face my test with courage,
To make my final journey
To see through my place of darkness,
And release what is old and unneeded any longer
    here on our Mother Earth.
I know that you bring not death but spiritual rebirth.
May I be renewed as a child from this white man's
    prison,
And on to the great circle of life whether it be
    difficult or easy
My spirit will know that it is good . . .

# 5

## SHORT STORIES

*One is absolutely sickened, not by the crimes*
*that the wicked have committed, but by the*
*punishments that the good have inflicted; and a*
*community is infinitely more brutalized by the*
*habitual employment of punishment than it is*
*by the occasional occurrence of crime.*

　　—Oscar Wilde

## A DAY IN THE LIFE

### Michael Wayne Hunter, Death Row, California

It's just another day on a death row exercise yard, another day of pumping iron, exactly like the more than 3,000 days I have already spent here at San Quentin State Prison awaiting my execution. As I stand in line for my turn at the weights, my eyes wander to that nearby cinder-block wall that separates me from the rest of the world. The yellow wall contrasts sharply with my blue prison clothing, making me an excellent target for the guards' assault rifles. My eyes linger on the wall, stopping to note the marks left by bullets that have banged off its imposing surface. I see that no two bullets have hit precisely the same place. Perhaps to stand in front of a previously scarred spot on the wall will keep me safe from future bullets. I smile and shake my head at such an absurd notion. There is no safe place when a guard pulls a trigger, sending a bullet careering around the yard. If the bullet doesn't immediately hit a prisoner, it will impact and fragment on the wall, ricocheting randomly, often stopping only when it finds the flesh of an inmate. It's almost simultaneous—the crack of the rifle and the moan of the struck man.

My eyes travel up the yellow wall to the blue sky above and join the seabirds wheeling about the sky, surfing in the wind. Their piercing cries mock me as they invite me to join their dance in the freedom of the world beyond the barbed and razor wire that confines me. After a moment, I've had enough and look around the yard at the other condemned men who have chosen to come to the exercise yard today. We are like hamsters running merrily on a wheel, enjoying the illusion that movement is freedom.

As I watch the condemned men sweating in the sunlight, I begin to imagine the marbled headstones bearing the chiseled names of murdered victims scattered about the yard. Suddenly, the exercise yard becomes more crowded as we are joined by the ghosts of the victims of the violence that led to death row. I see one man followed by more than a dozen crying and sobbing boys, asking why he had to take their lives after he raped them. The condemned man tries to ignore them, but they crowd around demanding an answer. I see another man haunted by his father, his dad screaming that he will beat him bloody when he gets his hands on him. The condemned man answers quietly, "No, you won't touch me again, because you're dead and I killed you." But there is no hint of triumph in the condemned man's voice regarding his Pyrrhic victory over his father, as he turns and walks sadly away from the ghost. I see a security guard in uniform asking a condemned man, "Why did you kill me? I gave you the money." There is no answer for a moment, then the condemned man tries to talk about his panic during the robbery and how things just spun out of control. The condemned man tries to find the words that will satisfy the ghostly guard but fails. All through the yard I see the ghosts of victims screaming, crying, threatening, and imploring condemned men for an explanation of why they had to die. Some prisoners try to walk away while others try to communicate an answer, only to discover that for some actions, perhaps, there are no explanations, no second chances, no resolutions. Over in the corner a condemned man stands all alone. No ghosts approach him to ask unanswerable questions. Although a prosecutor persuaded a jury that this man is guilty of murder, he has in fact killed no one. The man will make the final walk to the gas chamber alone in the knowledge of his innocence.

Suddenly, I hear my name called and look up blinking my eyes as the apparitions disappear. A lieutenant stands looking at me from the far side of a chain-link fence. He has deigned to call my name. I reluctantly approach the fence and say nothing, waiting for him to deliver his orders. "Place your belongings under your bunk tomorrow. We will be painting your cell." I deeply resent the idea of green uniforms invading the only space that provides me any sanctuary and barely restrain myself from screaming, "Stay out of my cell, Lieutenant!"

In my years locked in the box that I call home, I've come to know every flaw in the paint, every crevice on the floor and walls. Whatever the season I know how the light filters through the filthy windows of the cell block. Don't change my world, Lieutenant. Because on death row, change is almost always for the worse. As the silence lengthens between us, the lieutenant says sharply, "Do you understand me? What's wrong with you?" I'm tempted to respond, "What's wrong with you? Can't you comprehend that people like me are your job security? Without people like me, people like you couldn't saunter about in ugly uniforms with an aura of baseless superiority." But as these thoughts race through my head, I reply in an outwardly calm manner. "I understand you, and I'm just fine, Lieutenant."

I push away from frustration and walk away. I sit down. Feeling the solidity of the wall at my back, I wonder what an earthquake would do to this wall. Would it fall, allowing me to travel in freedom like the birds above me? I laugh at my thoughts, as I know I wouldn't know what to do with my freedom. After a decade of guards delivering meals to my cell, I'd starve to death in an apartment waiting for food to arrive. I'd be incapable of opening the door and walking out. I'd just sit there waiting for a guard to search me, place chains on my body, and escort me into the daylight. I've changed from when I first arrived at San Quentin. Now, when friends come to visit me, I ask them to come one at a time. I find it difficult to converse with more than one person at a time from the outside world unless I know them quite well. To meet more than one person for the first time is almost too much; I feel on edge, panicked.

Looking into the sky, I see the birds have gone; it will soon be time for the guards to lock me into my cell. I worry for a moment that the ghosts will return, but glancing around, I see no sign of them. The ghosts must be off doing whatever ghosts do when they aren't haunting the damned. My mind drifts to the words of another condemned man. He once told me this story:

> The mother of the man I killed sat with my mom in the courtroom during my trial. It started when she came to my mother to let her know that she didn't hold her responsible for the death of her son. My mother cried, and they spent the rest of the day whispering together. The next day the prosecutor asked the woman to move. He said it didn't look good to the jury that she was sitting with my mother, and it might hurt his efforts in trying to obtain a death verdict. The woman told him that she knew what it was like to bury her own son, and she wasn't going to help the prosecutor kill me so my mother would have to bury her son. The jury came back with death. As the deputies escorted me out of the courtroom, I looked back and saw this woman hugging my mother. They were both crying. That picture is engraved in my mind. I think about it every day.

He sat in silence for a moment and then added, "I didn't know there were people like that woman in this world. I was so wrapped up in my own rage, in my own pain, I couldn't think about anything except what her son had done to me. Now, it just seems like what he did was really unimportant. I wish I would have realized then how much my actions hurt this woman and the other people who loved this man. My actions echoed through so many lives, bringing loss and tremendous pain to everyone I touched. I really didn't understand at the height of my rage the enormity of the simple act of pulling a trigger. I'd do anything to give this woman back her son, but now it's just too late."

I understand this man's emotions. My personal ghosts remind me daily of what a shallow, immature, self-hating boy I was a decade ago when I was arrested for murder. Sometimes, I yearn for the death the state of California has promised me, but I also wake up in the early morning hours fearing death in the gas chamber. In truth, I fear equally living and dying. The guards begin to call our names. It's time to return to our cells until tomorrow. I reach out and rub a bullet mark on the wall. It occurs to me that if I attempt to climb over the wall, the guards will shoot me, and the wait for my execution will be over. Finally, I will join the ghosts. But then, perhaps, the bullet will simply paralyze me and the guards will wheel me into the gas chamber on a gurney. I'll be drooling and unable to control my bodily functions as they prepare me for the cyanide gas. Fear of dying or fear of paralysis? I don't know which, but today I don't climb the wall for the sole purpose of inviting a bullet. I walk to the gate, the guards place chains on my body, and I trudge toward my cell.

## CAT J

Michael Wayne Hunter, Death Row, California

"Chrysler!"

The strange word rocked me awake at 2 A.M., my reeling sleep-drunk mind mistaking "Chrysler" for "Christ." I cursed at what I imagined was another Jesus freak, hiding behind the Bible to excuse every wicked whim that led him again and again to San Quentin Prison.

"Chrysler Newport 61!" the Cat J bellowed again at 108-plus decibels, his voice booming about the condemned housing unit, hammering into my head, rocking through my ear canals before crashing to a fishtailing stop deep inside my skull.

"That's a damn car," I chuckled. I was amused by this strange change from the usual Cat J nuttiness that abounds in the dungeon I call home.

My housing unit at San Quentin holds about 500 men, the majority of them on death row. An exception is the Cat (Category) J prisoner who is housed on the first couple of tiers. Cat Js are the unbathed, unshaven, aggressive panhandlers who ramble about the world, talking and babbling, mostly to themselves. They sleep under bridges or on park benches and use the streets for toilets. Cat Js pretty much wander aimlessly until they get into the face of the wrong taxpayer, the one who runs screaming to the boys in blue. The police snatch the Cat Jaying madmen off the streets and pass them on to San Quentin's boys in green to warehouse them for a while.

Just as Cat Js fail in the society outside the walls, they fail in the general population inside the walls of San Quentin. As you may have guessed, Cat Js have severe psychiatric problems, so the prison stuffs them full of psychotropic drugs. The drugs aren't to help them with their mental illness (San Quentin isn't about helping anyone with anything), they're simply to dope them up, to cut down on the erratic Cat-J static. But the chemical solution doesn't seem to be working too well this early morning on Mr. Chrysler Newport 61. Pulling my body out of bed, I listen to the Cat J beating his cell bars with something dense and heavy, perhaps his head, accompanied by this perfect rhythm with his Chrysler chant. Bouncing out from the cells around me are evil threats directed at the madman deep in the throes of a mental meltdown.

I call out softly: "Since you're all awake, get your butts outta bed and work out with me." I laugh as my neighbors assault my ears but not my soul. I know they're really angry with the Cat J, not me. Lacing on my running shoes, I stretch out slowly and then fold up towels, placing them on the floor to muffle the sound of my feet. Putting on my headphones, I leave the Cat J cawing behind, masked by the sound of Pearl Jam rocking in my Walkman. The volume cranked to full, I'm running in place to "Once," the first song on the first side of "Ten." Running in place in the morning takes me far away from the craziness of just trying to survive another day on death row. Racing to "Kamikaze," epinephrine fills my adrenals, making me feel higher than any drug I ever took on the outside. Pumping my body to the slamming tune of "Even Flow," I find myself frequently going high to touch my hands on the ceiling. The music keeps pounding away, beating into my ears, my brain, filling my soul. Endorphins flow into my bloodstream, shutting out the pain, no matter if it's physical, emotional, mental, or spiritual. For just a little while on this glorious day, I feel FINE! All too soon, "Release," the last song on the last side, is gone and I reluctantly stop running and pull off my headphones. Glancing at my watch, I see it's a bit after 4 A.M. and time for a coffee break. Taking in the caffeine, I listen to another Cat J starting his lunatic solo on the first tier.

"Help me, help me! I need my medication," the Cat J calls to any damn fool who'll listen.

"What in the world do you want now?" growls a sleepy guard, frustrated that the wild man's wailing is keeping him from dozing at his post.

"I need my medication. I need help," the Cat J whimpers pathetically.

"The med tech will be in right after breakfast. Jus' hang 'till then," the guard responds, not unkindly, to the Cat J's pleas.

"Not the tech!" the Cat J cries out indignantly, his voice laced with surprise at the guard's naïveté. "I need a cigarette."

The suckered guard turns the air about him blue with curses, sounding for a moment on the edge of a Cat J mental meltdown himself. But, in the end, he shoves a cancer stick through the bars to pacify the madman and then there is SILENCE! Temporary for sure, but blessed quiet all the same. My coffee break over, its time for push-ups. As I shove my body up and down, I spy two guards with flashlights walking down the tier counting bodies in the cells. I shout, "Good morning!" Not that I give a damn about their morning—frankly, I couldn't care less about their very existence. I only say the words because one day, one or both of the guards might be on a catwalk with an assault rifle pointing at my bod. A "good morning" now might be the difference between a warning shot as opposed to a bullet fired unerringly into my skull. "DEAD DUE TO LACK OF SOCIAL GRACE" is a damn poor epitaph. A "good morning" is a cheap premium to pay, even if it doesn't ultimately garner a dividend.

Push-ups done, I bird-bathe in my sink and wash out my sweat-soaked gym clothes. Putting on a clean set of sweats, I settle down to my second cup of coffee. The loudspeaker in the housing unit squawks out the name of a Cat J, informing him it's time for him to parole. The crazy has just finished his wino time and he's free to rejoin the world for a beat or two, but not three, because he'll soon be back. I envy his release from the walls of San Quentin, but not his lifetime sentence trapped inside a brain that's more than a bit skewed, a mind incapable of coping in modern society.

Minutes later, incredibly, I hear the Cat J refuse to leave his cell for parole. The man states, with impeccable Cat J logic, that it's cold outside. No way he's going to leave a warm cell with breakfast about to arrive for the uncertain shuffle of the streets. The guards huddle to discuss their quandary. They could call an extraction team to Taser 50,000 volts into the madman and yank his body out of the cell by force. As much as they'd enjoy the spectacle, the "refusing movement" would void the Cat J's parole and they couldn't kick him out the front gate. Each and every day more Cat Js flood into San Quentin from the boys in blue. The guards are forced to move some bodies out to simply free up cells.

After some screaming, a lot of threats, and a little discussion, the Cat J agrees to leave if the guards will give him breakfast first. When the guards quickly agree, the Cat J senses he's on a roll and holds them up for more concessions. The condemned men in the unit listen in disbelief, many calling out, offering to take the Cat J's place on parole. The guards ignore the dead men as they continue their parley. Finally, the Cat J departs with breakfast in his belly, a bag lunch in his hands, a pack of cigarettes rolled up in his sleeve, and a triumphant grin on his face. The loony-toon will have a few weeks Cat Jaying around in the world before the boys in blue ship him back to continue his life sentence on the installment plan. After the housing unit eats breakfast, it's time for exercise yard. There are six small concrete yards for the housing unit, each so small they resemble dog runs. The yards are side by side, separated from each other by fences. Four of the yards are for condemned prisoners. The other two are disciplinary yards for non-condemned prisoners from the general population who have received a rules violation report from some guard, so they're sent to security housing for punishment. The rules violation could be as serious as mayhem, or as silly as going through the chow line twice. One guy was written up for aggressive eye contact with a guard, whatever that means. Though most of the men in the disciplinary yards are not Cat Js, the disciplinary yards are where the Cat J's are assigned to exercise.

Arriving on my yard, I enjoy the early morning sunshine while starting to work on my biceps with a curl bar. Idly glancing through the fence, I spot a young guy that I mentally mark down as trouble-looking-for-a-place-to-happen. He looks about sixteen (they seem to get younger every year), and he's proudly flashing his first prison tattoo. It's scabbed, still healing from the needle.

Across the yard from the youngster is a Cat J doing the Thorazine shuffle, head down looking in the gutter for cigarette butts to take home and fire up in his cell. The kid steals up behind the Cat J and punches him in the skull, right behind the ear. Down to the ground goes the Cat J, but like most lunatics, he seems impervious to pain and leaps back to his feet and the fight commences. I carefully place the weight bar on the ground. I don't want to make any noise that would attract the attention of the guards. Glancing at the catwalk, I intently watch the guard assigned to the disciplinary yard. The green-garbed man has just spotted the altercation. Leaping from his chair, he fumbles at his assault rifle in a panicky manner. At last, he chambers a bullet and his weapon is ready to fire, to kill.

Backing away from the fence, I watch the guard swing the business end of his rifle toward the combatants pounding away at each other. I glance at the hands of the prisoners and feel reassured by the absence of weapons. San Quentin policy requires a warning in a non-life-threatening situation. I feel confident that the guard won't shoot, at least not yet. The rifle finishes its arc, the barrel staring down at the two combatants, and a sharp crack echoes in my ears. A cloud of red mist explodes in the air, surrounding the two fighters as they crumble to the ground. Fragments from the bullet rattle past me, sounding like gravel kicked up from the spinning wheels of a car skidding down a country road. Men on my side of the fence fall to the ground, clutching their suddenly bleeding legs.

The guard on the catwalk over my yard joins the scene. Taking charge, he chambers a bullet in his rifle with a mechanical clack and bellows: "Onthemotherfuckinground RIGHT NOW!" Then he blows his whistle to summon help. My casual assurance long gone, my body is hugging concrete. Reluctantly raising my head, I see the guard on the catwalk above me. He's swinging his rifle around randomly. I wonder if he'll join the [in]sanity and shoot, too. For a fleeting moment our eyes meet. I see he's pumped up, his eyes bulging with adrenaline. But panic is absent. He's in control. Looking closer, I can see disbelief in his eyes in response to the quick shot fired by his fellow guard. The disbelief overflows, spilling out of his eyes and taking over his face, generating an expression of contempt for the other guard's inability to control himself and the situation. I begin to feel confident that this guard won't fire his rifle, sending another bullet ricocheting randomly about my yard.

My eyes click back through the fence to the two combatants. I note that the guard has not only shot without warning, he's shot the wrong prisoner! The victim, the Cat J, is shot just above the elbow. As I watch, the Cat J calmly wraps a sock around his arm just above the meaty gash where blood is pumping freely, splattering onto the concrete. The Cat J finally pulls the sock tight with a feral tug of his teeth and the blood flows to a trickle. I shake my head in amazement, thinking that this Cat J is one tough sonofabitch.

Guards come running with a stretcher and unlock the gate. The Cat J rolls through and is tossed onto the stretcher for the ride to the hospital. I can already hear the scream of an ambulance in the distance. As the stretcher passes my yard, I see the Cat J's blood-soaked blue prison clothing contrasting beautifully, hideously, with a face that's growing increasingly white. The wannabe tough guy who through dumb luck has just escaped unscathed from the violence scene is ordered to the gate. I watch the youngster show his new tattoos in defiance while the guards roughly slap chains onto his body and lead him away. As he passes my yard, I hear him snarl to the escort guard, "I kicked his ass. I'll kick yours too!" the guard simply shakes his head wearily and sighs.

Guards begin to remove the wounded men from my yard. They've been hit by lead fragments that splintered off the bullet as it passed through the Cat J's elbow. The wounds look superficial to me. But after years in this house of pain, my definition of a superficial wound is any wound on someone else's body. After the bleeding men are led off to the hospital, the guards call the rest of us, one by one, to the gate. We're chained, taken to locked cages, and strip-searched for weapons.

The guard watching me asks, "What happened out there?"

"Don't know," I answer warily. "Some canine got it into his head to bust a cap."

"Yeah, bad luck for Johnson."

"Is he going to be okay?" I ask.

"Don't know. He didn't follow procedure. Bad shooting could cost him his chance to make sergeant."

Spinning the words through my head, it dawns on me that Johnson is the guard who pulled the trigger, not the Cat J.

"How's the Cat J?" I ask softly, trying to keep my voice casual, disinterested.

"The med tech said they're going to whack off the arm for sure." With an absent, careless shrug of his shoulders, the guard added, "Maybe we'll get lucky and he'll just die."

## FAKE IDENTITY

### William Van Poyck, Sussex I State Prison, Virginia

On a quiet, humid night framed by a rising gunner's moon, Percy Brown— of dark hair, bright eyes, and reasonable intelligence, formerly of sound mind and spirit—was questioning his judgment, if not yet his sanity. *Swish, swash. Swish, swash.* Back and forth, four strides to the stretch, Percy paced the concrete floor of the small room situated in the hulking red building, laid brick upon brick among the sprawling assembly of like structures. The dark complex lay huddled like a sad story, deep in the pine tree forests skirting the Alabama state line. *Swish, swash. Swish, swash.* He felt his bare, calloused feet rhythmically chafing like dry bark on the worn floor.

Percy paused, his eye catching one of the hundreds of lines of graffiti drawn, burned, scratched, and gouged into the concrete and stonework: *Today a rooster, tomorrow a feather duster.* His brief smile was interrupted by a noise. Percy hurried to the solid steel door, cocking his head attentively to listen through the chest-level, steel-barred opening. Voices. The clank of heavy steel. The jangle of large, brass keys. Leather soles squeaking on linoleum. Percy's gut leaped. It was almost time. He again checked the position of the towel on the floor at the base of the door. Surely nobody on the other side would be able to see it. He dodged to the rear of the room, banged hard on the wall several times, and scrambled up on the ancient, stained porcelain toilet, then up on an equally ancient sink. Whispering hoarsely he spoke into the grimy wire mesh welded across the air vent.

"Winky. Winky!"

"Yeah," came a muted reply after a long moment. "Who's calling my name?"

"It's me. Listen—"

"Is that you Sheila? Sheila? Sheeeeila. Help me, Sheila." The voice was distant, lost, as though spoken from a deep well.

"Winky! Damn-it, it's me, Percy. Listen to me!"

"Yeah." There was a long pause. "Percy." Another pause. "OK . . . Yeah . . . I know you, Percy. Is that you, Percy?" The voice was monotone, flat.

"The cart is coming. Don't forget what I told you. When I give the signal, you do your thing. Don't forget. It's important. You remember what to do, Winky? You hear me, Winky?" Percy balanced on the rim of the sink, stretching up, turning his ear to the vent, wincing as he felt his stitches pull taut.

"Is that you Sheila? Help me, Sheila." The keening wail echoed from the well. Percy cursed under his breath. It was time. His wrenching gut tightened another notch. Climbing down, his foot slipped on the wet enamel and he lost his balance, falling backwards, windmilling. He hit the floor hard.

The cart slid up in front of the door, pushed by a heavy-set, grey-haired female nurse shadowed by a very large man in a tight-fitting white uniform. Both stared at Percy.

"What's wrong with you," the orderly wondered loudly. "Why did you jump off the sink?"

"I fell. I didn't jump." His leg hurt where it had hit the floor.

"You jumped. I saw you."

"So did I," the nurse added, nodding her head.

"You trying to kill yourself again, boy?"

"I fell."

"What were you doing up on that sink?" the nurse asked, pointing with her chin. "Yeah. What were you doing on the sink?"

"Nothing."

"Nothing?"

"Nothing. Look, just give me my stuff. I wanna go to sleep." Percy forced a crooked smile.

"I think maybe you need a shot. To calm you down. You look excited. Doesn't he look excited?"

"Yes. Looks upset and excited to me," the orderly agreed, fingering his brass keys.

Percy's stomach knotted up even more. "I ain't excited. I'm calm as the goddamn Rock of Gibraltar. Now give me my goddamn medication so I can go to sleep." Percy did not want a shot.

"Don't you cuss me," the nurse said.

"Don't you cuss her," The orderly took a heavy step forward.

"I won't take sass from you. You're excited. You need a shot."

"Look. I am *not* excited. I do not need a shot of Thorazine." Percy was breathing harder.

The nurse began pulling out drawers, searching for one of her pre-loaded syringes. Percy licked his lips. It was a salient moment, loaded with danger, and he stood still as a fence post, sorting his options.

"With thee all night I mean to stay,
And wrestle till the break of day"

Percy blurted out the words in a sing-song voice, even as he wondered where they came from. Both the nurse and orderly looked up, staring at Percy. "Look, I ain't taking no shot. I'm not one of these lame-ass crazies you love to jump on, tie down, beat up, and shoot full of Thorazine." Percy backed up, spreading his feet. Thorazine shots were very painful and knocked you out for two days. Percy's butt cheek still ached from the last shot. He was determined to take no more. "You'll have to go get the goon squad 'cuz I ain't taking no damn shot. I know damn well you aren't even supposed to be giving those shots without prior written authorization from a doctor. Ain't no doctor here." Percy paused, leaned forward slightly and lowered his voice. "And, let me tell you something, I don't have no public defender, I have a *real* lawyer, and if I get a shot I'll be reporting both of you, and my lawyer will be down here raising hell. I know what you two have been doing around here and I'm just dying for an excuse to tell it all to the Department of Professional Regulation, the Inspector General's Office and the damn newspapers. Just try me."

Percy stood firmly, feet braced, heart pounding. He was wary, upset, angry. He was excited. The nurse and orderly exchanged glances. In the silence Percy heard her labored breathing. Next door, Winky was mumbling, talking to someone or something. This was dangerous, Percy knew, for he had seen what they could do. Percy felt as though he was posted at life's window, watching a scene unfold. Abruptly he thrust his hand forward, palm up. Finally, the nurse handed him a paper cup containing his pre-scribed psychotropic cocktail of Haldol, Stellazine, Mellaril, and grapefruit juice. Powerful drugs. He, like everyone else, was also supposed to receive Benadryl, to counter the horrendous physical side effects, but it was seldom administered. Percy took the cup. The nurse and orderly stared at him, eyes glittering in the fluorescent light. "THANKS FOR MY MEDICATION, BOSS MAN!" Percy shouted out the agreed-upon signal, while slowly rais-ing the cup to his lips. He waited for Winky to scream, the agreed-upon re-sponse to distract the nurse and orderly, permitting Percy to surreptitiously spit the medication onto the towel . . . Nothing . . . The cup touched his lips . . . The nurse wrote something in Percy's chart, but the glaring orderly locked eyes, his face flushed red, neck bulging. Percy took the liquid into his mouth, feeling the bitterness wash over the back of his throat. He made an exaggerated swallowing gesture, tried to smile at the orderly. Silence filled the hallway as the orderly scowled back. Percy felt like a chipmunk.

"Swallow!"

The liquid burned all the way down as Percy reluctantly swallowed. "Step closer! Open up!"

Percy stepped forward. He knew the drill. Percy opened his mouth, stuck his tongue out and rolled it around in the standard fashion. He never saw the orderly's nightstick shoot through the door opening, only felt the impact at the base of his throat, driving him backwards, leaving a choking gasp in his wake.

"Punk!"

When Percy, back against the wall, looked up, they were gone. He gin-gerly felt the soft spot just below his Adam's apple, swallowing tentatively. When he heard the cart leave Winky's cell, Percy crouched at the toilet and jammed two fingers down his throat. He gagged, coughed, sputtered—but did not vomit. After a time he gave up. Cursing to himself he slumped down upon the sagging bunk. The cold fingers of resignation pulled at his spirit as he anticipated the medication's inevitable course, flowing and whistling down the staircases of his body, through the corridors of his mind, seeping into his psyche like red-eye gravy on cat head biscuits. Within an hour Percy would be unconscious. Tomorrow, after perhaps sixteen hours of sleep, he would awake, spacey, groggy, lethargic. Later, the terrible muscle cramps and spasms would humble him further.

Percy's gaze slid around the bare cell, gliding over the cobbled graffiti, the variegated stains impregnating walls and ceiling, the naked, solitary light bulb defiantly clawing at the pressing darkness. Cast shadows abounded, mottled, leavening the air with a weighted, tangible scent of bleakness. Only the tired floor, worn smooth by legions of shuffling feet, remained free of blemish, save for the rough corner patch bearing the unmistakable marks of some desperate soul sharpening steel. Percy sighed.

At least, Percy reflected, it was not Prolixin. Six months earlier, following his arrest, when he first purposed to play crazy, he was strenuously warned by fellow prisoners to avoid Prolixin shots at all costs. When Percy was, in fact, given a shot, he learned why. Each shot, he was duly advised, lasts two full weeks. The first three days were uneventful but on the fourth, like clockwork, the drug kicked him like a government mule. At once, Percy felt the change. It began with horrific muscle contractions and spasms, locking his jaw in a clenched position and pinning his head to his left shoulder. His arms drew up like a spastic's and he drooled uncontrollably. Prolixin's side effects, he was told, were known to kill, and Percy became a believer. The prisoners called patients on Prolixin "crispy critters," or "bacon," for the way their bodies drew up, making them choke and gag like epileptic hunch-backs. Percy, too, drew up, slobbering and gagging on his thick tongue, certain of the nearness of death in that solitary cell. Sometimes the nurses would give him a shot of Benadryl or Akinaton, bringing quick relief for a few hours; more often he was ignored, and, occasionally, mocked.

As terrible as the physical side effects were, the mental ones were worse. The drug changed the very way Percy thought, the mental process itself, shaking his concept of who he was, in a manner impossible to articulate to others. Percy became agitated, restless, unable to sleep, unable to sit still, unable to concentrate on any task. A void filled his mind, crowding out all desire for anything, leaving behind only a frightened husk. Like a detached spectator observing a distant phenomenon, some part of Percy recognized that his mind itself, the most basic essence of who he was, had been altered. The fear that the change was permanent terrified Percy. By the tenth day he was debating suicide to escape the unbearable mental anguish. Only the faint, desperate hope that he might return to normal in due time kept him alive. On the fourteenth day, as sure as if a switch was thrown, Percy was suddenly normal again. He was back. At that moment he vowed to die before accepting another Prolixin shot.

Percy blinked hard, fighting the medicine. He ached for a cigarette. Slowly, he lay back, stretching out his frame. His rancid pillow stunk, even through the two T-shirts wrapped around it. But now it did not matter to him. At that moment the moon became visible in the small slit window high up on the back wall. Percy considered standing up on his bunk, stretching up to take in the vast yellow orb. He had always considered the moon to be a friend, sharing his private solitude with a perfect understanding, devoid of judgment, eager to loan out its soft, limpid light to the whole round earth . . . Percy blinked again. He was weary. He struggled to keep his eyes open . . . Having feigned insanity with sufficient dexterity to secure a 120–day order of commitment to the forensic unit of the state hospital, he still had almost sixty more days to go. He wondered if he could make it, wondered if he should. The price was high.

Upon arrival Percy had been placed in an open bay ward with sixty other nut cases, mostly pre-trial detainees awaiting competency examinations. Some were there for degrees of homicide, others for relatively petty crimes like Percy's—a drunken encounter with a convenience store clerk over some shoplifted pastries that somehow escalated into a felony battery when Percy pushed and ran. Because it would be his third conviction, it was a very serious matter to Percy. At the hospital he quickly learned that prisoners from the nearby state penitentiary, called runners, ran the place with a casual brutality alarming in its arbitrariness. It was a zoo, raw survival of the fittest, pitiless and cruel for those patients genuinely mentally ill and unsophisticated in the ways of doing time. The rank scent of quiet desperation clung to everything.

Late one night, shortly after his arrival, Percy awoke with a start. He stared up into the darkness. Percy disliked going into the large communal bathroom after lights out. Strange things occurred in there, and hearing them was bad enough. On that night, though, his bladder insisted. Treading through the dim dormitory, he stepped into the expansive bathroom, passed the gang showers, and stood at one of the urinals. He thought he was alone.

A low, moaning sort of sound cut Percy off in mid-stream. He looked around, saw nothing. Percy strained at the urinal, staring at the wall. The sound returned, sliding along the tiles, echoing off the porcelain, spiraling into a guttural, animalistic quaver that made his neck hairs stand on end. Percy wheeled about, eyes wide, searching the darkness. There, barely discernible in the corner, was a shadowy figure, hunkered down, squatting atop a toilet like a perched bird poised to lay an egg, one foot on each side of the rim. Percy strained to see. The figure appeared to be staring upward, as though lost in a trance. As Percy watched, a long, horrible groan escaped from the figure's lips, a cry of anguish so wrenching that it seemed torn from his very soul. At that moment an orderly opened a door across the hall and a shaft of light fell through a bathroom window, across the tile floor, and fully illuminated the corner for an awful instant. The horrific scene revealed to Percy would be forever burned into his mind. In that moment of terrible recognition Percy saw Benjamin, a seriously disturbed young man charged with murdering his own mother. Percy's numb mind struggled to comprehend the scene. Benjamin's entire hand was inserted into his rectum, his face turned upwards, twisted in torment. Before Percy's shocked eyes Benjamin pulled out his hand, tightly gripping a handful of bloody offal and intestines. Benjamin's howl of agony pierced the night air, striking to the quick of Percy's soul.

Percy ran. He confronted an orderly, yelled, pointed. No big deal, he was told. Benjamin had done this before. He was punishing himself. They took Benjamin away and Percy never saw him again. Percy was not easily shocked, but he found no sleep that night, and for the first time in years he prayed.

The next week an elderly patient supposedly hanged himself, but the word was that the two runners who were terrorizing and extorting money from him had hung him up. The circumstances were very suspicious, but there was no investigation. Percy watched, saw, recognizing that in this place death was just a word.

A few weeks later Percy stepped into the shower only to slip and fall. Bracing his hand on the floor to get up, he found himself covered in semi-coagulated blood, a shocking amount coating the entire floor like a fetid varnish of claret putrescence. A patient, he learned, had castrated himself with a razor blade. The incident had not even caused a ripple on the ward.

For Percy, though, the final denouement came several weeks later. In a semiprivate room attached to the ward lay Harold, a state prisoner who, some years earlier, had climbed inside an industrial soap-making machine to clean it. Somehow, the machine was switched on, mangling Harold, cutting off both arms, one leg, and knocking a patch out of his skull. Harold was a mess. Invalid, a little bit retarded, he resided permanently at the hospital.

One afternoon Percy was peering through the small patch of bare glass in the painted-over window separating ward from room. It was his daily custom to tap on the glass and call a few words of encouragement to Harold, to try to make him smile. On that day, though, Percy was shocked to see Harold being raped by two runners, his feeble struggles for naught. Percy would never forget the forlorn look of resignation seared on Harold's turned face, the tears streaking down his cheek. The scene sent an arrow into Percy's heart.

Percy snapped. Picking up a wooden bench from the dayroom, he threw it through the window into Harold's room. Before the shattered glass finished falling Percy broke off a chair leg and charged through the opening, clubbing the runners with unbridled ferocity. Within moments Percy, too, was beaten down by a flood of orderlies and runners, bound in leather handcuffs and injected with a massive dose of Thorazine. Then, he was thrown into the solitary confinement cell where the friendly lemon moon was smiling down through his narrow slit window.

Percy sighed again. The medication was on him. His eyes fluttered, closed. He was tired of fighting against the drugs. There was so much he was tired of. With a final effort he struggled to stand, looking up through his window, smiling at the broad-faced moon. Percy reflected on his situation, wondering how best to measure the value of this journey. The things he had seen were beyond belief, taxing his spirit, perhaps more than he was willing to pay. Prison now seemed a reasonable alternative, a place he at least understood, not one beyond belief. Percy watched the pine trees swaying in the darkness, rooted in red clay, reaching up to the bright stars. *Your heart decides what your head will believe,* he decided. *Perhaps the brightest and darkest lie next to each other in all of our souls.* For the second time in recent memory Percy prayed, this time with a sincerity so direct and strong that it cut itself, like the facets of a diamond, into the deepest chambers of his heart. Then, Percy Brown lay on his bunk and fell into a deep, yet troubled, sleep.

The following afternoon, per his request, Percy Brown was escorted to the office of the chief psychiatrist, a short, elderly, balding Vietnamese man wearing thick, heavy-framed glasses topping a heavily scarred face. As Percy, in handcuffs and leg irons, entered the office, it occurred to him that in all his years in jails and prisons he had never met an American doctor. Percy sat in the hard plastic chair. The conditioned air felt barely cool and smelled stale. A lone window, covered by a heavy gauge grey steel wire screen, was tightly sealed against the dense rain silently sheeting down the glass. A low, leaden sky seemed to press its weight down upon the building itself. Across from Percy the doctor sat at his desk, ignoring him, reading a case file. It was very quiet except for the loud ticking of an unseen clock. The doctor's pen scratched as he wrote in the file. Percy glanced around, unable to locate the clock. The doctor, Percy noted, was absently toying with a pair of shiny, stainless steel tweezers. The doctor looked up, staring at Percy as though surprised to find him there.

"I want to go back to the jail."

"Oh?"

The ticking expanded to fill the small room. Percy looked around again, uncertain of words or thoughts. He knew he was sweating. Where was that damn clock, anyway? "I . . . I can't take this place anymore."

"I see." The doctor slowly twirled the needle-nosed tweezers while staring at Percy.

"Look," Percy said, exhaling loudly, "I don't belong here. I'm not crazy. Not at all. In fact, I'm just playing crazy, see? Playing. I fooled the doctor at the jail. I was just trying to beat my case."

"Fooled the doctor?"

"Yeah."

"Fooled Dr. Trung?"

"Yeah. I'm facing the third strike. Automatic life, you know? For a lousy box of Little Debbie snack cakes."

"So, you fooled him, you think?"

"Yeah, I think." The clock ticked away. Percy wiped the sweat from his brow. His thigh muscle spasmed and the leg jumped involuntarily.

The doctor eyed him closely, then wrote something in his chart. "No need to beat your case now?"

"Man, I don't care now." Percy vigorously rubbed his eyes with both palms. The medication made his eyes itch and water. "I'll go crazy if I stay here."

"Go crazy?"

"Yeah."

"Your medication will prevent that."

"Shit. I don't take that junk."

"Oh?"

"That's only for crazy guys." Percy's eyes itched terribly and he rubbed them again. "I just told you, I'm not crazy."

"I see." The doctor scribbled something else in the file. "Why do you believe you will go crazy here?"

"The shit I've seen here, it's unbelievable. I've never seen shit like this, not even in jail or prison. This place is evil. Needs to be closed down, you ask me. Crazy shit."

"Crazy?"

Percy arched his back suddenly, then shook out his cramping leg. He ached all over. He was very tired. Percy wanted out. Now. So, he told the doctor everything he had seen. Percy spoke of beatings and rapes, of knight-sticks and cattle prods, and of runners amok. He told about suicides and castrations, of poor Benjamin and retarded Harold. He omitted nothing. He spoke of his friend, the moon, with its perfect understanding. He told how he had prayed, really prayed, until the gates of hell itself felt the ponderous stroke, prayed with a sincerity as certain as God's promises to Abraham and his seed. He explained God's promise that he was covered in mercies, a promise that now shone bright and perfect in its execution. And that, Percy explained, was why he could now return to the jail, shedding this fraud, this deception, like an old, ragged coat.

"And you believe all those things occurred here?"

"Sure. I saw them with my own eyes."

The doctor stared, toying with the tweezers. "And tell me, Mr. Nelson, do you still believe that your name is—" the doctor glanced at the open file—"Percy Brown?"

"Yeah. It is. I told you last time, I had fake ID. Nelson is just an alias, to fool the police. 'Course, it didn't work. Fingerprints, you know?" Percy offered up his hands. "Since they booked me under Nelson, Nelson it is."

"Fake?"

"Yeah."

"To fool them?"

"Yeah."

The clock continued ticking away, louder than ever. Percy squinted his eyes, blinking rapidly. His leg jumped again. Sweat slid down his cheek.

"I see." The doctor scribbled more words, continuing to the next page.

"And your suicide attempt?" The doctor nodded at the long cut navigating across Percy's neck like black railroad tracks.

"Fake." Percy smiled weakly.

"Fake?"

"Yeah. Fake. Fake. Fake." Percy waved his cuffed hands like a conductor, emphasizing each word.

"To fool us?"

"Yeah."

"And last night, that was fake also?"

"Last night?"

"You dove off your sink." The doctor idly tapped the tweezers against a coffee mug.

"No. No, I didn't."

"I have the report."

"It's a lie."

"Both the nurse and the orderly witnessed it."

"They're lying. They just don't like me."

"Are they plotting against you?"

"Yeah, you can say that."

"I see." The doctor held the tweezers up, like a heron poised to spear an unsuspecting fish. "You may return to your cell, Mr. Nelson. Don't worry, I will arrange everything."

"That's it? I'll be going back to the jail?"

"I'll arrange everything, do not worry." The doctor smiled reassuringly.

"Thanks, doc. I'll be glad to get out of here, I'll tell you. Get visits. Cigarettes, canteen, telephone, recreation." Percy stood up, elated.

"Yes, I'm sure. Goodbye now." The doctor remained seated.

"Bye. Thanks again, doc." Percy left the office, his leg chains tinkling and scraping the shiny waxed floor.

The doctor stared out the window, then swiveled in his chair, turning on a tape recorder. After a moment he spoke into the machine, twirling the tweezers absently:

Patient is superficially persuasive, adept at faking sanity through innovative masking strategy of claiming he only feigns his psychosis. Diagnosis: patient is severely delusional with confirmed identity crisis, demonstrating psychotic thought process and exhibiting paranoid personality disorder . . . Chronic suicidal tendencies noted . . . Probable psychoactive substance dependence . . . Prognosis: poor. Recommend petitioning court for six-month extension of commitment order for long-term treatment . . . Increase dosages of current medications, institute regimen of Prolixin injections.

William Van Poyck has been transferred to Sussex I State Prison at Waverly, from Virginia's Death Row.

## BURNT ALMONDS

### Steven King Ainsworth, Death Row, California

A burst of color and the vortex began to spin, a jumbled mass of scattered thoughts shot through my mind at incredible speed, my breathing became ragged and labored. Then as I gained some control of the quickly tripping synapse a picture began to emerge. The image cleared at the back of my skull.

There was no dignity in dying at the hands of a state, any state! But it was my turn. I had exhausted all avenues of appeal. They had moved me to the death cell just hours before; the death watch took over, guards I have never seen before, none I knew, all seemed so much larger than my six-foot frame. The one outside the cell staring in intently, watching my every move. Another to the right by the death chamber door, sipping coffee from a styrofoam cup, nonetheless alert and glancing up to peer at me. They did not try to talk to me, as if I was a pariah, laying there on my last bed, my hands behind my head planning my last moves. Through the upper bars and across the way, the deadly eye of the gunrail's weapon, casually pointed my way, its deadly menace well known to me, the man's face hidden in the shadows behind the rifle's stock, the black eye raising and lowering minutely in mimic of the hidden gunner's respiration.

Buzzing, ringing, clangs, and muted shouts came through the thick cement walls. The sounds that bothered me the many years of delay. Keys turning, food slots banging, Spanish, English, Swahili, and other dialects of many voices shouting out in defiance from the cell blocks. A cacophony muffled and distant now from where I lay not fifteen feet from the gas chamber's door. Acrid smells of antiseptic wash surrounded me. The death cell area was in full swing and I was just one of three who would go this week. There had been two before and now it was my turn to take center stage in the ritual of death.

The two days before had gone quietly with little fuss. Their final statements of inane remarks. Meaningless gestures to victims and families. One's heartfelt reach for God no doubt fell on deaf ears, and, with tears, he precedes me to ash. I had decided that I would not go numbly down the path. I would not make a statement nor plea for clemency from the very system that had produced me as fodder for its now vast machine. My final moves, actions, would speak louder than words. With my state-issued five witnesses, I had provided the executioner's act with an audience that would not let this dance of death remain surreptitious from most. They would not allow the events of this morbid week to go unnoticed in the back pages of time. Where, in ignorance, the public could skip the account and not really think of the state that has to resort to killing its own citizens to address its social deficiencies.

The hours, minutes, and seconds of this final day were tick-tocking away with speed. At some time, they brought my last meal and I wolfed down the gastronomical surprise, belching as the last remnants slid down to my stomach. When in death's grip my sphincter relaxed and the contents of my viscera spilled out, the stench of feces would add a sinister bouquet to assault the players in this rite when they entered the chamber after the deed was done. They were a pungent reminder of their part in the macabre.

Already the rubber tube protruded from my shirt front. Beneath where the medico had taped to my chest the stethoscope which would reverberate the sounds and finality of my demise. The criss-cross of adhesive tape exing me out. Pacing back and forth to the hubbub around me, the time was coming close. The studied and practiced procedures of the death watch were in progress. Behind the death chamber door, the executioner was preparing the elements of the final brew. Little thuds and muted sounds filtered through the steel door. Pacing back and forth, the cold cement chilling my stockinged feet. The black eye of the gunrail's rifle muzzle following my movement. Back and forth, the death watch eyes followed me. Back and forth, back and forth. "Calm down," I told myself albeit in these moments of absolute terror, it was hard to do.

The Catholic priest came in, said some words, a jumble to me as the thudding of my heart became louder in my ears. "It's time, it's time," the death commander intoned. I stopped and made my move. The secreted razor blade came out and slashed my throat, and blood spurted as the jugular parted! Now my wrist and red appeared! Inside my arms, the blade rode, nipping the junctions of life's road there. Slinging my arms about, I flung the juice, splashing and splattering everyone, the walls and all. Splotches of blood on the uniform of the minions of death as they charged into the cell to stop my act. I smeared the blood on their skins, hair, and all over myself. Subdued, they cuffed me up. The medico wrapped the slashes up. They were pissed! Their nostrils flared in anger as they rushed me through the door into the chamber itself. They strapped me in quickly, as I spat on each. The blinds on the windows flew up as they retreated out the gas chamber's door. Aghast, the witnesses gaped at the sight as the door shut and clamped tight. I swiveled my head to and fro to make the blood flow. It seeped through the wraps, darkening them with a moist red stain and dripping to the floor their eyes wide in horror, mine with madness.

Suddenly, my head sprang back as the gas hit my nose. I stiffened, my hands in fists, the knuckles white! I slumped forward and a shudder ran through my body; the blood stopped, my struggle had ceased, my eyes closed. I relaxed, the bittersweet gas overtaking me: peaches, apricots. No! Burnt almonds more like. This my last sense as my breathing ceased and life left me a shattered surreal hulk: red, white, and institutional green.

The vortex stopped spinning and the voices cleared.

"Brewster! Brewster!" my name was called!

"What? What?" I gruffly replied.

"Brewster, Brewster, get four! Get four!" the voice yelled.

"Get four? Get four?" confusedly I queried.

"Channel Four, they got you on Channel Four!" the voice screamed.

Automatically I sprang to the selector knob. The TV tube brightened, my mug shot appeared, the newscaster's voice rang in my ear. I was given a full reversal today by the United States Supreme Court, ending a fifteen-year legal battle to execute me.

# INTERVIEWING
# PRISONERS

*It is well-nigh obvious that those who are in
favor of the death penalty have more affinities
with murderers than those who oppose it.*
   —Rémy de Gourmont

*The gallows is not only a machine of death but
a symbol. It is the symbol of terror, cruelty, and
irreverence for life; the common denominator of
primitive savagery, mediaeval fanaticism and
modern totalitarianism. It stands for everything
that mankind must reject, if mankind is to
survive the present crisis.*
   —Arthur Koestler

# INTERVIEW WITH MUMIA ABU-JAMAL

## Interview by Allen Houghland

Pennsylvania's new "control unit" prison, the State Correctional Institution at Waynesburg (SCI Greene), hides in rural hills just fifteen miles from the West Virginia border. Its low earth-toned block walls blend into the grassy clearing where it furtively crouches, surrounded by multiple layers of green metal fences ringed with double-edged razor wire. Once inside, video producer Thomas Filmyer and I follow a genial female administrator through the stark bright corridors, passing through a series of sliding metal security doors to a cubicle where we will spend ninety minutes with Mumia Abu-Jamal.

As we enter the little cinderblock room, the official places herself outside; the door remains open during the interview. Mumia is already seated, wearing a blue cotton shirt and steel handcuffs, long dreadlocks hanging over his shoulders. Appearing healthy and relaxed, he seems eager to begin talking. His deep voice echoes as it filters through narrow strips of screen at the ends of the thick Plexiglas barrier that separates him from us.

ALLEN HOUGHLAND: Can you tell us who you are, in your own words?

MUMIA: My name is Mumia Abu-Jamal. I'm in my early forties. I've been on death row since July of 1982.

AH: Mumia, about the death penalty—with which you're well acquainted—you have said that, "where the death penalty is concerned, law follows politics." And we have seen a change, an evolution—if you want to call it that—in death penalty law over the last twenty or twenty-five years.

MUMIA: It might best be called "devolution."

AH: Yes—from the U.S. Supreme Court case *Furman v. Georgia,* which declared the death penalty unconstitutional as it was being applied at that time, 1972;

through *Gregg v. Georgia* in 1976, which declared the death penalty would be constitutional if "guided discretion" were used in sentencing, requiring "objective standards" to be followed. Since then there has been a new tide of capital punishment in this country, with over three thousand condemned now. And the current Supreme Court seems inclined to curb the rights of appeal of the condemned. This is happening at the same time that other industrialized nations have all backed away from capital punishment. Can you talk about why you think it is that this country has devoted itself so wholeheartedly to executions at this point in time?

MUMIA: I think the impetus for that reality arises from the same source from which arises the impetus for the unprecedented levels of incarceration of African-Americans, as compared with other sectors of the American population. I don't think it's a coincidence that this is happening in the United States of America. If you look at another North American society that is very, very similar in its history, you find a completely different reality. The society I'm speaking of, of course, is Canada. We share the same temporal space, the same continent, for the most part (except for Quebec) the same language, the same general Anglo-oriented legal traditions. Yet there you find no capital punishment. There you find a completely different perspective when one talks about the penal system—the so-called correctional system. There it's almost unheard of for a man to be sentenced to more than twenty years in prison—it has to be a mass ax-murder type of situation. And when you look at Canada and you examine it, and you look at the United States and you examine it, the elements that differ between those two societies cohere, I think, around the issue of race, around the issue of this country's history as a slave society, who relegated an entire people to a sub-human status. In the infamous *Dred Scott* opinion of 1857, U.S. Chief Justice Roger Brooks Taney said: "A Negro has no rights that a white man is bound to respect."[1] In that seminal case, the Supreme Court denied a petition of a slave for his freedom. He said: "I live in a free state, where there is no slavery, and therefore my slave status should be invalidated as a matter of law."[2] The overwhelming majority of the United States Supreme Court, of Justice Taney's Court said: "Uh-uh, you're wrong." What they said was: "When the Constitution and the Declaration of Independence were written, Africans were perceived as three-fifths of a person. When one speaks of 'we the people,' we were certainly not speaking of you. And therefore we cannot now give you the rights and appurtenances that apply to 'we the people.' The Constitution has no relevance to you and your kind, or to your descendants should they ever become free."[3] That's in the words of the *Dred Scott* opinion. And that spirit continues to resonate throughout American law.

People who are sticklers would say: "Well, the Fourteenth Amendment surely overruled that case." But if you look at that case and you examine its precedent, you will find that to this day, that case has yet to be *judicially* overruled. And where humans actually come in contact with their government is not in the voting booth—I mean, that's an empty formality for many—but it's in the courtroom. That's where most people literally meet their government. And it's in that courtroom where people find whether the rights they're told about truly exist, or don't exist. And for all intents and purposes, if one is poor, if one is African-American, if one lacks influence and power, then you come into that courtroom without the hope that you will walk out a free man. That is the undeniable reality in America.

The death penalty is unique in American law, in that if you really examine the process, you'll come away with a lot of curious ideas about how it works in reality, as opposed to how it's supposed to work in theory. I'll tell you why. In capital case law, unlike any other law, from the very beginning, under the case *Wainright v. Witt,* a juror can be excluded if he or she has any opinion against capital punishment. So therefore you have what's called a pro-prosecution jury—from the beginning—who must swear that they can give the death penalty before they hear one word of evidence. Studies have shown this jury is prone to convict, that it is pro-prosecution and anti-defendant in the extreme, compared to any other jury in American jurisprudence. That's how you begin the process.

Isn't it also odd that at this stage of the process, where you're under the threat of having not just your liberty but your life stolen by the State, you're equipped with the worst counsel the system provides—court-appointed counsel, with no financial resources. Often, while they may have good hearts, they have the least training, because capital case law is distinct from any other kind of law. In Philadelphia, if a person is charged with a capital offense, he gets a court-appointed lawyer. At the time of my trial, the fee for the lawyer was only $2,500. Out of that, he was supposed to provide investigators, ballisticians, forensic experts, psychologists, whatever. He was a sole practitioner—he had no investigator, no paralegal—he had a secretary and himself. We had absolutely no resources. We had nothing. I didn't have to be a wild-eyed, raving, Black Panther or MOVE maniac to say: "Fuck, I'll represent myself." If all he could do was get a motion denied, I could do that. But the court denied me my constitutional right to represent myself. They insisted this guy take over my defense, first as backup counsel and later as lead counsel. I didn't want him as lead counsel—or backup counsel, for that matter.

AH: Tell us about a typical day here.

MUMIA: A typical day begins at 6:25 A.M. A guard enters a "pod" of twenty-four men and announces "yard." "Yard list! Yard list!" If you're up, you can sign up by shouting out your number or your name. By 6:35, the morning meal arrives—a tray is delivered to your door. By 7:05, "yard" is allowed. "Yard" is a euphemism—it actually means "cage," because men go out into the cages here, being counted. You can go one, two, three, four at a time. That "yard" or "cage" period lasts for one hour. Then one goes back into his cell, and unless you have a visitor, you don't leave that cell until 7:05 the next morning. It's twenty-three hours lock-in, one hour outside, five days a week. On weekends, it's twenty-four hours lock-in. If you don't have a visitor, if you don't go to the law library—which is two hours, once or twice a week—you're in that cell.

AH: And nothing happens?

MUMIA: Nothing happens unless you make it happen. Other than that, you're in that cell.

AH: So what do you do to hold up under those conditions?

MUMIA: I'm an addicted writer and reader. I try to read everything I can get my paws on. I just finished reading two books by Alice Walker—*The Temple of My Familiar,* and her most recent book. I've read Toni Morrison's *Jazz.* I've also read *Strange Justice* by Jane Mayer and Jill Abramson, on the confirmation hearings of Justice Clarence Thomas. I try to read as much as I can.

AH: How do you deal with the fact that you may be executed?

MUMIA: I deal with it day to day. I mean, you can't, obviously, just dwell on that reality. You do the best you can every day to transform that reality into a new reality. Luckily, thanks to my book *Live from Death Row,* I have lawyers, very good lawyers, working on my case for the first time. So, you do your daily thing to keep well, to keep sane, to keep strong—to stay human.

AH: Do you feel that you've had an unusual share of bad luck?

MUMIA: No, I really don't.

AH: Why have you attracted this fate, if I may put it that way?

MUMIA: I think that I have a certain history, and because of my history, I have my share of enemies—political, governmental. How many people can brag—and I use that term with a little humor—about having an FBI file from the time they were fourteen? I have. Phone calls, mail, the whole deal—I've been tracked by the FBI since I was a child. Dogged by them for my political beliefs, my political expressions, my political associations. If you were to review my FBI file, of course you'd find a lot of nonsense in it because that's what FBI files have in them. But you'd find an attempt by the government, when I was perhaps seventeen or eighteen years old, to frame me for two murders in another country. What saved me was my work record—my hourly work record showed that I not only wasn't in that country, but that I was at work doing what I was supposed to be doing. They also tried to frame me when I went to college in Vermont for a robbery of some sort. And I'm finding this out reading these records years later.

AH: You have said that you "live in the fastest-growing public housing tract in America."

MUMIA: I do.

AH: You've described torture, theft, terror, humiliation, degradation, brutality. Do you stand by all that?

MUMIA: Absolutely. A lot of people who don't know this reality have perhaps read my book *Live from Death Row* and reacted to it with complete incredulity. The reality is that my book is a toned-down, stripped, bare-bones, objective version of the reality I'm living on death row, in the hole—of what I've seen, what I've smelt; the bodies I've seen carried out of here. If I wrote pure stream of consciousness, no publisher would publish it, and any reader would say it's fiction. The reality is that this is a world that is, by design, closed. Were it not for a court order and our civil action, this very interview would not have transpired. Six months ago, it would not have been allowed. As we speak, the state of California has announced a moratorium on all interviews with all prisoners throughout the penal system. There's a reason for that. It's to keep people in the dark.

AH: Mumia, thank you for talking with us today.

The prison official signals that our time is up; then a guard comes into Mumia's side of the cubicle and motions for him to follow. Mumia raises his cuffed hands in a kind of salute, his eyes fixed on us, and says in a loud, cheerful voice: "Ona move!" He then turns and goes out. As do all Pennsylvania death row inmates before and after a visit, Mumia will endure a body-cavity strip search before returning to the isolation of his cell. Meanwhile, we banter with the prison administrator as we pack up our gear and walk back through the quiet, lonely corridors. She tells us of her twelve-year-old son, and how she does not want him to ever work in prisons.

## Notes

1. *Dred Scott versus Sandford,* 1857, quoted by Mumia Abu-Jamal, *Death Blossoms: Reflections from a Prisoner of Conscience* (Robertsbridge E. Sussex: Plough Publishing House, 1997), 139.
2. Ibid.
3. Ibid.

## PRISONER INTERVIEWING PRISONER

### Martin A. Draughton, Death Row, Texas

A fellow death row prisoner asked me to participate in a book he is putting together. Here is the "interview" he conducted. Please remember, we are still always separated in here. This interview was conducted on paper, although we did get a chance or two to speak when he was recreating in the dayroom in my section of the pod. Anyway, I thought this might all be worth sharing with you folks. (M.A.D.)

NW: How are you feeling today?

MARTIN: Today? I'd have to say that at this moment, June 4, 2000, I'm not feeling all that stressed out. Seems a good day so far, but that might be 'cause I kept my ass in bed all day 'til now.

NW: I certainly appreciate you sharing your thoughts for the purpose of this book, so you say what you want, however you wish to say it.

MARTIN: Don't worry. I plan on just being me. And thanks for asking me to be a part of the book, as most days are mentally and spiritually exhausting. This is no way for a human being to have to live.

NW: Let's start off with you telling me your age and how long you've been locked up.

MARTIN: I am uh . . . hmmmm . . . thirty-six years old. I don't try to keep up with birthdays, in here it's just another day you know. So I had to think on that one for a second. I have been locked up about thirteen years or so.

NW: You gave me two pictures of yourself. In one picture you're smiling and you have no tattoos. In the other photo you have a bald head, you're riddled with tattoos, and your features look hardened, which is how you look now. Explain how you felt when each photo was taken.

MARTIN: The first photo of me was taken after being on death row only about four years. I still had a gleam in my eye and there was still the ability to experience joy in my life. I still looked like "the guy next door" and I was a different person. What happened is, I've taken on the characteristics of your stereotypical "convict" complete with twenty-eight tattoos and a hard stare. These incarcerated years have hardened me and limited my scope on the future.

NW: What do you mean when you say "limiting your scope on the future"?

MARTIN: That is when your mind stays within these walls and the only future is your next prison experience. Something just short of being institutionalized. I think all the tattoos I have probably make me look hard. There's a "shock value" in that. Looking the way I do lots of times helps me get through tough situations, but eventually it's no longer about adapting to your environment because prison does harden you . . . literally. Prison has drastically changed me and I sometimes analyze how and when that change took place in me.

NW: Let's go through the years and tell me what you felt during those time periods.

MARTIN: All of them?

NW: No, let's do it in stages. What were the first four years like?

MARTIN: I think the first few years of being on death row I was still innocent and naive to prison life. I was still learning, growing, educating myself, maturing and searching for the good in all this bad. Each new experience I attempted to learn from to the fullest.

NW: How about after seven or eight years; what was that like?

MARTIN: At some point in time, be it seven, eight, nine or however many years . . . I had already experienced all there was to experience on death row. At this point I had already grown, matured, and gotten all the good I would ever get out of this place, this experience. The first few years refined me and made me a better person through all the hardships and negativity.

These last few years have seemed to erode the good I have gotten from this whole experience.

NW: After almost fourteen years, what is it like now?

MARTIN: The longer I am here now, the more mentally, spiritually, and socially disconnected I become. There seem to be mostly only negative experiences anymore. I'm self-aware enough to recognize the great change in myself, from the person who came into this place and the person I have evolved into through the years. Yet none of the good I've imbibed has made any difference it seems. Apathy seems to be the rule of the day anymore.

NW: In all these years, what experience sticks in your mind the most?

MARTIN: Mid-June 1995. I just finished a handball game with this guy. (This was, of course, before we were all transferred to this super seg prison.) I was getting a drink from the water fountain in the dayroom and when I turned around I was slammed into by these three guys. One of them was the guy I had been playing ball with. My eyes never left the long shiny steel rod in each of their hands as I bobbed and weaved to get untangled from this nightmare. These two guys were stabbing the guy I had been playing ball with. I made my way outside and stood there in a daze against the wall next to my departed friend Frank McFarland. Frank looks up at me and says, "You might want to get that off you," as he points. I didn't have a shirt on and when I looked where he was pointing, the entire left side of my body was smeared with blood. It was after that incident that I swore to myself I would never get caught so unaware again. And I think that was when my mind really started staying locked within these walls, focusing only on what is happening around me.

NW: Why didn't you help the guy getting stabbed? And did the guy die?

MARTIN: Hey man, I was in a mild state of shock from getting caught in the middle of that shit! I was thinking about self-preservation first and foremost! Looking back in retrospect though: Man you mind your own business in prison. I didn't know what that guy had done (I do now) to warrant having that done to him by two other guys. Odds are, had I stepped in to assist I would've been stuck myself. Besides, that dude had friends and associates out there and they didn't even step in. He got what he had coming. Seems coldhearted but that's the unyielding world of a prisoner's existence. And besides, that guy didn't die. If they were really trying to kill him they would've been holding those thirteen-inch-long steel rods at the end instead of holding it three inches from the point. That observation did not go unnoticed. I can't say, however, whether or not the lesson was learned.

NW: You said your "departed" friend Frank McFarland. What happened to Frank?

MARTIN: Executed.

NW: How many executions have taken place since you've been incarcerated?

MARTIN: More than I can keep up with. I know it's more than a hundred. Hell, it's more than a hundred and fifty, I'm sure. I didn't know all of them but I knew most.

NW: How do you deal with the executions of close friends?

MARTIN: Quietly. Inwardly. I write about it to my family and friends mostly. In a few instances I have known family members and/or close pen pals or the wife of a departed friend and a correspondence with them would bloom and grow for a while. Seems to be a healing process for each of us I think. I don't want to talk about executions.

NW: Okay cool. Let's talk about your pending execution. How does your family deal with it?

MARTIN: DENIAL I think.

NW: How do you deal with it?

MARTIN: DENIAL I think. No really, I just take it a day at a time and I try to keep busy writing to leave as much of me behind as I can. I know my words have touched many hearts since I have been locked up. That's my legacy. It's all I can do really. Guess it's a redemption of sorts.

NW: What about dreams?

MARTIN: What about them?

NW: Do you have dreams that bother you?

MARTIN: No. Never. My dreams are uplifting for me. I get many messages from my dreams as well as visits from family, relatives, and friends. I dream of getting out of prison one day. I have never dreamed of being executed or dying. I've had dreams of being in wars, and gun battles, etc., and of being wounded, but never of dying. I often write significant dreams in my journal.

NW: You've mentioned the word "spirituality" twice. Do you believe in God?

MARTIN: I have always believed in God. I was first baptized at eleven years old in Crystal River, Florida, at an ancient Indian burial ground. When I first arrived on death row I was placed next to a practicing Christian fellow. We became very good friends and brothers in Christ. But as to why I came to God . . . I think it was basically a refusal to believe that THIS was all my life is and would ever be. Therefore I had to look to an afterlife. It was with Christ in my life that I walked the most straight and narrow path I ever walked in my life right here on death row.

NW: You talk of your views of Christianity as in the past tense. Have your views changed?

MARTIN: I stopped progressing in my spiritual growth. I also began to resent more and more the fact that of all the people in this world who would have anything to do with a death row prisoner, it seems it was from the "Christians" that I received the most condemnation. That simply did not and could not mesh with my concept, understanding, and experience of Jesus and Christianity. Therefore I gradually backed away from the Christian fellowship and continued to walk with God personally, privately. I need to point out also that my fellowship pretty much ceased anyway, when one by one all of the death row "church" that I grew in walked away, never to be seen again. Now I keep my thoughts of God and religion mostly to myself.

NW: Have you ever looked up to anyone as a role model?

MARTIN: The only person I can think of is my Aunt Faith. She rose up out of the drug environment I also once lived in, went to college as an adult with a family, home, husband, and job to look after, and graduated at the top of her class. She is now a second-grade teacher at a Christian school. To me Aunt Faith bettered herself against the odds. During my aimless, drug-filled teen years she really was the only adult that would "connect" with me and really listen and try to help me with my life.

NW: You have used drugs most of your life too. Is that why you look up to her?

MARTIN: Yeah. She did it, she bettered herself on her own, without having to go to prison to clean herself up, as happened to me.

NW: You once or twice overdosed on drugs. Were you trying to kill yourself, or have you ever been suicidal?

MARTIN: I don't know that I ever tried to o.d. and kill myself that way, that was basically just trying to get higher and higher, of not caring about myself. As for being suicidal, yeah, but not since I have been on the row. While I was still in the county jail, I knew that my life as I had known it, was OVER: Twice I held a razor blade to my neck. Then right after I was sentenced to death the bailiff took me out the back of the courtroom and down the fire escape stairs. We were standing on the outside landing waiting for someone inside to open the door and as I stood there handcuffed behind my back, looking down six stories to the street below . . . mind racing so fast . . . it was like I emptied myself. Once I accepted the fact that I was going to jump, my mind went blank and I was a split second from throwing myself over the edge when CRASH the door opened up and the bailiff grabbed my arm and led me inside. I think in that instant I was closer to killing myself than I was the two times with the razor blade to my throat. But I haven't been suicidal since then.

NW: What would you say replaced those suicidal thoughts?

MARTIN: God I believe . . . Yeah. But now it's the anger.

NW: Tell me about your anger.

MARTIN: Before prison I had always been a person very slow to anger. These years in prison, being treated worse than an animal has changed all that. My "punishment" is to be "held in custody until such time as my death can be carried out." Being treated like shit and harassed in the meantime is uncalled for. But I digress from the question. Anyway, my resolve to maintain [my life] has increased exponentially over the years. It seems the older I get the more determined I am to stay "with it" and live at all cost. And I get some of that resolve from the anger over the treatment I receive, when I haven't done anything in here to warrant it. It kind of energizes me. I just have to quickly get a grip on that anger and channel it into something constructive and not let it eat at me inside too much. And for the most part I do that. I should point out, that not once in all my years of being locked up here have I let that anger seduce me into physically lashing out at a guard or prisoner. Yes, I've had words with a couple but that's as far as it went. And they were not "an innocent" in the particular situation either.

NW: What type of people do you think become prison guards?

MARTIN: Well, not all prison guards are the same. Most I think are just plain ol' blue collar working stiffs, usually of the lower-middle class to lower class of society, just literate enough to function. Some of them however are truly mean-spirited and hateful people who allow the false sense of power and authority they have to go to their heads. They come in here and try to be the "boss" of prisoners, just swelling up their egos. A lot of the guards are prejudiced and some of them are downright sadistic. These type of guards are the ones who breed and feed that anger and racial prejudice that exist in prison today. In my observations a lot of the problems that occur in prison are created and manipulated by immature and/or hateful, prejudiced guards.

NW: Now that we're on the subject of racism, tell me more about what you think causes it to thrive.

MARTIN: That's a good question. I like to think that for the most part it's merely people sticking with their own kind. The old axiom of "birds of a feather flock together." I have however met some truly racist people since I've been locked up. People who really hate other races for no reason. I don't like being around those kind of people. I can understand sticking with your own kind because you can relate to each other. But personally, I give each man I encounter a clean slate and even break. Everyone gets the same respect, until they prove they don't deserve it. I can also understand those that stick with their own race for the "safety in numbers" it provides the individual prisoner. Prison is not a kind place for the weak of mind, body, or spirit.

NW: Racism plays a factor in rapes that occur in prison. What about sex in prison; how do you see it?

MARTIN: In prison we call these people homosexuals or punks. Personally I don't have anything against homosexuals. What I don't like, though, is a guy turning to homosexuality (becoming a punk) because he's in the joint. Coming in here being gay and continuing to be is one thing; becoming someone's punk 'cause they are too weak to make it any other way . . . I don't have the time of day for these people. Most prisoners are young, healthy men in prime physical condition. If one of these guys gets his dick sucked to get his rocks off, that's his business. What puzzles me though are the guys who really fall in love with their punk because they're sexually deprived. Guess I'll never understand that. And as far as rape is concerned, it happens. Like I said, prison is no place for the weak of mind, body, or spirit. You don't have to stand as tall as King Kong to get through prison; but you do have to at least stand!

NW: Do you wish anything for yourself, or for the other prisoners?

MARTIN: For myself, I wish I would get a new trial and be found guilty of a lesser offense and get something less than a life sentence to do so I would at least have some hope of one day getting out of prison. As for my fellow prisoners . . . I hope the death penalty is abolished and everyone could be a part of the general population in prison.

NW: Have you attempted to do anything for the wrong you've done in life?

MARTIN: Absolutely! For one thing, I write and share my "hard-learned" wisdom with the youth of today. I respond to the e-mails that are sent to me
honestly and openly, and many times these e-mails come from teenagers
who ask legitimate questions. I give them honest answers as one who's been
there, who's made the fuck ups, but who now has the presence and clarity of
mind to be able to speak candidly about my past and what led me to death
row. I guess the best thing I can do is reach out to younger people so they
won't walk the same path through life that I did. Also, about six or seven
years ago, a private investigator tried to locate the family of the deceased in
my case. I wanted to contact them and try to express my sorrow and regret.
This investigator went to Mexico and even all the way to Illinois trying to
find them but struck out.

NW: If you were to die this moment, as if saying your final words to the world,
what would you say?

MARTIN: To my family, my mother and sisters, to my friends, relatives and
those who know me . . . You know me. You know that I am a good man,
that I have a good heart. I am not deserving of this cruel, premeditated act
of murder by the state of Texas. Please believe in your hearts and minds
that I love you all beyond what I could express in words. Hopefully we
will meet up again in a place much better than this. I've already apologized
repeatedly, in many forums, for my stupid and foolish and hurtful past. So I
won't again here. Instead, to all of you who support this I quote Sister Helen
Prejean: "A person is more than the worst thing he or she has ever done."
Killing me is a far more deliberate murder than what I am guilty of! As I
have said from the beginning; I am not guilty of a capital murder. Having
so much hate in your hearts to want me dead is not solving anything, is
not going to bring back the dead, is not going to make the victims' family
feel any better. Capital punishment is supposed to be reserved for the most
sadistic and heinous murders . . . That is not my case at all.

NW: Do you want to say anything in closing this interview?

MARTIN: I was a young man, who had never been in any serious trouble with
the law; I had never been to juvenile detention, never been to prison, never
had a felony, never been on probation for anything . . . I had some kind of
mental, moral, and rational breakdown and committed several crimes, while
having never done so before in my life! In theory, I should have been a prime

candidate for "rehabilitation." (Unfortunately that has not been a part of the criminal justice system in this country for the past twenty years!) Indeed I should be punished for fucking up so badly and for hurting people. I agree I should do prison time, but. . . . NOT PUT TO DEATH! A first-time felon! I've said since day one; I did not knowingly kill anyone. It'd be a lot different if I had purposely taken someone's life but I did not. Had I been fortunate enough to be able to obtain decent counsel the odds are very likely that I would NOT have been sentenced to death. But, as are most death-sentenced prisoners, I am merely a poor nobody. As far as the government and society is concerned, I'm easily disposable. No one but family and friends will miss me. Money and politics and social standing dictate what justice one receives in this American judicial system. And that simply is not right, especially when it comes to a life hanging in the balance. Our government should not have the power to exterminate its citizens, period!!

# CORRESPONDENCE, JOURNALS, AND A PRISON REPORT

*I watched a man die once. There was no question that everyone concerned knew this to be a dreadful unnatural action. I believe it is always the same—the whole jail, wardens and prisoners alike are upset when there is an execution. It is probably the fact that capital punishment is accepted as necessary, and yet instinctively felt to be wrong, that gives so many descriptions of executions their tragic atmosphere.*

—George Orwell

# FROM CONVENT TO PRISON: A CORRESPONDENCE

## Sister Ruth Evans, member, Life Lines

My interest in the American death penalty became a preoccupation after Nicholas Ingram, a British subject on Georgia's death row, was electrocuted in April 1995. During the run-up to the execution the hopes of Nicky and his family were raised again and again only to be dashed. I felt forced into the role of onlooker at a savage spectacle. America was openly tormenting a human being before the eyes of Britain, and all I could do was watch.

I will never forget the silence of the morning of April 8, 1995, after I heard on the radio that Nicky had been killed. I made myself do what I had planned to do; I cleaned some outdoor windows. It was a beautiful, sunny day. I tried to understand that Nicky had been here and was no longer here. I wanted to write a letter to him and it could never be written. Ever since then I find it difficult to clean windows.

When I heard of another British prisoner, a Scotsman, Kenneth Richey, on death row in Ohio, I felt anxious about his fate. In January 1998, I read that Kenny's mother had tried to visit her son and had been turned away by the prison. I began to feel that I could not and should not remain a spectator. A couple of weeks later I wrote to Kenny for the first time. He was then thirty-three years old. In Glasgow, Karen Torley, a mother of four children, was leading a campaign on his behalf. She had been prompted to correspond with Kenny by her outrage at the Nicholas Ingram execution. Three years later her campaign had drawn media attention to the many unanswered questions in Kenny's case and to the fact that time was running out. People in the United Kingdom were becoming aware of the fact that Ohio had held a Scotsman on death row for eleven years after a travesty of a trial, without sound evidence of guilt.

Writing to Kenny required patience I did not know I had. Sometimes the prison delayed giving mail to him for weeks. Sometimes they would suddenly give him a pile of letters, written by one of his pen pals over an extended period. Some letters never reached him at all. His replies were also subject to delays. I found it hard to give hours and thought to letters which I knew he might never see. Frequently, I felt that I was writing into a void. At these times to write became a simple act of perseverance, a refusal to abandon someone who was abandoned. When I did receive replies, they acted as a tremendous spur.

"Yes, it was very difficult not getting to see my mum," he wrote on February 19, 1998, "when she came over to visit and was turned away by the prison. She was terribly hurt over it, which really upset me. There was no call for what they did. They just did it to get to me. It's just one of the many games they enjoy playing with me. They are determined to break me! Unfortunately for them, I'm even more determined that they don't!"

On April 22, 1998, he wrote, "Glad to hear that Karen sent you two photos of me. The photo of me wearing the pendant and standing before a blue background was taken about two and a half years ago. I don't like the more recent one as I look a lot older in it. (I have a thing about looking and growing old.) (Smile)"

Kenny was twenty-one when he was sentenced to death. He has a horror of the ageing process because he has not been allowed to possess his youth. The annihilation of his choices makes it hard for him to understand a voluntary curtailment of freedom. "I can't understand how you could choose life as a nun. There's not much difference between that and being in prison."

I see the enclosure of my convent as a place where I can be united to some of the terrible enclosed places in our world. The reason an enclosed sister accepts the conditioning of her freedom is to live in deeper union with Christ. To pray for death row inmates and write to one of them is for me an extension of my original commitment to the crucified Christ. I believe that Christianity and the death penalty are irreconcilable in the modern era, where secure penal institutions can offer all that is necessary for the protection of society. Jesus was a victim of the death penalty. Jesus lived under the shadow of his own execution. He sweated blood at the prospect of execution. He forgave the violent men who killed him. His last companion was a criminal on a cross. Christians owe their salvation to an executed man. They offer their hymns of thanksgiving to Christ, the executed God.

The longer I wrote to Kenny the more conscious I became of how relentless the odds against him were. Months passed and developments occurred in my life and the lives of my associates. But whenever I heard from Kenny his situation was always the same. He was always waiting to hear whether he was going to live or die. I felt sad when I told Kenny about the activity in my life, although I knew he needed stimulation. There is a lot more variety in the life of an enclosed nun than in the life of a death row inmate.

Death row sets out to destroy the resources of the inmates. Enormous strength and courage are needed to tolerate the futility and terror. The prisoners have to endure the greatest stress imaginable for an indefinite length of time, every day of their lives. In the eyes of society the significance of their existence is that they are condemned to die. They are not fed and clothed in order to live, but to die. Most of us ease ourselves through life by looking forward to times of pleasure, relaxation, and sleep. We are not forced to endlessly contemplate the event that we dread most, the way that we will die. For the inmates on death row there is no lulling of the harsh edges of existence. They have few pleasures, no release from tension. Often sleep deserts them. They are sentenced to reality.

The case against Kenny was being exposed to the world at large as false. However, the courts in Ohio remained obdurate in their refusal to review his case. "We've finally got the evidence through hard work to prove he is innocent and we can't get anyone to listen," Kenny's lawyer, Ken Parsigian, commented to the TV program "World in Action." The documentary was broadcast in January 1998. In March 1998, the Supreme Court of Ohio denied Kenny's appeal, without opinion. His case then moved into the federal court. Every time an appeal is denied, Kenny says, something in you dies.

In June 1999, Kenny was very ill and nearly died. For twenty-four hours the prison did not respond to his complaints. Finally, he was given oxygen in his cell and was chained to a trolley. Kenny was hospitalized for two weeks with bronchitis, kidney dysfunction, and severe dehydration. For all this time he was chained to a bed. No one in his family was informed.

After months of silence, Kenny wrote to me on October 15, 1999.

> Sorry about the long delay in my reply. I haven't been myself for quite some time now. It wasn't just being ill of health though. I have been suffering severe depression and anxiety. . . . After 13 ½ years of being on

Death Row, watching the years and my life pass me by, all for a crime that I didn't commit, everything just seemed a little bit too much for me to handle. Fortunately, however, a voice inside of me reminded me of all the friends and supporters I have, who are fighting for me and counting on me to keep fighting myself and it cried out for me to keep going. Through that, I have somehow managed to get up and push on again.

In November 1999, Pope John Paul II made an appeal to the authorities in Ohio on Kenny Richey's behalf.

## WHEN AND WHERE WILL IT END?

William (Bill) Clark, Death Row, California

Dear Traci,

I'm sure you've had your share of nightmares, but what if you woke up one morning, in a cold sweat, after dreaming you had been wrongfully convicted and sentenced to death?

Imagine the actual process of being arrested, fingerprinted, strip-searched, photographed and slammed in a cold, dry cell! Imagine being formally charged with murder, transferred back and forth to court each day and going through a preliminary hearing and trial! After all the above, imagine being convicted and sentenced to death at a trial where police and civilian witnesses committed numerous acts of perjury and where prosecutors manufactured, concealed, destroyed, altered and consistently lied about evidence!

Have you ever thought about how such a chain of events would effect your life and the lives of your family and friends? Well, for a moment, I'd like you to think about such a shocking and unbelievable predicament! Imagine the police coming to your home in the middle of the night, waking you and your family, frightening both you and them by yelling at you, placing you in handcuffs, arresting you for a horrific crime and taking you to jail! Think about the terrifying, confused, agitated state you'd be in. Think about your family, your friends, and your employer as you try to figure out a way to explain to him or her what happened.

Think about the realities of life in jail: the intense loneliness, the staggering depression, the agonizing stress, the gross mistreatment, etc. Imagine the drastic change in your diet and living conditions. Your health begins to suffer both physically and mentally. You will no longer be able to go to your favorite restaurants, to your favorite night clubs, to the theater, etc. No longer will you be able to enjoy the comfort of your nice, warm bed, your private bath or your computer games. No longer will you be able to go for a walk along the beach, for a drive in the country, window shopping in the mall or simply to your refrigerator to grab a snack.

While sitting in jail awaiting trial, imagine having the judge appoint you an attorney [to whom] you are just another "paycheck," as he has bought into the prosecution's theory that you are indeed the culprit. Imagine this attorney, who's supposed to be working on your behalf, thumbing his nose at your claims of innocence. Imagine giving this same court-appointed attorney information and instructions on how to locate evidence that could and would prove your innocence, yet he takes little or no steps to follow up on what you've provided. Imagine telling this attorney that the prosecution's theory and evidence are indeed false, yet this attorney makes no attempt to object, disprove, or challenge either.

Imagine the beginning of your trial, you're supposed to be selecting a jury of your "peers," yet not one of the people sitting in the jury box when your trial begins is a member of your race. And what led to this injustice was the fact that the prosecutor "deliberately removed" any and all the people of your race from the original jury pool.

Imagine the blank, insensitive stares on the jury members' faces as the prosecutor presents his fabricated evidence, points at you and urges them to find you guilty. Imagine what you'd be thinking and feeling as you see your family and friends shaking their heads with disgust as the police and prosecutor's "hand-picked" witnesses commit numerous acts of perjury, admit it, get right back on the witness stand, change their story and continue to perjure themselves.

Imagine your thoughts and feelings as your attorney comes to your holding cell to tell you that the jury has reached a verdict. You're wrought with terror because you know the jury's verdict will not be based on fairness and impartiality. Imagine yourself being led into the courtroom, sitting down, and listening as the guilty verdict is announced.

Imagine watching yourself on television being labeled a "monster," a menace to society, a person who should never be allowed back in the free world. Imagine going back to court the day you are sentenced and as the judge hands down the harshest sentence he can, he refers to you using the same vile, evil, sinister epithets you previously heard on television.

Imagine the bus ride to prison, more specifically to death row. Here you are on the bus with guys who have lived the majority of their lives in the revolving doors of penal institutions. These are now your peers; murderers, rapists, child molesters, psychopaths, drug addicts, etc. Imagine not having anything in common with these guys, yet here you are living with and interacting with them.

Imagine being locked in a six-by-nine foot cell twenty hours per day, with no means or method to alleviate the depression, the loneliness, the boredom or the stress that has enveloped you. Imagine the only things you have to look forward to are five hours of outdoor recreation, a quarterly package of food and personal items, a letter, a telephone call or a visit from a loved one.

At this point, you've obviously lost your job, your savings account has been depleted and you are left with no means of financial support. You have no money to hire a competent, experienced, compassionate appellate attorney, which means the State may appoint you another attorney like the one you had at your original trial.

Finally, imagine your mental and emotional state after years of deprivation and neglect, after years of degrading and dehumanizing treatment, after years of living your worse nightmare! However, for me, this is certainly no nightmare! It's a reality, something I live and deal with every day of my life. And for me, the nightmare began September 22nd, 1991, in the Orange County Jail located at 550 North Flower Street in Santa Ana, California. When and where will it end?

This letter was written to Traci W. Lister who founded Surviving the System (see Organizations and Prison Writing Web Sites).

## OPEN LETTER FROM IDAHO'S ONLY FEMALE DEATH ROW PRISONER

### Robin Lee Row, Death Row, Idaho

Greetings All,

Can you imagine losing your family all in one night? I couldn't until it happened to me. I lost my husband, Randy, age thirty-four, my ten-year-old son Joshua, and my eight-year-old daughter Tabitha in a house fire. I wanted to die with them when I heard. The pain I felt was excruciating. It felt as if my heart had been ripped out of my chest and stomped on, tearing it to shreds. Then the numbness settled in and then the denial. Not me, not my children. No way that this could happen to me. At first the memories would come rushing through my mind and they were so hard to handle. A commercial that would remind me of my son or I'd hear a song that was my daughter's favorite. All over I'd see them or think I hear them. The agony was unbearable.

Why them and not me? I felt like I was in a nightmare I couldn't wake up from, but it was nothing compared with what was to come. I was arrested and charged with their deaths. Three counts of First Degree Murder. How could this be happening? Couldn't anyone see I was in agony? Couldn't anyone see that I was dying inside? Couldn't anyone see my children were my life? No, all anyone could see was that justice had to be served.

I went through a five week trial, February 1–March 5th. Half the time I was there physically, but not mentally, and when I was there I was a basket case. I sat there while the prosecutor took sentences or incidents and twisted and turned them, until even I thought I was guilty. I found out that all a trial was were two stories being told and the jury believing the better story. The story my jury liked most was the prosecutor's. They found me guilty on all counts. Then I was escorted back to county jail, where I was for over a year.

I learned firsthand that our justice system needs some serious changes, but it won't change in my lifetime. Police, prosecutors, lawyers, and judges are all people and they lie, just as people do. After nine months in county jail, wondering if I'd go insane from the grief of losing my family, I was taken before the judge once more. In a twenty-one page facts and findings for the death penalty brief, which he passed out to the media, this judge proceeded to tell me, in a standing-room-only courtroom, what a monster I was and that I wasn't fit to live. Then he sentenced me to Death.

For months before my sentence was handed down, I tried to prepare myself for a death sentence that I knew I was going to receive. Though I thought I was ready for it, when the judge actually said it, my knees buckled, my eyes welled up with tears and I started to shake uncontrollably. I was taken straight to the men's institution from the courtroom. On the way there, I began to believe this was a blessing. I would be with my family, my precious children. I was sentenced at the Ada County courthouse. Directly after my death sentence was handed down, I was escorted to the men's maximum-security prison in Boise, Idaho, where I spent one night. Then reality set in, as we drove through those prison's gates. When I heard those gates close behind me, in my mind I knew I was trapped forever. I couldn't turn around and say "Open sesame." I was in prison and I was going to death row. Me, yes really, me.

First I went through an embarrassing and absolutely humiliating experience. I was strip searched, which has never happened to me before. When the officers told me to bend over, spread my cheeks and cough twice, I started to cry. This can't be real. Then I had to stand before two female officers, completely nude, while they went over my body inch by inch, writing down and describing every mark, blemish, birthmark, scar, tattoo, etc., I had. Before the strip search, I was processed in. Filled out various paperwork, had my picture taken and was fingerprinted. Then in handcuffs, these same officers watched me take a shower. Can you imagine taking a shower in handcuffs? It's not easy. Then the officer poured lice shampoo all over my hair. I was so upset that I again started shaking. After my "shower" I was given white coveralls, that were more grey than white, to put on with no underclothes. The coveralls were several inches too long and several sizes too big. I was given a pair of men's shower shoes size ten. I wore a women's size six. I had trouble keeping them on my feet. Once I was "dressed," they put leg irons on me and belly chains and removed the handcuffs. Trying to dress with them on was a real challenge. It was a long walk to isolation. If the officers weren't holding my elbows I would have fallen many times, as I kept tripping on the coveralls. As I walked, each step that fell led me to a place that would be my "home" for years to come until the authorities felt it was my time to die.

At the time, I didn't know that I was going to be moved to another prison the next morning. I got to my cell and was shocked to hear "strip," after they took the restraints off through a slot in the door, which I now know is called a bean slot. I now was dealing with another female officer. I looked at her and said, "I just did." She told me I would be wise to do as I was told. So, once again I went through that humiliating ordeal. I learned that it would be a daily event for me to go through, as well as my cell being searched every day. I was told the rules, given an orientation booklet and learned I could be pat or strip searched on demand, for no reason. I have been strip searched more times than you can imagine and it's still a humiliating experience and the officers know it.

I was sentenced on December 16, 1993, and taken to the men's maximum-security prison, as I previously stated. On December 17, 1993, I was moved to another men's prison, in Orofino, Idaho. At this time, Idaho DOC [Department of Corrections] was in the process of finishing the women's prison in Pocatello. It would be named the Pocatello's Women's Correction Center (PWCC). Until PWCC was opened, women serving stiff sentences were housed at Orofino. When I got there, there were approximately fifty-five women—I was there from December 17, 1993 to April 24, 1994. The prison officers took total control of my life. They would tell me when to get up, when to go to bed, when my bed had to be made, when I ate, when I'd shower, what I'd wear, when I'd go to recreation, and on and on. I had no privacy. The first time I had a "UA" I thought this is the absolute worst. My mail was (and still is) opened, scanned, or read. My telephone calls are recorded and monitored. During cell searches, my room was torn apart and no respect was given to my property. I was strip searched every day while I was in Orofino, sometimes more than once. I definitely had to be [searched] ANY time I left my room. I was allowed three showers a week. Each time I was strip-searched before and after. I have to wear a towel around me, I couldn't take any clothes to the shower with me. Every time I left my cell I had to be escorted by two officers, including going to the shower. Most of the time one of the officers was male.

Once I had to see the doctor. Even though I was in restraints, handcuffs, and leg irons, and I had two officers with me, I still had to be strip searched, although I was never out of their presence. I even had to wear restraints when being seen by medical staff. This is also true here at PWCC. While in Orofino, I didn't have many privileges, but since I have moved to PWCC, I was granted more, on good behavior of course.

After the women's prison was finished and opened, I was sent there. Things weren't much better. Some of the officers were more humane, and they would talk to me for a few minutes. The staff is the only contact I have with people. When first coming to PWCC, I wasn't permitted to communicate with any of the other women. Now I am permitted to talk to the women who come back to this area, usually for behavior problems. However, I am still not permitted contact with any of the other inmates. Before I am moved from my tier, I must be in restraints, no leg irons unless I leave the institution, and the halls must be empty. Here at PWCC, I am usually moved with one escort. I am still strip searched, but only if I am out of the direct supervision of a security officer. Even when I have Bible Study, I must be searched, even though it is non-contact and there isn't any way to pass anything.

I know you must be thinking it can't be all that bad, well try this one: I am only allowed two rolls of bathroom tissue a week. I had something happen in my family, and I cried for days, I was so distraught. I ran out of bathroom tissue because of the crying and I needed another roll. The male officer asked why I needed another roll, since I had already been issued two that week. I am frightened of this particular officer and I couldn't answer him. He came back to my cell and proceeded to give me a lecture on waste. At about that time the Sergeant walked back to my cell, and saw me crying. When he asked what was up, the officer told him. The Sergeant told him, "give her a roll, she's having a rough time now." I thanked him, and he stayed with me until I could bring myself under control. This officer is no longer employed here. His leaving did not have anything to do with me. There are now no limits on bathroom tissue. A little human kindness isn't hard to give. I starve for human touch, but touching is forbidden. Is it too much to ask for a little compassion?

My day to day routine rarely changes. There are certain days to do my laundry and certain days to clean my cell. The isolation, the solitary confinement, the loneliness, and the boredom are all a constant part of my life. I am only allowed to have non-contact visits with my immediate family, and due to health reasons and distance, visits aren't possible. I live for my mail and telephone calls. When I first came to prison, I received a lot of mail, but as time goes by, people get busy with their lives and I fade into the background. I don't call many people, because nothing changes in my life, so what do I have to talk about? It's also depressing for them too. I leave them alone, unless I hear from them.

Since I am able to talk to the other women housed back here, I am no longer considered to be in isolation, [though] I am still in solitary confinement, because I am housed by myself. I do have one constant thing in my life. By State Statute, I am permitted to have a spiritual advisor of my own choosing. Jackie comes in once a week for one hour of non-contact Bible Study. The staff even messes with her. There have been times that they made her wait up to an hour to see me. She has also been turned away a few times. Once because she wore a pair of sandals and another time for having a sleeveless blouse on. She has also been turned away if they are too busy to come and get me. The officers have been rude to her on more than one occasion, and this woman comes in as a volunteer.

If an officer doesn't like you, he/she could make your life miserable. I happen to have a male officer who does just that. I hear you say "what can be harder than death row," well let me tell you. This officer will call me at 6:30 A.M. to take a shower, and if I want a shower that day I go. The officer offers something once and if I refuse, that's it for the day. I am allowed to shower for fifteen minutes. If I go one minute over, believe me he will give me a warning slip. When I get out of the shower, he doesn't even give me time to get dressed before he calls me to take my one hour of recreation time. If it is warm out, that is not a problem, but I won't go out in cold weather with my hair wet. At those times I refuse. Too many of those days and I will then go out anyway, because I have cabin fever. This officer no longer is employed here. His leaving did not have anything to do with me. I usually, during the week, take my shower at 6:00 A.M., however, if possible, I like to sleep in until 8:00 A.M. on the weekends. Most officers start showers at 7:00 A.M. and on weekends at 8:00 A.M.

The officer will ask you once if you want a shower, recreation, supplies, etc. Supplies are forms, bathroom tissue, and things of that nature. If you refuse, you will not be asked again. My meals will come and he will let them sit there. This causes the food to either get cold or warm, if it's supposed to be cold. My ice cream has melted, my gravy congeals, pasta will stick together, etc. As I said, this officer is no longer here. Most of the staff is really good about getting the food trays passed out as soon as they arrive on the unit.

The mail will come at 4:00 P.M., and [the officer] will give it out at 9:00 P.M., even when he is not busy. If I have a telephone call scheduled at 7:00 P.M., he will let me make it at 8:00 P.M. He will withhold my supplies, search my room, more than once, etc. Oh yes, my life can be worse. Recently the mail system has changed. I never know when it will arrive on the unit. Sometimes it comes early in the day, and other days it arrives late. Depending on when it arrives, and who the officer is, depends on how soon I will receive my mail. We have one officer who doesn't like to do the mail. She brought it in with her at 6:30 A.M., and didn't sort it and pass it out until after count cleared at 4:30 P.M.

The darkness and despair overwhelms me. It gets to the point when my little cell becomes my haven, where I am safe, at least for a little bit. Before I leave my room to go to another section of the institution, it's once again strip search time (when I come back to my cell), restraints and clear the halls. Everyone knows I am being moved. The officer will announce "escorting one death row inmate." I'm the only death row inmate.

On June 3, 1998, at approximately 1:00 P.M. [an officer] came to my room and told me the Deputy Warden requested my presence. When I put my back to the door, to be handcuffed, [the officer] said "No, in front." I should have known then that something was up. I'm never handcuffed in front. When I walked into the common area, not only was the Deputy Warden waiting, but also the institution's counselor. Neither would look me in the eye when I addressed them. They escorted me to the counseling room and told me to take a seat. [The counselor] sat to my left and the Deputy Warden sat across from me. He slid a document across the table to me. I picked it up and saw in bold type, the words "DEATH WARRANT." My eyes teared up and my throat choked me. The Deputy Warden commenced to read it to me. Although I knew the Death Warrant was coming and had decided not to appeal to the Federal Courts, I felt I had been punched in the stomach. I was led to believe it would be thirty to sixty days before the Death Warrant came.

The date of my execution was set for June 18, 1998. In less than fifteen days I would be dead. That was a real eye opener. When the Deputy Warden finished, he looked up at me and I could see the compassion in his eyes. By then the tears were flowing down my cheeks. [The counselor] gave me a Kleenex. As the Deputy Warden commented that he heard that I didn't wish to appeal, I nodded to confirm that because I couldn't speak. He told me he felt I should take the appeal to give myself more time to think this through more as fifteen days wasn't a lot of time to make a major life or death decision. I asked if he could make arrangements for me to call my attorney from a private telephone. He said he would and left the room. [The counselor] reached over and touched my hand. That was the first time in over four years that someone touched me without putting restraints on me. At the time that was a lifeline for me. I so desperately, at that point, needed to be hugged. But I knew that was forbidden.

I was taken back to my room, as [the counselor] had a group to attend, but she said she'd come back. I was so numb that all I could do was just sit on my bunk and stare at the walls, something I'm accustomed to doing. All kinds of thoughts were running through my mind. But one in particular kept coming back. How would my execution affect my family and friends. It's always the ones left behind who suffer most. Myself, I'm not afraid to die. True to his word, the Deputy Warden made arrangements for me to call my attorney. When speaking with him I told him "No stay, I want out." My next words were, " . . . I'm just so tired, and I don't have anything left in me to fight." [My attorney] said, "I'm saddened to hear this."

By now it had hit the media. Not only has the only woman on death row in the state of Idaho received an execution date, but she is not appealing. My attorney and the institution were flooded with calls. The media was out in full force and all wanted an interview. I was given unlimited access to the telephone. I tried to reach my family and friends, to tell them myself, before they heard it on the news. Most didn't agree with my decision, but accepted it. A couple of them saw my way of thinking and gave their full support. Only one said, "No!" He has a great impact on my life and he's close to my heart. He said, "Fight this." He also was the only one I could cry with—with all the others I had to be the strong one.

On June 4th, my attorney flew up to see me. We did a great deal of talking. [He] said he wouldn't leave me until I signed the "Application for a Stay." I finally did, but requested that he give me some time to think before filing it with the court.

During the next week the staff [at the prison] was really supportive. I spent a great deal of time with [the counselor]. Many of the [officers] came to see me, one even had tears in his eyes. He said he believed in the death penalty, but with me it was different. He knew me. I wasn't a faceless person to be executed. How many other people feel that way? Remember we may be inmates, but we are people, just like you. . . . I also received cards and letters from friends. One wrote, "Knowing you as I do, I know you are more concerned about your family and friends than you are about yourself. I don't believe in the death penalty, but I will support your decision because I love you." Another writes, "I will miss you, but I'm not going to be selfish. I'll let you go so you can be free." Another wrote, "I wish you would fight this for Joshua and Tabitha (my children). They wouldn't want this for you." I also received cards and letters of support from people I don't know. Most of them said the same. "You aren't alone. You are in the thoughts of many. I give you strength, courage, and faith." They came from the United States and many other countries, such as Switzerland, the Netherlands, Holland, Ireland, Great Britain, Italy, and others. I wrote back to all who wrote me. I wish to publicly thank these individuals and others who held me in their hearts, thought and prayers.

Since I am writing this it's obvious that I wasn't executed on June 18th. I did receive a stay from the U.S. District Court in Boise, Idaho. Why? I changed my mind. What led me to that decision when I was determined to die? One reason was a conversation I had with my attorney. I asked him honestly what he thought my chances were if I went into the Federal System. He said he has clients that he knows are just passing time and going through their appeals even though they are helpless. The difference between them and myself, beside our genders, is they are guilty. I'm not! I know most of you think that everyone on death row claims to be innocent. In my case, it is true!

[My attorney] feels that my chances are very good once I reach the Ninth Circuit Court of Appeals in San Francisco. My next question was how long? He said about two years. I gave that considerable thought, as I did other conversations with family and a particular friend. . . . He gave good arguments. Also, I couldn't leave behind the legacy that if I died everyone would think that my children's mother killed them. That really bothered me and I couldn't let that thought go.

So, with that, my friend's arguments and my attorney's words, I decided I've come this far, I can go another two years if it will accomplish something. I can always re-examine my options again in two years. I then met my federal attorneys and they gave me something else—Hope!! Now I feel like I made the right choice—Life!! Many wonder how someone can want to die. My reasons may sound minor to most of you, but to me they are very real:

1. I'm tired. Emotionally drained.
2. I'm lonely. Living in isolation is a hard life. Not the picnic most people believe. I never thought I would crave human contact. Other women alone on death row can relate to this. My heart goes out to them.
3. Boredom. Contrary to popular belief, I do not have exercise equipment, a pool table, or cable television to entertain me.
4. Finances. Most months I can't afford a bottle of shampoo. No, the state doesn't provide me with all my hygiene items.
5. I want out of here and saw execution as a way out.

For now I will think positively. I know the next two years will drag by. There are times that I wonder if I made the right choice. I guess only time will tell.

> Happy Endings,
> Robin Lee Row

## JOURNAL FROM DEATH ROW MISSISSIPPI

Tracy A. Hansen, Death Row, Mississippi

OCTOBER 18, 2001, 4:20 A.M.

Hi, I'm Tracy A. Hansen, Unit 32–C, # 46404, Parchman, MS 38738. My date of birth is 05/25/63, and I was born and brought up in a small town outside Orlando, Florida. I'm a white man, raised in a middle-class family. I was arrested in April 1987 and put on death row six months later for the shooting death of a highway patrol officer. On death row I remain, presently on my last meaningful appeal.

In 1987 I was pulled over by Highway Patrol, and because of a situation ended up pulling a pistol on the officer. He panicked and went for his gun. I panicked and shot. I disarmed him and let him go to a stopped vehicle to get a ride to the hospital. A female companion and I fled. The woman and I were arrested a number of hours later. The officer died thirty-six hours later. Here I am, and the woman was given a life sentence, which I'm not sure whether she's yet paroled or not. Much apologies if this description sounds mechanical . . . I care, I hurt about it, I can cry about it, but there is nothing I can do to change that day fourteen and a half years ago. I don't claim to really know the pain of any of the family, but having corresponded with the victim's daughter for a length of time, I certainly know of the pain I caused, and also care and hurt for that.

In a way, I want to scream that I am a good person. Please don't judge me by my wors[t] mistake so many years ago. In other ways, it's like that crime is never away from me—the victim never returns to life, and it's almost as if I can feel I have no right to ask anyone to consider me good. Still, I do believe life comes with a responsibility to give according to our utmost ability to do so—I care about yesterday, but I have to learn from it in ways which don't disable what potential I have to give in some way today. I might try and minimize things to myself by saying it wasn't a woman or a child, it was panic rather than malicious intent, there was no intent to kill, etc. I know none of this brings the man back to life and gives him back his family, who miss him and hurt over the way he was taken from them.

I don't mean to take from the victims of our crime by saying that there is much pain involved with being on death row. People here are put into a room about the size of most folk's bathroom, with a bed in place of a tub, and are here to stay for many, many years. Here we know that maybe as much as eighty percent of our country hates us—we're rejected to the point that they want to kill us. In many phases of the experience we hate ourselves just as much. We know the hurt of the family and friends of our victims, and if we truly care, then we truly feel their pain—we feel the pain of those who hate us, and of those who may love us. If I'm executed in six months from now, people I love, who love me, are going to have their heart torn sharply—I love deeply, and my friends love deeply, and the hurt they will feel . . . it will be intense and I'll not be here to even try and comfort them.

Night-time is the only time there's possibly any sense of quiet, and it's when I usually try and stay up. I spend most of my time writing.

**OCTOBER 19, 2001**
Good morning! 5:39 A.M. and I'm feeling a bit rushed this morning. Visiting for death row is over a telephone, for only one hour, once every two

weeks. This last month they've decided attorney visits can no longer be face to face, so, the last civilian life you see which may be on "your side," you don't even get a handshake with anymore, nor are able to really talk freely with them. They do like to harass attorneys who help death row prisoners. I'd had one drive a couple hundred miles to be barred from the prison for having had their work camera with them, had them get stuff stolen up here, had one who was inappropriately touched when being searched.

I could seem to complain a lot, but most things are opinion, and not like an emotion I carry around with me. After a while, one eventually learns that you have the choice to let something bother you or not, and I'm pleased I recognize this free will. On the more outstanding side, I've had an officer who was a gang member have a prisoner gang member prompt him to assault me, and so he did, removing my eyeglasses that I had on at the time (my hands and feet were chained as I sat there), then he turned and kicked me squarely in the face. I was a bit angry at first, but I was already on the way to the hospital at the time because a gang member had scalded me with hot water when an officer made me walk by that cell on the opposite side of the hall, and by the time I was in the van on the way to the hospital, I felt forgiveness. Forgiveness seems to come fairly easy for me, and I'm glad of this—certainly much more peace in forgiveness [than] resentment.

I expect my own situation contributes a lot toward me being forgiving. I've violated well beyond my share in the past . . . so, I need a lot of forgiveness for things I did when I was free. I've worked hard to grow to a better understanding in life, to follow good, not violate others, mature love in my heart and have something good to give unto others, and like to believe I deserve some degree of being seen as something more than my worst mistakes in life. Anyway, running out of room, so, more tomorrow . . .

**OCTOBER 20, 2001, 12:30 A.M.**
Well, beyond the day to day routines, is how being here touches the person—that is, the experience isn't really the external things going on around you but rather how the internal person is affected by it all . . . same as with anywhere else in life.

Wednesday was an hour of recreation in a one-man pen, about 9 x 16. I run in tight circles. After recreation I do my laundry. If you send something white out to be washed, it's a drab gray within two to three washes and comes back smelling rather foul. If you wash your own laundry and hang it in your cell to dry, then they can write you a rule violation for doing that. So, anyway, I clean the toilet and wash my clothes there since it's easier to rinse them there with more water to flow. I sometimes use a catheter hose connected to my sink while I stand in the toilet, getting a shower this way after recreation. Being searched Thursday, they took my shower hose and wrote me a discipline report for it (possession of contraband). Over six months ago they took all my appliances (TV, radio, fan, and typewriter) for possession of contraband (tobacco and nail clippers, then silly things like empty plastic containers and a turtle that had wandered into my cell to visit) and say I can now never again have any appliances.

They move me from cell to cell once a week. This is ordered by officials in the capitol who never consider it being an entirely different social system in here—how one is accepted, or rejected, in a social system very different from free society, which administrators a couple hundred miles from here don't understand. They also don't realize the importance of letting us display family pictures on our walls.

### OCTOBER 21, 2001, 2:43 A.M.

Supper last night was the normal for Saturday night—soybean by-product meat, vegetables, rice, and rice pudding for dessert. Breakfast in the morning will be biscuits with either jelly or prunes, gravy with potatoes or rice, and either grits or oatmeal. Not necessarily complaining—except for what may be stolen, since we are given a meal to meet certain dietary standards (sometimes twice since trays are cleaned so poorly there's scum built up in them). We get far more then many millions of other people in this world, and I am truly very grateful for the food we receive, though I'd complain that the prison gets tons of fresh fruit, and will only serve canned fruit to this unit, and deprive us of food they serve the other units such as government surplus cheese, peanuts, butter, raisins, honey and the like which we never see.

Friday was especially annoying; the guard passing out the mail was giving it to the wrong people. The Superintendent was in the building today, telling that all shoes and drinking cups would be taken and state issue "flip flops" and drinking cups would be the only kind we could have. The shoe situation annoys me personally since I like to jog, and it will annoy everyone having to wear only those when going outside in freezing weather. Such things can be very annoying if you let yourself think about it. So you try and block out that such changes are "forever." For example, they once came through and cut all the toothbrushes in half, and now only tiny toothbrushes can be possessed, under three inches long. This isn't saying it's only another convenience to deal with, but it's saying that for the rest of your life, you can never again use a normal-size toothbrush; you can never again wear tennis shoes; you can never again have this drinking cup which has sentimental value. I'm thirty-eight years old, and if I could have a teddy bear that came from someone I love, I would sleep with it every night. If I could have a small little plant, I would talk with it all the time and treasure the opportunity to care for it.

On a happy note, I have a pet turtle about three inches long, which I've had since July 1, 2001. Her name is Shy because she always stayed in her shell when I picked her up. She drinks from the palm of my hand, and eats from my fingers when I hold tuna in the water as she swims in the sink . . . Well . . . you get the picture . . . we fell in love and my turtle still remains with me. I do very much appreciate being able to care for her. If only things could always be as peaceful.

For instance, when I saw a friend murdered outside my cell door, knew I was an intended victim, and knew how poor security here is, how officers set up prisoners, and the fact that one always has one's hands cuffed behind their back when out of the cell, it scared me in ways. As for being hand-cuffed when leaving your cell, you're to back up to the bars, for hands to be cuffed behind your back, often having the legs shackled. Worse part of that is all the times when someone has the wrong door opened, gets cuffs off by officers not paying attention or meaning to set someone up—as when someone goes to stab someone else, who is helpless because they have trusted this guard who has cuffed their hands behind their back, making them defenseless as they're stabbed. I've seen a couple of guards stand and watch, ask the stabber to stop, while doing nothing, and saw the guard actually run the other way when my friend was murdered outside my door, stabbed all along the hallways as he ran down the hall with hands cuffed behind his back, yelling for the officer to use his shield and to please help him . . . I will try and be more cheerful tomorrow. Sorry to close on a blah note . . . good night for now.

**OCTOBER 22, 2001, 2:20 A.M.**

I was feeling a bit blah about ten minutes ago, but I'm feeling a bit more chipper now. The weekdays I can look forward to because mail will be running again or maybe go to the clinic to have x-rays on a shoulder which is bothering me and I've pushed for years to get something done or get to the dentist for dental problems which are several years old. Several years I've tried to get them to replace a partial plate a dentist broke while trying to clean it. I'd also like to get attention for cavities which they ignore for years until they claim they can only extract the tooth, though once in a while they squeeze some rubber-like stuff in there which stays for about a year and then falls out. Worse experience was once making it clear I didn't want any teeth pulled, the dentist agreed, I close my eyes and . . . then open my eyes when he starts prying. He breaks the tooth, which he is indeed trying to pull. He then tries to put a sort of screw into it since there's nothing to grab a hold of, slips, cuts me, blood everywhere, no assistant, has me holding a suction hose and mirror while he tries to clean up . . . More cutting . . . More blood . . . Unconscious for a minute . . . Back to work . . . I was too sick to walk back to my room for about an hour after I finally get out of the chair. Not the only horror story but on to other things.

Sometimes it can feel lonely and hurt to know I can't even see things such as the ocean, or feel such when I clean my nails, trim my beard and such. I've not always been as stable as I am now, and used to be a bit more explosive at times. Rarely all that angry, but I used to have a lot more frustration. Thoughts, memories, worries, etc. return to haunt you again later if you suppress them, but if you face them head on, you arrive at peace. For me, if something bothers me, I almost welcome it these days as an adventure, for I can exercise free will in how I may interpret it, with the expectation of learning something constructive from it. Obstacles or trials become something I can appreciate for whatever constructive growth it may give to the heart.

I've not always had such peace, and I give very much credit to friends who have contributed in a lot of ways in making me who I am today . . . but who is still a person who complains and such. I'll be back in about twenty-four hours from now . . .

**OCTOBER 24, 2001, 1:53 A.M.**

Update on the day's events??? Hmmm . . . exercise, a shower, some sleep, writing, rolling, and here I am. Exercise was outside, running in circles for forty minutes, then about twenty minutes of upper body exercise. They stopped exercise equipment for this unit years ago to appease the public during election time by getting rid of exercise equipment and air conditioning for prisoners for their "tough on crime" policy . . . I heard this other unit about a mile from here has had problems with people "gang banging" for the last couple of weeks. Among other things, this place is a sort of farming plantation. Laws on the books say slavery is still allowed in this state as long as the slaves are prisoners.

Sometimes I wonder how blind I am to people. I've always felt that I could connect well with people, and understand fairly well. I know I never believed that twelve out of twelve people would vote for me to be killed. I looked like a teenager though I had committed a very terrible crime, I still just couldn't imagine that each and every one of them would vote me to literally be dead. For me, I know there is more to me than my worst action I ever did in my life—I know that I care about other people, truly appreciate people, don't want to violate even those who stand against me as an enemy, and have a sense of love for others I'm very pleased with but they really saw none of this—only the crime, which is all that most of the world would see of me.

During showers today a man was throwing human waste. He is one of three very severe psychiatric patients they try to hide because it would be inconvenient to have them more directly under psychiatric care. They give them drugs, ignore them, and bathe them when too many people start complaining about the odor of them not washing or refusing to flush their waste for WEEKS at a time. No wonder my neighbor is so sick, the one directly beside me, and a couple others within a few doors of him, all with fever. It's doubtful they will see the doctor. You could tell an officer that you have extreme chest pain and half your body has gone numb, and they would call the clinic (inmate hospital) for a nurse to diagnose you over the phone. I'd think the deaths would speak volumes about the medical care here such as the eight deaths at Parchman in one month.

I hear Loreena McKennitt singing in the background tonight. I think I could hear this tape a thousand times without tiring of it . . . very peaceful,

seems to take you to a completely other world . . . Good night for now . . .
zzzzzzzzz . . .

Feeling a bit exhausted this morning, just cleared up a bit, in anticipation of moving to another room tomorrow. Last week when I moved, they wanted me to pull my shorts down before coming out, and since I had some tobacco held there, I had to flush it. Sometimes they will pour out everything from your cell, even things like toothpaste into plastic bags, then dump something like coffee over all your personal belongings, making a mess of everything.

Hopefully I'll move into a clean room tomorrow. I always clean a little anyway, though some rooms you really need to scrub in order to find the actual floor, There can be toothpaste all over the walls where they have had pornography posted on the wall, etc. along with a really filthy toilet and sink. I very much hate having to clean up after another grown man!

Good morning to you. New cell and pleased to be out of the front cell where doors were banging during all hours of the day and night. Pleased this new cell was clean when I came into it. Janice Joplin singing . . . *freedom's just another word for . . . nothing left to lose* . . . Hmmmmm . . . Bad side to this cell is the people above me. I'm back in an area where the people upstairs beat on the floor and kick the walls all day—very annoying that they're inconsiderate enough to carry on like that, and annoying that I could bang for five minutes where officers would want to write me up. But they don't want to enforce rules against someone carrying on in a way which annoys others pretty much all day.

Sometimes annoying in the front cell was the way guards were laughing, playing, running around screaming with people sleeping during the wee hours of the morning, they will carry on like they are hanging out on the street somewhere, yelling and screaming, beating on the walls. So off for now, goodnight with a hug and with love always . . .

I suppose the excitement for the day was being able to have about two to three hours outside, and I'm quite pleased with that. I also ate lunch when

I came back in. It was cold. We have bread with every meal and it's either stale, outdated, or even moldy, though for breakfast it is baked biscuits which are rather good. You can't have butter though unless you pay someone to steal you some.

They assure us the heating is on, only it's blowing cold air—that's why people are complaining that it isn't on and officers wrap up in heavy coats even for a couple of minutes' walk to make count.

Think good thoughts that keep good feelings growing in the heart, share some smiles and hugs.

NOVEMBER 07, 2001, 12:06 A.M.

Well, not all that thrilling of a day today. I had a hearing for the write up I received over a shower hose and a couple pieces of magnet someone before me left in the cell. Used to always be ten days loss of privileges but it seems they have now upped it to thirty days. Anyway, they found me guilty—I'm not allowed canteen, which I've not ordered for over a year anyway, not allowed visits for thirty days, which I've had none of in the last fourteen years anyway and I lose phone privileges, which I'm not all that pleased about.

Today's memo reads: "It has been brought to my attention that several offenders are sliding their trays across the floor instead of using the porthole. The porthole is being utilized for this purpose and should be treated as such. In order to prevent this from happening, any offender caught sliding his tray across the floor will be placed on alternative meals for a period of one week. If the problem still exists the alternative meals will be extended indefinitely." I corrected the spelling errors for them. The problem is that when you set food trays in the door, they frequently get bumped by someone in the hall, then you have all the left-over food splash all over your floor, perhaps on your bed as well, and then of course you can't get anything to clean your cell with, and laundry is only done twice a week, you can't even get cleaning materials when someone upstairs pours urine down your back wall. So anyway, now they will try and use what they feed you as leverage.

Today I enjoyed making six kitties. I've molded them out of bread I turned into dough. They have dried quite solid. They dry with cracks so I'll make some thinner dough to fill in the cracks, then melt some plastic over them. I'd like seeing if I could make a whole "cat" chess set before they decide there's a rule against molding my bread into the shape of animals.

**NOVEMBER 08, 2001, 2:34 A.M.**

And big news for the day is that the court has denied my appeal. Not sure how to describe how it really feels . . .

**NOVEMBER 09, 2001, 6:21 A.M.**

Sleep hasn't been all that easy lately, but I did get in a couple hours last night. Right after searching me with moving yesterday, which included them pulling my pants down when they got done, then having me go into the hall again with them still down then came another search, with them taking all shoes, and leaving everyone with only a pair of flip flops—should be fun to run in those. Temperatures are in the 40s today and I don't want to get sick. Trying to talk with my friend yesterday was blah in many ways as it's quite likely I have only four to six months left before they execute me. Blah to have the phone disconnect five times in an effort to talk only fifteen minutes. This is a problem we ALL have here and something that has continued for years without them correcting it probably on purpose in view of the money they make from it. It cost a dollar a minute to call my friend, and they also charge a $6.00 connection fee for the first minute each time so there was $30.00 for probably not even a full fifteen minutes!!

By the way, I do consider the victim's family, there's just not a lot I can say with that—I think about them, feel for them in ways, caring about all that pain I gave to their lives, etc . . .

**NOVEMBER 10, 2001, 9:18 P.M.**

Welcome to Noise World! Seems some of those people upstairs are sick of those beating and banging, so they beat and banged all night to keep them up . . . and then someone barely pushes in their water button so that it sounds like a fog horn throughout this whole side of the building, trying to drown out others making noise and *la la la* . . .

I do consider that it has been ten years since Mississippi executed anyone. It somehow seems bizarre that I could be the first to go in so many years.

**NOVEMBER 13, 2001, 8:02 P.M.**

Hello again. It doesn't look like I'll be sleeping this evening, so I thought I would drop in again now. I tried to catch a short nap earlier, thinking about the ocean, but I kept getting interrupted.

I did go to court today—about an hour's drive from here. In some ways it was nice being out, and in some ways not. I had a fair walk before I got to where they change clothes, and so my ankles were bleeding from shackles and they only had filthy shoes to give me, leather work boots with no socks, making me wonder whose filthy, perhaps bloody feet had been in them before. The pants were about five sizes too large and the white shirt was filthy. Then they added these sort of tubes that they lock over my hands so that I'm unable to mess with the locks on the cuffs/waist chain. So anyway, I'm uncomfortable, no legal papers, and go in looking like a clown. They do remove everything except the shackles as I go into the courtroom. No attorneys, clerks nor judge, just a room full of potential jurors, and I walk in wearing shackles, trying to hold my pants up and sit down and close my eyes trying to look more peaceful than criminal, knowing they must be looking at me sitting there in the center of them all. They tell me I'm to be seen in the judge's chambers and I rightly assumed that was the end of the show. The judge explained how they "forgot" to serve defendants with the complaints and "forgot" to subpoena my witnesses but did I want to go ahead with trial against one defendant? Basically I had no choice, but to choose for it all to be postponed once again.

I did show the judge my ankles, clothes falling down, etc. and told him it defeats the purpose to let someone dress up before a jury to show a sense of dignity and present themselves as a gentleman when one is dressed like that. On the way in, I had been forced to put my nose to the wall on the elevator, but I decided I wasn't going to do so on the way out. I maintained more dignity and self respect like that, than agreeing to put my nose in the wall like a naughty child dressed in filthy shoes, baggy-ass fucking clown pants, filthy-ass shirt, and with stupid-ass clown mittens on my hands because I'm the animal that no one should look at, and I'm not good enough to see other people.

On the journey back, the guards stopped to pick up real food and then sat there in the van eating for about thirty minutes. It smelled strong enough for me to taste it and I appreciated that, though somehow it seemed very inconsiderate. I did enjoy the sights on the way there. The cars I saw seem much smaller than what I remember and many more places seem to have bars on the windows. I mainly wanted to see people but didn't see too many of them. The "thrill" when I got back was receiving a copy of the court denying my appeal. I'm not sure what I felt reading that. I feel a lot when reading about me having killed someone and of course feel a lot when reading how they are intending to kill me.

### JANUARY 7, 2002, 5:48 A.M.

Blah news for today is I was called to the law library to call my attorney today and he tells me of the state moving to have an execution date set. Lying here, the mind doesn't want to rest . . . should I fight and let them know it's murder they're doing, and I'm not laying down my life. Should I be more willing and attempt to excuse them and encourage peace of mind for them? Should last words be about murder, or be about love?

I was thinking about execution as I ate. The stew had real meat, and actually I'd prefer not to eat meat. I considered how we raise and kill such animals for food—animals which are clearly capable of emotions, demonstrations of affection to their young and such. And then I thought about people of course—how they will strap me to a table, making me even more helpless than I am in this cell, and as I lay there, strapped down and helpless, they will intentionally kill me to show that killing is wrong.

Quite possible that the Mississippi Supreme Court could end up setting an execution date within thirty days. Is that the time to panic, or does that come later?

### JANUARY 11, 2002, 7:21 P.M.

Biggest news is they are now saying that starting February 1st, 2002, we can no longer write to people overseas and we can no longer receive mail from there either.

Several have written and thanked me for sharing my life with them. Be assured that I'm also very grateful to have you to share with. Hunger strike seems to be staggering a bit, kind of sad to look at it. There's people starving themselves to try and get someone to care about the way they're being treated.

### MARCH 31, 2002, 5:45 A.M.

Blah news yesterday—Shy was expiring. Someone held her for me when I changed cells last week, and when I retrieved her she floated very lopsided. The man said he didn't accidentally step on her, but it seemed one of her air pouches burst and the next day her shell was very soft, almost soggy. I warmed some paper on the light to give her a warmer place to lie and she wasn't very responsive at all and the last movement I saw from her was her front legs going up like saying goodbye.

I think a fair bit about being "set free." I do appreciate that if it's my time, a part of me can welcome being free from here at last and if it's by execution, then at least I don't have to deal with this damned prison anymore and all their senseless rules that are running so rampant lately.

JULY 1ST, 2002

I don't like not knowing the time. I'm not sure when I last wrote my journal but I think it was after a shakedown when I lost my little watch. The officers will keep me in this front cell until I go to another unit sometime in the last week before the 17th. I still don't feel it in my bones that the 17th will be my last day.

It seems odd writing to some of my friends overseas, knowing that I may never receive their responses. The superintendent assures me that I would not be allowed to place or receive international calls on the 17th either. Anyway I am still peaceful at this time, in a way more aware that I may never have the time to get to this and that but don't let such thoughts stop me from accomplishing what I can. And now I'm off to see what I may get to do.

A big hug and kindly love

Tracy

Tracy A. Hansen was executed by the State of Mississippi on July 17, 2002.

## PRISON MADNESS IN MISSISSIPPI

Dr. Terry Kupers, School of Psychology
of the Wright Institute in Berkeley

I toured death row at Mississippi State Penitentiary, Parchman, on August 8, 2002, in the company of American Civil Liberties Union (ACLU) and Mississippi Department of Corrections (MDOC), attorneys, the Warden and Associate Warden of Unit 32, and Corrections staff. . . . It was abundantly obvious that MDOC had made efforts to improve appearances in the days immediately preceding our tour. In the three days preceding our tour, . . .

the psychiatry department had posted quite a few "90–day Comprehensive Mental Health reviews" in the inmates' medical charts. Shortly before our tour, some of the prisoners' televisions and fans had been returned to them. The outdoor areas surrounding C Building had been sprayed for insects within hours of our visit. Parts of Tier 1 had been freshly painted. Staff had given showers to psychotic prisoners and had cleaned their cells shortly before we arrived.

Parchman's death row rivals any prison I have seen for cruel, harsh, and inhumane conditions of confinement, even compared with super-maximum facilities. These conditions are not warranted on penological grounds, and they cause the death row prisoners at Parchman intense and needless pain and suffering. These conditions are virtually certain to cause medical illness and destruction of mental stability and functioning. It is probable that as a result of these conditions, a significant proportion of the prisoners have developed or will develop psychiatric conditions that interfere with their ability to cope with life in prison and in the community, and that many have suffered or will suffer breakdowns that become chronic and chronically disabling.

But in any event, in our society, even a prisoner condemned to execution may not be incarcerated in cruelly inhumane conditions, or allowed to suffer severe pain and illness without basic treatment for his serious medical and psychiatric needs. A high percentage of the prisoners I interviewed clearly suffer from severe mental illness. At least six suffer from obvious psychosis with current signs including auditory hallucinations and delusions. At least another six suffer from severe depression and other mood disorders. I also discovered several cases each of severe anxiety, panic disorder, post-traumatic stress disorder, and other significant mental illnesses. In all likelihood there are many more prisoners suffering from serious mental illness beyond the ones I happened to interview.

The very serious mental health needs of these prisoners are not being addressed. The mental health care available to prisoners on death row is grossly inadequate. Most of the prisoners who suffer from mental illness, including those who are prescribed psychiatric medications, tell me that besides their occasional visits with the psychiatrist they have no other contact with mental health personnel. Several prisoners who are taking psychiatric medications told me that on more than a few occasions they were given the wrong medications, and others told me that their medications are frequently discontinued for days or longer for reasons unknown to them.

While the mental health care is inadequate in general, the care provided to extremely disturbed individuals is shockingly deficient, and creates a threat to the well-being of all prisoners on death row. Just about every prisoner I interviewed discussed the presence on death row of severely psychotic prisoners who cannot control themselves, foul their cells, stop up their toilets, flood the tiers with excrement which they also throw, and keep the others up day and night with their loud noises and hollering. Prisoners in neighboring cells suffer immense pain, discomfort, and psychiatric breakdown because of this. The seriously disturbed prisoners are left to deteriorate even further because of the severe idleness and isolation on death row.

One prisoner who has been diagnosed paranoid schizophrenic and is prescribed Haldol, a strong anti-psychotic medication, hears voices that order him "to do things" (command hallucinations). He tells me that he sleeps much of every day, he cannot afford a television so when he is awake he sits and stares or tries to read, but he cannot remember what he reads and cannot concentrate on the pages. His cell was next door to that of a prisoner in a filthy cell that stank, causing many bugs, which made him extremely anxious and the voices in his head louder. These are entirely unacceptable conditions of confinement and psychiatric treatment for a prisoner who suffers from this degree of serious mental illness. There are many more prisoners on death row who suffer from serious mental illness and are receiving far from adequate mental health treatment.

Corrections staff tell me that their strategy for managing death row prisoners whom they consider to be high security risks is to constantly move them to a new cell, on average once every week. Of course, this means that other prisoners must be moved to accommodate the movement of the high-risk prisoners; thus, there is frequent and widespread cell movement. Security expert Vincent Nathan questions the necessity of this procedure in his report. The consequence, whether intended or unintended, is that prisoners live with the omnipresent possibility that they will be placed in a filthy, foul-smelling cell that had been occupied by one of the very disturbed prisoners who smeared feces or fouled the cell, or a cell in which the window mechanism is broken or the electrical outlet has been destroyed. When the unlucky prisoner who is moved into a filthy cell requests cleaning supplies to make the cell habitable, the staff cannot or will not provide adequate supplies.

This technique for managing security risks constitutes a kind of physical and psychological punishment that can drive men stark raving mad, or to suicide. A letter from one prisoner describes the effect on him of a recent move of this kind:

> They moved me into Cell #13, which had been another prisoner's cell. Cell #13 has no electrical outlet or TV hook-up. I couldn't use any of my electrical appliances. My fan was sorely missed! The cell was full of mosquitoes, as the window was open and the screen has a huge gash in it. There was feces and dried urine all over the floor and walls, as well as the bars and the bed. I asked officers for a broom and mop for five hours, but all they gave me was a piece of a towel and a little disinfectant, which I used on the bars as my food had to pass through them. The heat and mosquitoes were too bad to sleep, so I spent most of that night [the 24th] scrubbing that cell. You may recall that I weigh 320 lbs. The only way I could scrub the floor with that piece of towel was to get down on my hands and knees. I tried to lie on the bed and clean a spot on the floor to begin on my hands and knees. I wanted to keep from getting the feces and urine all over me, but I failed miserably! When I had the cell as clean as I could get it, I washed myself, and then my boxers. A sergeant came along and told me to take the clothesline down or get written up. It just seemed that everything was working on me as punishment.

Health care for death row prisoners is as glaringly deficient as mental health care. Besides the gross deficiencies in medical and mental health care, I observed first-hand a number of the other inhumane conditions of which the prisoners complain, including the "ping pong toilets." When a prisoner flushes his toilet, the waste backs up into his neighbor's toilet. Many of the prisoners cover their toilet bowl with a towel in order to slow the overflow of waste from their neighbor, but this is likely to leave them without a clean towel. Worse, if a prisoner suffering from serious mental illness stuffs something down his toilet in order to stop it up, the toilets up and down the tier back up and waste overflows onto the floor in all the cells. Environmental expert James Balsamo summarizes his findings: "Conditions in this facility, including excessive heat, filth, uncontrolled insect and mosquito infestations with attendant risk of West Nile infection, inadequate water supply, water leaks, impaired ventilation, uncontrolled water temperatures, malfunctioning toilets, the apparent lack of adequate cleaning supplies, food being held and served at unsafe temperatures, unsanitary laundry, broken automatic fire detection and alarm system, excessive noise, and extremely poor lighting, all combine to seriously jeopardize the health and safety of the inmates and the correctional officers who live and work in Unit C-32, Death Row."

The high risk of morbidity and mortality on Parchman's death row due to extremes of heat and humidity requires urgent attention. Many of the prisoners are at particularly heightened risk of serious heat-related illness and permanent injury. I had myself locked for a few minutes into Willie Russell's "special management" cell, which has a Plexiglas cover over the metal door, and experienced even more discomfort than I felt in the regular cells. Even being locked in the cell for a few minutes I could feel the temperature and humidity rise. This kind of punishment is well known to cause intense anxiety and rage, psychiatric breakdown, and in a large proportion of cases, suicide. For example, Jimmy Mack waived all further appeals while he was confined for a long time behind a plastic-covered door in a special management cell. He explained to me, "If I'm going to have to live like that, you might as well just kill me." Recently he was removed from that cell and decided to permit his appeals to go forward. Willie Russell continues to be incarcerated in this kind of cell, where he has been for two years.

A certain modicum of dignity and self-respect is a requirement for the maintenance of sound mental health. Most of the prisoners I spoke to were very upset by what they consider arbitrary rules that inflict unnecessary pain and deprivations. For example, policy prohibits prisoners from moving their mattresses from the concrete slabs under the window. There are several reasons why prisoners urgently want to move from under their windows. When state prisoners in cells above flood their toilets, or when rainwater pours in along the outer cell wall onto the bed, the prisoner is not allowed to move his bed away from the water. In many cells, the afternoon sun shines through the windows directly onto the prisoners' bunks, yet policy prohibits the prisoners from covering their window to avoid the sun's glare. Several inmates spoke of their attempts to lie on the floor in order to gain relief from the excruciating heat, only to be told by officers that they will be given a disciplinary write-up if they lie on the floor. While prisoners are required to keep their cells clean, the officers do not bring them sufficient cleaning materials. A prisoner explains: "They bring a bucket of water and a mop to the first cell on the tier, and then when that guy's finished cleaning his cell they take it to the next cell. By the time the bucket gets to the third cell the water is filthy, and they never even bother taking it past the first few cells on the tier. So the guys in the further back cells never get a chance to clean their cells." MDOC recently instituted a policy that the men on death row must wear other inmates' used underwear. Many of the prisoners I interviewed felt that being forced to wear another man's used underclothes, which they have no way of sanitizing, was so repugnant, humiliating and demeaning, that they would rather incur discipline than obey orders to do so.

Most of the prisoners feel that the rules are enforced in erratic and unpredictable ways. I asked some prisoners why they did not purchase a television or radio when they are permitted to do so, and was told by several prisoners that a television costs over $300, and they can never know when it will be taken away from them for purely arbitrary reasons. The attitude of many prisoners was summed up by one man: "What's the use? Why purchase a television when it can be taken from you in a minute and you may or may not get it back?"

The perception among prisoners is of incessant, unrelenting and arbitrary deprivations and punishments. According to Steve Knox: "Every rule change is for the worse: they took our shoes and we have to go out on the yard in the rain and get our feet wet, and we can't even run and get any exercise in those shower clogs; then in April (2002) they took most of our photographs and limited us to keeping only ten letters from loved ones in our cells, I don't know why, but it was hurtful, those letters are all I have from my sister and others I love; then they stopped stamps from coming in through the mail, you have to buy them in commissary—I don't have money, I was broke for two months and that meant I couldn't write to anyone." According to another prisoner, "It seems like everything they do around here is aimed at driving you crazy."

A certain amount of sadness is obviously to be expected in a death row setting, but at Parchman I discovered rampant depression, hopelessness, and suicidal ideation, far beyond what I have observed on death rows in other states. The prisoners connect their sense of despair and lack of hope to the harsh conditions and incremental deprivations they feel are unfairly forced upon them. The prisoners' gloomy characterization of the incremental deprivations is borne out by my observations. Things are taken away, things are never given. There are no programs and few if any opportunities for the prisoners to improve their situation by behaving well. Hope fades of ever being treated like a human being again. Despair sets in.

I saw much evidence of psychiatric breakdown. Continued isolated confinement is very likely to cause further deterioration of prisoners' psychiatric conditions, and they require more intensive treatment than can be administered in the death row setting. A secure treatment facility must be established that provides necessary therapeutic programs in a setting that will not increase psychiatric illness. Many prisoners told me about the rage they feel, in spite of their every effort to remain peaceful. One prisoner confides: "I'm always afraid something bad's going to happen to me." It is very clear that while isolation and idleness alone would cause many troubling psychiatric symptoms, the other harsh conditions in effect on Parchman's death row—including but not limited to the extremes of heat and humidity, the grossly unsanitary environment, the vermin, the arbitrary and punitive disciplinary policies, and inadequate health and mental health care significantly increase the risk of prisoners developing major psychiatric problems and increase the severity of despair and psychiatric morbidity that plague these prisoners. The presence of severely disturbed prisoners on the tiers decidedly worsens the psychiatric symptoms of other prisoners. It is likewise highly anxiety-producing for prisoners to watch as a neighbor suffers seemingly life-threatening medical symptoms and yet is left entirely unattended by medical staff. According to the prisoners with whom I spoke, when staff eventually do get around to responding, they pay more attention to the fact that the prisoner is making noise than to the emergency needs that led the prisoner to try so hard to get the staff's attention. Again, as in many other instances, the staff's response is likely to be limited to punishment, a disciplinary infraction perhaps, and meanwhile the prisoners' concerns about the lack of emergency response go unheard.

All the inhumane conditions I have described combine to make life unbearable on death row at Parchman. Even well behaved prisoners are forced to endure permanent and almost total isolation and idleness. There is no reason for all death row prisoners to be kept in their cells twenty-three or twenty-four hours per day. They need a modicum of hope that through good behavior they can positively affect their situation. Human beings are most likely to respond positively to punishments that are specific to their offenses and time-limited, so they can feel some hope that with better behavior they can earn a better situation for themselves. On death row at Parchman, the punishments are so severe and often so arbitrary, and the length of many of the deprivations or punishments is so long or indeterminate, that the prisoner despairs of ever alleviating his suffering.

This is an abridged version of the report.

## AN AMERICAN CHRONICLE

### Rogelio Reyes Cannady, Death Row, Texas

JANUARY 4, 1999

I have written to you twice since my last conversation with you but decided to tear them up because the letters confused me too. I just hobbled on about subjects that either made no sense or should not have. Remember that I told you before that I would not like to be anyone's friend here not because I don't like people but losing a friend is not so easy. This is what I've tried to write about but confused myself while I got lost in my thoughts. I'm not making any sense, am I?

Regardless how hard I try, I can't do anything without thinking about my neighbor. The days go by and slowly the 10th of February inches closer. This day is George Cordova's date. His appeals are exhausted and his day is inching closer; somehow I started speaking to him about sports. It was the morning after I posted your letter. He called me to the heating ventilation and we started exchanging ideas and opinions about football teams. It was real quiet, so everyone must have been asleep and so suddenly after we were getting done talking sports, a wave of these emotions caught me off guard.

I couldn't just leave him in such a depressed state so I sat and listened to him. I tried to understand him and still do. It has been a week now and he feels comfortable speaking to me about his life's tribulations and anguish. It seems that his life runs at a parallel to mine at times. I understand where he is coming from. I can see that like me he has never expressed his deepest fears and shame to anyone for fear of a critical individual repeating it. I have you . . . he has never trusted anyone that I know of. This is where I have had trouble when I wrote to you.

After telling me of shameful situations that he experienced as a kid, he asks me not to ever tell anybody, as if somehow it came out involuntary in a moment of weakness? His suffering is great, I can understand . . . Sometimes I'm confused and don't know what to respond so I just sit and listen. What can I do? I've told you about what he told me in the letters I tore up, because I don't know who to ask but I also promised him not to ever repeat what he said. If I had no one in the world that I could truly trust, I know it would all just pressurize inside so I'm very grateful to have you. You know Isabelle, I don't think that Cordova would mind if I asked for your opinion on this. I have tried to put myself in his situation as hard as it is but he has cut his family off and will not tell them of his date. I asked him why and he only says that he does not want to hurt them. So his family does not know about his date. What do you think about this? It confuses me. I can understand that he does not want his mother to suffer any over him but to not tell his brothers? I'm sorry. I really can't do much without thinking of his situation. It won't be long before he calls me . . .

## JANUARY 9, 1999

. . . I spoke to Cordova this morning and what he said really disgusted me. I doubt that he would mind if I told you this. Can you believe that people have solicited him to attend and be present in the chamber on the day of his execution? It sounds sick to even repeat this. These people who have asked do not even know him! I sense a circus that is coming around him . . . we spoke today for sometime. It seems that now he confides in me without a second's hesitation.

## JANUARY 12, 1999

. . . You know, yesterday the property officer brought my neighbor Cordova all the property that had been confiscated so that he could sort through it all and pack the stuff he wants to send home. Anyway his radio was included and he sent it to me. I have been listening to it. Life has been good but only for a bit. I should send it back soon.

## JANUARY 20, 1999

. . . I wish that I could tell you all about him and you would better understand why he has buried a lot of guilt for so long. Only now that he realizes how serious this date is, he's in a state of mind that . . . well it's only my guess but reflecting on his life. Have you ever heard that when one is close to death, it is said that there are life flashes before one's eyes?

## JANUARY 26, 1999

. . . about George. His attorney is just done filing an appeal but we just don't know. He's been doing a lot of writing lately. He has been putting all those that asked to attend his date to the wayside. He does have a right to say that they cannot attend with some exceptions (that being victims' relatives who want to attend and a crop, hand picked by the State prosecutor who put him on death row).

## FEBRUARY 3, 1999

Today Cordova went out to visit with a media group. The reporter was taken aback on some of our circumstances here. George said that she fought back tears too. He's almost forty years old but if you saw him you'd swear that he was around my age (twenty-six).

## FEBRUARY 6, 1999

His family was turned back from the visit because he had already a visit that day. His brother, who he hadn't seen in years, came and was turned away. Also one of his sisters came to visit but was turned away. Another of his friends from out of state dropped by and, well, the same.

## FEBRUARY 9, 1999, EARLY IN THE MORNING

They came and told George to pack up because he was being moved into what is called the death watch cell on a lock down wing. I used to be several cells down from the cell where he will be tonight. I can't explain in words how it is that I feel inside right now. There is somehow inside of me a feeling of trying to distance myself away but the reality is that he will leave tonight and I'll never converse with him again. Don't imagine me in a very depressed state of mind. I'm not so depressed that I cannot function but sad . . . yes. In any time he'll be gone. . . . Inside I wish that I could run and hide but there's nowhere to go. Is there?

## FEBRUARY 9, 1999, DURING THE DAY

I'm just sitting here. Didn't expect to write today but I feel really low. I would rather express and release my thoughts. I hardly slept last night, well this morning I should say. Last night I stayed up with George and didn't get but about a half hour of sleep this morning. They woke me at 7:40 A.M. for recreation.

I knew that George would be gone to visit all day because of his status and would probably be moved to the death watch cell . . . I would see him before I left for recreation so I woke him up and pulled away from the escorting officers, got to his cell and shook his hand. I looked him in the face . . . got up. I had to get on my knees to shake his hand. You know, there is a type of metal grill on the bars except on the lowest section of the cell bars. I had to kneel down so I could shake his hand also because I am handcuffed behind my back wherever I go.

I was told: "Cannady, what do you think you're doing?" I was then escorted to recreation. . . . When I was back on the block, I kept walking past my cell to George's knowing that he would not be there but I had to see! Only his mattress, neatly made, remained . . . I wonder to myself why George was made to remain in a solitary cell these last days. Everyone else is always put on the regular wing about a week before their date.

At least they can be distracted by the television or even a small meal delivered from friends, got from the commissary, my God something! Here in the solitary cell block, he can see nothing, do nothing, eat nothing, just think. I believe he's now been moved to a death watch cell. How can these people be so inhumane? Wow! I'll be with you in a bit, George has just come back!

**FEBRUARY 9, 1999, A MOMENT LATER**

He was brought back but was actually supposed to be escorted to another cell. Isabelle, I had never imagined him with the concerned expression he showed right now. He just came back from his visit. He stopped in front of my cell, looked at me and just said: "*Ojala que nunca pases por esto!*" (I hope that you never pass through this.) He repeated this several times from his cell. He was visibly shaken and called me.

After his time ran out visiting with his sister and nephew and nieces, the roaming officer who was working visitation started telling George's people that they had to leave. The escort officers were not even present to take him back! George said that he had a grin on his face and looked as though he were enjoying the moment because the family was crying. The officer kept telling his people to leave but his little nephew stood fast refusing to leave!

His nephew grabbed the chair and his nieces came to their brother's side, all children crying for their uncle! My heart goes out to them . . .

Again, George's waiting to be moved. Someone is in the death watch cell he is to be housed in. He just left again. This time for good. When George asked if he could please have permission to see his mother, the captain said "no," that she was not on the list. So then he went out and told George's mother that George did not want to see her! I swear it angers me! That snake! Why does he insist on adding sorrow to that poor lady? George says that he never had bad words with him. That worm just is no good.

While the commotion happened in the visiting room, the inmate janitor even left the room, it was too much for him. After they were escorted out and the officers left, the inmate janitor walked up to George and told him that he did not know how he kept from shedding tears but that he shed some for him . . . That's George. He does believe in strength and not showing the system that they have defeated him. His sister had asked her employer for time off because she would be seeing her brother and explained the situation. She had been promoted to assistant manager not long ago but has now lost her job.

Friar Walsh has been coming to visit George. A while ago, I saw him passing in front of my cell and heard George say from inside his cell, "It was hard, they were crying." What purpose does all this serve? Who wins from George's death? It is only a legal tool for the vengeance of a few! Those who suffer are family left behind. How can someone feel good about inflicting pain on a woman (a mother) and kids, inflict the same pain as they feel? Families are the ones who suffer most.

I really don't know what to do, think, or feel. I know now that when I told you before that I would never get so close to anyone in here because of what has now happened. It will happen regardless if I realize it, when it happens or not. Guess that I may have been naïve. I can say that I've attained a better understanding of everything.

**FEBRUARY 11, 1999**
Hello! I left this letter open because I knew that I would be back before I mailed it out. It's after breakfast. I didn't get to eat but that's OK because I didn't much feel hungry. I was hoping for some good news or that maybe I could hear someone next door but it's not to be. I have just found out for

sure that George was executed yesterday. . . . Isabelle, as much as I'm trying to block out what is happening in my life at this time, it's not working. I think I'll sleep now OK? I know things won't change but somehow I need a different mind set!

## FEBRUARY 14, 1999

I spent the whole day cleaning and tossing out some paperwork that was of no use. I got some more of my property back because of my promotion in level status. Also George left me some of his property too . . . I find myself thinking about these past few months and a dark cloud of sadness creeps over me. I have a radio now (George's) but don't even turn it on . . . When George came back from his visit, one thing he kept repeating was: "*Ojala que nunca pases por esto!*" (I hope that you never pass through this.) I'm more determined now not to let it happen. I'm running into some obstacles but will figure out a way somehow!

## MARCH 6, 1999

George would totally agree for you to translate this and make the public aware of our situation. He was always compassionate, so much that he would take the shirt off his back and give it to one still more unfortunate than him. His execution makes no sense! He had so much to give . . . You know, I found out that on the 9th of February his sister was put on the ground and restrained at the Walls. I doubt people realize the whole truth. A lot of people just seem to think that an execution consists of murdering an inmate but what of all others involved? It shatters mothers, brothers, sisters . . . just family members generally!

This business (executions) that Texas sees as beneficial, is really a no-win situation. Unless it is a vengeful act but they try to avoid this in saying that it is "closure" for the victims. Who do the victims' family members think of? Certainly not about other families, the kids, etc. It is not like an act out of passion or one just losing it or something. Their act is one of true premeditation to murder another when other alternatives exist.

## MARCH 13, 1999

It has now been some time since George was murdered to extinguish a few individuals' desires. I can honestly say that this experience has been a rude awakening for me and my situation. No longer am I lax about my own future nor legal representation. I have learned from George's mistakes. Our situation in Texas is desperate.

These are excerpts of Rogelio's letters to his Swiss pen pal, Isabelle.

## BEING RUSHED TO DEATH

### Richard Rossi, Death Row, Arizona

JUNE 12, 1996

I just received notice that the state is seeking an execution warrant for me. It will be my first one. I do not have much to worry about because I still have my *Habeas* appeal in the federal court before they can execute me, but it shows how they are pushing to eliminate us.

JUNE 30, 1996

Yesterday, I was surprised to receive the Warrant for Execution reproduced below. The date is for July 24th. There is no way I should have received this now. I am just in the door of the Federal District Court and so I have my entire *Habeas Corpus* petition left to go before I have to start worrying about death warrants. Although I know this to be an error, I wonder if it is not a result of them wanting to stick it to me for all the anti-prison articles I write. Only time will tell. However, I must tell you that I am at a loss and feel disoriented at the prospect of having only a month to live. It makes me realize how little I have prepared for this eventuality. If I don't get my stay in a week or so, I will frantically race to get everything in order.

THE EXECUTION WARRANT—Filed June 25, 1996

NOW THEREFORE, IT IS ORDERED, that Wednesday, the 24th day of July, 1996, be and the same is hereby fixed as the time when the judgment and sentence of death pronounced upon the appellant, RICHARD MICHAEL ROSSI, by the Superior Court of Maricopa County, State of Arizona, shall be executed by administering to RICH-ARD MICHAEL ROSSI an intravenous injection of a substance or substances in a lethal quantity sufficient to cause death, except that RICHARD MICHAEL ROSSI shall have the choice of either lethal injection or lethal gas.

JULY 4, 1996

Well, the emergency has been averted. I heard from my lawyer yesterday that the federal judge had signed the order to stay my execution. I cannot say that I was not concerned about this whole turn of events. I was getting all kinds of signs from the administration here that plans were being readied for my demise.

I was served with all the appropriate forms to be filled out: such things as my last meal, who will attend hearings, disposition of my property, etc. I had deadlines for each form and some I had to already hand in. I was going to be moved Tuesday to an observation cell for the remaining two weeks until forty-eight hours before the actual time. Then I would be transported to the death house.

It has never been the thought of death that has bothered me. However, when this warrant came down unexpectedly as it did, I was taken off balance. The reason being that at the proper time when I know all my avenues of appeal are finished, I will have said my goodbyes and had everything in order. I was simply not ready. So the thought of my life ending in thirty days was startling. I am sure you can understand what I am saying. How does one cram forty-nine years of life into thirty days? It certainly displayed the cold-hearted nature of the system and how prepared they are to bring life to an end in an organized and efficient manner. I guess I can consider this a wake up call.

When discussing this incident with my attorney, I asked her if she had found out why this warrant was issued in the first place. She spoke to the death penalty clerk (at the federal court), who was as surprised to hear about the warrant as we were. The only reason she came away with for the issuance of the warrant is that it was the state's way of putting the pressure on me. As if to say that after all these years, they want me to know they intend to kill me. And also so as to require a federal judge to stay the execution so that later on the state can claim that I was not executed because some liberal federal judge got in the way and stayed my execution. This takes the heat off the Attorney General. Thus politics go on as usual with human lives their pawns of power.

What I did find ironic is that we had just reviewed the Antonio James execution (*Forum,* July, 1996), and if you remember, I had remarked to you that this had all caused me some problems. Then like *déjà vu,* I find myself in the same situation. I wonder if all my anti-establishment articles had anything to do with their desire to be rid of me? It doesn't matter, because the articles will continue to come forth until I am no longer.

## AUGUST 15, 1996

Two weeks ago on July 30, I received a personal letter from one of the victims of my crime. There were two immediate victims, the man who died and a woman neighbor who was shot and thankfully survived. This note was hand-delivered to me by the administrator of my cell block. Since there are restrictions on communications between us and our victims, the note was delivered in a sealed envelope after making its way through the proper channels at the Department of Corrections in Phoenix. I was told it was from a victim of my crime and did I want to accept it. Without hesitation, I said yes. The odd part about this was that by the time the department had processed the letter and delivered it to me, it was a week after the date I was due to be executed, so if I had been executed, I would never have had the opportunity to read it and that would have been quite an injustice and a major disappointment in itself. The letter was a hand-written note. It was obviously difficult to write to me and she didn't know if I would be receptive to it. But she felt after all these years compelled to write it, and was also afraid to write it. She had learned of my impending execution which was very emotional for her and did not know how to react to it. She explained that the Lord holds us accountable for our actions and we must pay for our sins as well as ask for forgiveness. She closed with the following: "Too many things go unsaid and then it's too late. I wanted you to know that I have forgiven you for your actions against me and hope in someway that this will bring peace to your heart as it also heals mine. God bless you."

I was emotionally rocked after I read this beautiful letter. For years I had wanted to reach out to her but was afraid to do so because of the strict rules about writing to one's victims and also because I didn't want to cause any more pain. It has been thirteen years since my crime, and I have long since asked God for forgiveness and many times wished I could tell victims how sorry I was to have inflicted the pain and suffering that was unnecessary and unwanted. Now the door has been opened.

Over the years, all of us prisoners on death row have come to experience the bitterness of a society that clamors for more punishment, speedier executions and their share of retribution. More sentences for more crimes, more years in prisons so that a person will never return to society: out of sight, out of mind. They feel that prison is the only way to deal with crime because if they release prisoners, they will just commit new crimes. In their eyes, few if any of us are good people and fewer yet are capable of rehabilitation. And the more prisoners we execute, the safer society will be. This is the most tragic commentary on modern society.

If you would travel down the roads I have walked in the past thirteen years, stand in my shoes, you would be very surprised. If you think it is easy to die a little bit each day, to see your loved ones pass away and not be able to commiserate with friends and family, to see how much we are condemned for all of society's ills, then you should take another look. Every individual on this troubled earth deserves to be touched by love as well as accorded the opportunity to express his/her feelings to others and to be able to touch another. Every person has the ability to change. We are not made of concrete. The feelings of compassion, love, the understanding of right from wrong, can reach us. We are affected by all that goes on around us. The greater crime is to lump us all together as failures and discard us all on the refuse pile. We must learn that every person has value and worth and each individual must be judged for who and what he/she is now and not what he/she was once. We as human beings have the ability to learn, adapt and change.

This short letter I received says volumes about love and understanding. She has shown me what a beautiful, caring and wonderful person she is. To reach out to me after thirteen years on the eve of my execution and express her forgiveness of me, allows me to have faith that compassion still exists in our world, no matter how limited it is. The politicians, the courts and the judges may not see any redeemable value in me, but the compassion of this one person says it all. We all wish that we could change the past, but since that is impossible, it is the present that confines and defines us. I must take solace in the knowledge that this letter has healed her heart as well as having brought peace to my own.

Richard Rossi died of natural causes while on Death Row in Texas on April 22, 2006.

## SCRAPPERS: GIVING IN TO LIFE

Sister Helen Prejean, Louisiana

Dear Kevin,

I got your letter last week and have been making my way to you ever since. First in prayer, now in writing to you and trying to see if a visit might be possible, or at least a phone call. In case our visit will happen by phone my number is ———. That's my private phone. If I'm not there, the answering machine takes a message (but you will be calling collect, so the answering machine will be of no help). Through [your lawyer] we'll set up a time so there are no mix-ups. When you call I want to be waiting for you.

I was so touched by your letter. Honored, really, that you as one of your last acts on this earth would want to talk to *me.* That's very humbling, Kevin. I keep looking at and re-reading your letter, noticing every word and how you say things. I sense a beautiful sensitivity in you, a goodness. You do know, don't you, that whatever you may have done— whatever—even if it was a terrible, heinous act—that you are more than that act. You are, you know, a son of God, and very precious to God and to others like me, who appreciate your goodness and so, naturally, want to see you live.

You gotta know, Kevin, that I'm a scrapper. I don't believe in giving in to the state's desire to kill you. I spend my life fighting state executions and working to change public consciousness about the death penalty so we can abolish it forever one day, I hope soon.

Why do you want to give up your appeals and let the state kill you? Is it a death wish? A suicide wish, and you're asking the state to help you do it? I don't know you yet, so don't have a clear sense of why you want to do this, Kevin. Don't you know that when you're gone from this earth there's *no* replacing you? I think of your poor mother's heart—you think that by doing this you will *ease* her pain? I am praying for your mother and your family.

What do you look like? I have a *great* desire to see your face. Can you send a picture? Do you know what I look like? Can I send you a photo? What's your personality like? Do you like jokes? (I do.) Have a good sense of humor? (I do.) Do you believe that love can live in the human heart?

Have you known love in your life? Whom do you love? Who loves you? Do you like to read? What's your favorite music? (Do you sing—even in the shower?) Kevin, I'm thinking . . . you must be in a lot of pain to want to end your life here. I wonder what your pain is and what I might do to ease it. Somehow, even with just your letter, your words to me, I am already drawn toward you. Already, Kevin, you have sneaked into my heart.

Already I have begun to care about you. So, what will it be like to hear your actual voice on the phone? Meeting Kevin Scutter—a new adventure in my life. What made you seek me out? Why do you want to meet *me?* I mean, there are a lot of people in the world. *A lot!* But, of all of them, you want to meet *me.* Of course, I'm honored. Do you realize how special that is?

I'm on a plane. These days I'm almost always on a plane, going somewhere to give a talk in a university or to a church group, telling stories about the death penalty and why we need to abolish it. Have you by any chance read *Dead Man Walking?* Can I send it to you? I'd love for you to read it. Can you put off dropping your appeals until *after* you have read my book? (Right, you got it, I'm trying to delay you, trying to hold you tight in the life web so you don't slip away.) I land at the St. Louis airport soon, and I'll set up our phone call. I look forward to hearing your voice for the first time.

Love and prayers,
Sister Helen

Sister Helen Prejean is a spiritual advisor on Death Row in Louisiana.

# Organizations and Prison Writing Web Sites

## Organizations

*Amicus* was set up in 1992 in memory of Andrew Lee Jones, who was executed in Louisiana in July 1991. The charity is designed to assist in the provision of legal representation for those awaiting capital trial and punishment in the U.S., and to raise awareness of potential abuses of their rights. This is done in a number of ways. Amicus trains U.K. lawyers and students to go and work in the U.S. alongside attorneys. Interns will investigate cases, undertake legal research and assist in trials and appeals. The charity also does casework, researching particular areas of law, and drafting amicus curiae briefs to be presented to U.S. courts. It has also made applications to the Inter-American Commission of Human Rights in Washington about breaches of the American Declaration of Human Rights in death penalty trials. The charity provides training on the death penalty several times a year which is essentially for anyone who would like to further their interest in the law and procedure surrounding the death penalty in the United States and around the world. President: Michael Mansfield QC
http://www.Amicus-alj.org

*LifeLines* supports and befriends prisoners on death row in the United States, through letter writing. It was set up in 1988 in Cambridge, England, and is the largest organization of its kind, having spread both nationally and internationally. Currently LifeLines has around 1700 members, mainly based in the U.K. but also in many parts of Europe, Australia, and some in the U.S.A. It organizes two annual conferences, has a quarterly newsletter and a system of state coordinators to provide its members with support. LifeLines is not actively involved in campaigning nor is it a political group.

Founder: Jan Arriens
http://www.lifelines.org

*Amnesty International,* founded in 1961, is a worldwide nonpartisan organization with more than 1.5 million members and supporters in over 150 countries and territories. It is independent of any government, political faction, ideology, economic interest, or religious creed. It is the winner of the 1977 Nobel Peace Prize for its efforts to promote global observance of the United Nations Universal Declaration of Human Rights. Amnesty International works specifically for the release of prisoners of conscience—men, women, and children imprisoned for their beliefs, color, sex, ethnic origin, language, religion, or sexual orientation, who have not used or advocated violence; fair and prompt trials for all political prisoners; an end to all torture, "disappearances," and executions.
http://www.amnesty.org

*The Texas Coalition to Abolish the Death Penalty (TCADP)* is a grassroots organization dedicated to abolishing the death penalty in Texas. We have chapters in Houston, Austin, Dallas/Fort Worth, San Antonio, and College Station. The Texas Moratorium Network and El Pasoans Against the Death Penalty are active organizational members of the TCADP. The TCADP is affiliated with the National Coalition to Abolish the Death Penalty and works with other organizations which oppose the death penalty including Amnesty International, American Civil Liberties Union, National Association for the Advancement of Colored People, American Friends Service Committee, the Moratorium Campaign, Equal Justice U.S.A, Murder Victims Families for Reconciliation, Texas Defender Services, University of Houston Innocence Project, Texas Criminal Defense Lawyers Association, Texas Conference of Churches, Texas Catholic Conference, Baptist Life Commission, and the StandDown Project.
http://www.tcadp.org

*The Centre for Capital Punishment Studies,* a project funded by the European Commission and based at the University of Westminster, London, undertakes research into a diverse range of issues concerning the death penalty. It has a growing specialist library on the death penalty that is open to all

with a scholarly interest in the subject. The CCPS was the first to establish what has become a thriving internship program providing opportunities for students and practitioners to work with capital defense lawyers in the U.S.A and Caribbean Commonwealth.
Founder: Peter Hodgkinson
http://www.wmin.ac.uk/ccps

*Human Writes* is a humanitarian nonprofit organization that befriends prisoners on death row throughout the United States. It is neither a campaigning nor political group. The organization has over 1,300 members whose non-judgmental friendship through letter writing has enriched the lives of many prisoners in their final years.
Patron: Charles Wheeler
http://www.humanwrites.com

*Southern Center for Human Rights* represents people facing the death penalty at trials, on appeals and in post-conviction proceedings. It documents and publicizes the denial of competent counsel for those facing death.
Director: Stephen B. Bright
http://www.schr.org

*Murder Victims' Families for Reconciliation* is a national organization of family members of victims of homicide and state killings who oppose the death penalty in all cases. Its mission is to abolish the death penalty. MVFR is an advocate for programs and policies that reduce the rate of homicide and promote crime prevention and alternatives to violence. It also supports programs that address the needs of victims, helping them to rebuild their lives.
http://www.mvfr.org

*Death Penalty Focus* is a non-profit organization, with more than 10,000 members nationwide, dedicated to the abolition of capital punishment through grassroots organizing, research, and the dissemination of information about the death penalty and its alternatives. It is governed by a volunteer board of directors comprising renowned political, religious, and civic leaders, along with legal scholars and attorneys involved in death penalty litigation. In addition, DPF has an Advisory Board composed of commu-

nity and religious leaders, celebrities, writers, and representatives of labor and human rights organizations.
President: Mike Farrell
http://www.deathpenalty.org

## Web Sites Containing Prison Writing

*Surviving the System* is a community of prisoners and their loved ones, as well as various activists, professionals and recovering persons who desire and see an absolute need for social change.
Founder: Traci W. Lister
http://www.SurvivingTheSystem.com

*The Other Side of the Wall* features news, writing, and information on prisons and the death penalty.
Founder: Arnold Erickson
http://www.prisonwall.org

*The Dark Faces of Justice,* a satellite of Project Hope to Abolish the Death Penalty, is an inmate-based group focused on issues concerning Alabama's death row. Our goals are to educate the public on the issues of the death penalty and the fight to have it abolished.
http:// www.darkfacesofjustice.org/html/about_us.html

*Lamp of Hope* was founded by Texas death row prisoners in order to educate the public about the death penalty and to support the families of both prisoners and victims.
http://www.lampofhope.org

*Reprieve* provides effective legal representation and humanitarian assistance to impoverished people facing the death penalty at the hands of the state in the U.S. and the Caribbean.
Founder: Clive Stafford Smith
http://www.reprieve.org.uk

# Further Reading

Arriens, Jan. *Welcome to Hell: Letters and Writings from Death Row.* Boston: Northeastern University Press, 1997.

Abu-Jamal, Mumia. *Death Blossoms: Reflections from a Prisoner of Conscience.* Robertsbridge E. Sussex: The Plough Publishing House, 1997.

———. *Live from Death Row.* New York: Addison-Wesley Publishing Company, 1995.

Amnesty International USA. *The Machinery of Death: A Shocking Indictment of Capital Punishment in the United States,* ed. Enid Harlow, David Matas, and Jane Rocamora. New York: Amnesty International USA, 1995.

Banner, Stuart. *The Death Penalty: An American History.* London: Harvard University Press, 2002.

Beccaria, Cesare. *On Crimes and Punishments,* ed. David Young. Indianapolis: [Hackett], 1986.

Bessler, John D. *Death in the Dark: Midnight Executions in America.* Boston: Northeastern University Press, 1997.

Bosco, Antoinette. *Choosing Mercy: A Mother of Murder Victims Pleads to End the Death Penalty.* Maryknoll, N.Y.: Orbis Books, 2001.

Bright, Stephen B. "Will the Death Penalty Remain Alive in the Twenty-first Century?: International Norms, Discrimination, Arbitrariness and the Risk of Executing the Innocent," *Wisconsin Law Review,* no.1 (2001): 1–27.

———. "Is Fairness Irrelevant? The Evisceration of Federal Habeas Corpus Review and Limits on the Ability of State Courts to Protect Fundamental Rights," *Washington and Lee Law Review* 54, no 1 (Winter 1997): 1–30.

Burnett, Cathleen. *Justice Denied: Clemency Appeals in Death Penalty Cases.* Boston: Northeastern University Press, 2002.

Cabana, Donald A. *Death at Midnight: The Confession of an Executioner.* Boston: Northeastern University Press, 1996.

Davies, Ioan. *Writers in Prison.* Oxford: Basil Blackwell, 1990.

Dow, David R. and Mark Dow, ed. *Machinery of Death: The Reality of America's Death Penalty Regime.* London: Routledge, 2002.

Dwyer, Jim, Peter Neufeld, and Barry Scheck. *Actual Innocence: Five Days to Execution and Other Dispatches from the Wrongly Convicted.* New York: Doubleday, 2000.

Elder, Joy. *Lethal Justice: One Man's Journey of Hope on Death Row.* New York: New City Press, 2002.

Gatrell, V. A. C. *The Hanging Tree: Execution and the English People 1770–1868.* Oxford: Oxford University Press, 1994.

Haines, Herbert. *Against Capital Punishment, the Anti-Death Penalty Movement in America 1972–1994.* Oxford: Oxford University Press, 1996.

Hood, Roger. *The Death Penalty: A Worldwide Perspective.* Oxford: Oxford University Press, 2002.

Ingle, Joseph, B. *Last Rights: 13 Fatal Encounters with the State's Justice.* Nashville: Abingdon Press, 1990.

Jackson, Rev. Jesse L., Rep. Jesse J. Jackson Jr, and Bruce Shapiro. *Legal Lynching: The Death Penalty and America's Future.* New York: The New Press, 2001.

James, Mike. *Women on Death Row.* London: True Crime Library, 1994.

Keenan, Brian. *An Evil Cradling.* London: Vintage, 1992.

Krishnamma, S. R. *The Ballad of the Lazy "L".* Corsham: Rani Press, 1994.

Kupers, Terry. *Prison Madness: The Mental Health Crisis Behind Bars and What We Must Do About It.* San Francisco: John Wiley and Son, 1999.

Lesser, Wendy. *Pictures at an Execution.* London: Harvard University Press, 1993.

Loney, Randolph. *A Dream of the Tattered Man: Stories from Georgia's Death Row.* Cambridge: William B. Eerdmans Publishing Company, 2001.

Mailer, Norman. *The Executioner's Song.* London: Hutchinson, 1979.

Masters, Jarvis. *Finding Freedom: Writings from Death Row.* Junction City, Calif.: Padma Publishing, 1997.

McFeely, William S. *Proximity to Death.* London: W. W. Norton, 2000.

Megivern, James J. *The Death Penalty: An Historical and Theological Survey.* New York: Paulist Press, 1997.

Mitford, Jessica. *Kind and Usual Punishment: The Prison Business.* New York: Vintage Books, 1973.

Morris, Norval and David J. Rothman. ed. *The Oxford History of the Prison: The Practice of Punishment in Western Society.* Oxford: Oxford University Press, 1995.

Mulvey-Roberts, Marie. ed. *Out of the Night: Writings from Death Row.* Cheltenham, U.K.: New Clarion Press, 1994.

Officer, Jane, ed. *If I Should Die . . . A Death Row Correspondence.* Cheltenham, U.K.: New Clarion Press, 1999.

O'Shea, Kathleen. *Women and the Death Penalty in the United States, 1900–1998.* London: Praeger, 1999.

Potter, Harry. *Hanging in Judgment: Religion and the Death Penalty in England.* London: SCM Press Ltd, 1993.

Poyck, William Van. *A Checkered Past: A Memoir.* Bloomington, Ind.: 1stBooks Library, 2003.

Prejean, Helen. *Dead Man Walking: An Eyewitness Account of the Death Penalty in the United States.* New York: Random House, 1993.

Radelet, Michael L., Hugo Adam Bedau, and Constance E. Putnam. *In Spite of Innocence: Erroneous Convictions in Capital Cases.* Boston: Northeastern University Press, 1992.

Russell, Sue. *Damsel of Death.* London: True Crime, 1992.

Sarat, Austin, ed. *The Killing State: Capital Punishment in Law, Politics and Culture.* Oxford: Oxford University Press, 1999.

Schabas, William A. *The Death Penalty as Cruel Treatment and Torture.* Boston: Northeastern University Press, 1996.

Solotaroff, Ivan. *The Last Face You'll Ever See: The Private Life of the American Death Penalty.* London: HarperCollins, 2001.

Thomas, Merrilyn. *Life on Death Row: One Man's Fight against Racism and the Death Penalty.* London: Piatkus, 1989.

Trombley, Stephen. *The Execution Protocol.* London: Century, 1993.

Vila, Bryan and Cynthia Morris, ed. *Capital Punishment in the United States: A Documentary History.* London: Greenwood Press, 1997.

Waite, Terry. *Taken on Trust.* London: Hodder and Stoughton, 1993.

# Filmography

*Monster,* dir. Patty Jenkins (2003)
Charlize Theron stars in this powerful and moving feature film about Aileen Wuornos, who was purported to be America's first female serial murderer. She is also the subject of two documentaries directed by Nick Broomfield: *Aileen Wuornos: The Selling of a Serial Killer* (1992) and *Aileen: The Life and Death of a Serial Killer* (2003).

*Monster's Ball,* dir. Marc Foster (2001)
In this sultry atmospheric feature film set in the Deep South, a racist prison guard re-examines his attitudes after falling in love with the African American wife of the last prisoner he executed.

*Dead Man Walking,* dir. Tim Robbins (1996)
Sister Helen Prejean's remarkable account of her experience as a spiritual advisor on death row in Louisiana is translated to film, starring Susan Sarandon.

*In the Blink of an Eye,* dir. Micki Dickoff (1996)
This feature film is based on the true story of filmmaker Micki Dickoff's mission to help prove the innocence of her childhood friend Sunni (Sonya Jacobs) who was wrongly imprisoned on Florida's death row.

*Paradise Lost: The Child Murders at Robin Hood Hills,* dir. Joe Berlinger and Bruce Sinofsky (1996)
Both sides of a murder trial in a case against three teenagers are investigated in this disturbing courtroom documentary.

*The Execution Protocol,* dir. Stephen Trombley (1993)
The procedures of execution are examined from different points of view,

including prison personnel and prisoners, in this film version of Trombley's book.

*The Thin Blue Line,* dir. Errol Morris (1988)
This is a classic documentary relating to the death row incarceration of an innocent man.

*14 Days in May* dir. Paul Hamman (1988)
This influential BBC documentary, which inspired Jan Arriens to found LifeLines, witnesses the run up to the execution of Edward Earl Johnson at Parchman, Mississippi. He is believed by many to have been innocent.

# Reading for Their Lives Projects

## Books to Death Row Project

This is a nonprofit plan for sending books into prisons at a very modest cost. If you would like to participate, get in touch with Sheena Dewan at the London-based book publisher Vision, 101 Southwark Street, London, SE1 0JF, UK.
Telephone: 0207 928 5599
Fax 0207 928 8822.
E-mail: info@visionpaperbacks.co.uk or sheenadewan@visionpaperbacks.co.uk

## Survival Yoga Handbook

Sunni Jacobs spent seventeen years in prison in Florida, five years of which were endured on death row, for a crime she did not commit. The story of her release is dramatized in the movie *In the Blink of an Eye* (1996). Her survival, she claims, was due to yoga. Since her exoneration and release, Sunni has written *Survival Yoga Handbook.* For every book sold at a cost of approximately $18, £10 or 15 EUR, she is able to send a copy to a prisoner. For further information please write to Human Kindness Foundation, P.O. Box 61619, Durham, N.C. 27715, USA

**MARIE MULVEY-ROBERTS** is a Reader in Literary Studies at the University of the West of England, Bristol, in England. She has produced over thirty books, including *Out of the Night: Writings from Death Row* (1994), and numerous articles in a wide range of areas, including the trials of Oscar Wilde and the suffragette Constance Lytton. She has taught in prisons in the U.K. and judged writing competitions for prisoners in the U.S.A., U.K., and Ireland, and is a member of both LifeLines and Amnesty International.

The University of Illinois Press
is a founding member of the
Association of American University Presses.

———————————————————

Composed in 10.5/14 Adobe Garamond
with Adrianna Extended display
by Type One, LLC
for the University of Illinois Press
Designed by Paula Newcomb
Manufactured by Sheridan Books, Inc.

University of Illinois Press
1325 South Oak Street
Champaign, IL 61820-6903
www.press.uillinois.edu